Where Do I Belong?

Sarah Carrington

For permission, please email the author at sarah.carrington.author@gmail.com

Bookstores and wholesale orders can be placed with the author at sarah.carrington.author@gmail.com

Website: sarahcarringtonauthor.com

Issued in print and electronic formats.
ISBN 978-1-7388423-0-8 (paperback)
ISBN 978-1-7388423-1-5 (epub)

Cover by: Palmer Halvorson

First Edition

DISCLAIMER
This work depicts actual events in the life of the author as truthfully as recollection permits and/or can be verified by research. Occasionally, dialogue consistent with the character or nature of the person speaking has been supplemented. All persons are actual individuals. There are no composite characters. The names of individuals have been changed to respect their privacy.

Dedication

This book is dedicated to Paula.

Paula, you were my family, the voice of reason,
unending love, and support. You were my sister,
mother, and friend all in one. You loved me just as
I am. You showed me possibilities for a
life I had never thought of.

#fuckcancer

A portion of the sales from each book
will be dontated to cancer research.

Table of Contents

Prologue

Every story has a beginning, a middle, and an end. My story begins with an American draft dodger (or conscientious objector, if you prefer), his Canadian wife, and my birth into a closed community based on the Seventh Day Adventist's beliefs. The adherents called their lifestyle self-supporting communities. I called them religious communes.

My father was born in the United States. He was in his last semester at university when the Vietnam War was in full swing. Dad didn't believe in the war. It was the mid-seventies, and the world was in turmoil. Reporting came from brave war correspondents, and the images they showed were horrific. During this time, the Ohio National Guard shot and killed unarmed students at Kent State University. The bombings by small groups of leftist extremists became so commonplace between the mid-sixties and seventies that the population became desensitized to it.

Dad left for Canada as soon as he graduated from university. He successfully dodged the draft but lost any hope of returning to his friends and family. Leaving was incredibly hard, and he was homesick. Dad questioned the world he lived in. He had a great job with limitless growth, yet he was unhappy and unfulfilled. Being a draft dodger was a lonely existence. He couldn't go back, or he would face prison time. It reinforced my father's disenchantment with the conventional world.

He longed for something more, something free from the weighty burden and the restlessness that grew as the outside world became more chaotic. He was without a country or a sense of purpose. He was a wanted man in the United States and stateless in Canada. In 1983, five years after Jimmy Carter became president, he issued a pardon for draft dodgers. My dad was finally allowed to go home, but Dad's Canadian immigration application was subsequently approved. It was a proud and happy moment when my father became a Canadian citizen.

Prior to the amnesty, my dad's big brother, Fred, came to visit. He fell in love with the beautiful country Dad called home. He loved the mountains, untamed rivers, and miles of long sandy beaches. He particularly loved what he believed to be the unspoiled wilderness.

During the visit, they ended up at a revival camp meeting—I think it was the camping that first got Dad interested. The whole experience was so riveting that they joined the movement.

The Bible-spouting idealists offered Dad what he was searching for. Upon conversion, he wanted to completely change his life and join this amazing religious family. He wanted to build a new life with them: a world of their own away from mainstream society.

Then Dad met Mom. She wasn't part of this new church, so when he proposed marriage, he also asked her to join his new church and the community they would help build. She said yes, and the rest, as they say, is history.

They were fresh new converts eager to build a better life. She laughed when she shared the story of how she had a list of things needed to set up the house and all the plans she had while not realizing how much her life would change.

I imagine them driving along in the forest-green International pickup with its handmade log camper on the back. The road curved and twisted as they drove farther and farther north. When she told her story, I could feel the excitement she must have felt going to see the home they would share. She had a new life with the man she loved above all others. On the drive to their new home, she reviewed her list with Dad. It was then she discovered only two items on her list were approved by the commune—salt and flour.

Over the years, they had me, my two brothers, and my sister. My childhood was different, very different. I wasn't raised to live in an open society. I was incredibly sheltered and innocent in the ways of the world. I was brought up to be a good submissive Christian daughter, child, woman, and wife. This is the story of how I left what I consider a cult and learned to navigate a life I was woefully unprepared for.

Chapter One: The Utopia I Was Born Into

My first childhood home was a big three-storey cedar house. In the basement, the large beams had obvious scorch marks created when a fire started in the furnace room and threatened to burn the house to the ground.

Our home had wood heat, hence the fire-breathing monster in the basement. As a child, it was a large black, scary, yet compelling contraption. Great red flames licked at the wood, with hot embers burning my face when I peered in. A great pile of firewood was stacked to the side of the wood chute that wood from the outside woodpile was chucked into for indoor storage to burn as needed.

The house had large windows that flooded the house with light. The view I had those first few years played a big part in shaping my love of nature. The house sat high up on the mountainside with a breathtaking view. I loved looking down at the lush green valley with the river snaking through it like a path to the outside world. Only a few houses were visible as far as the eye could see. It was untouched, beautiful nature.

Our house was a couple of miles up a curvy and bumpy dirt road that cut into the side of the mountain. There was a sharp turn dubbed "suicide corner." When the roads were really bad, my dad would have to drive the Volvo a mile or two backward up the hill with people sitting on the hood to give traction. Sometimes he would get halfway to the worst corner and have to drive back down to give it a better run.

It was scary, and I knew to keep my mouth shut so he could focus. When faced with fear, I learned to breathe through it until the worst was past.

The community had large homes that were expressly built to house several people. We had women living upstairs, sharing the five large bedrooms and the single bathroom. The main floor was for us, with three bedrooms and a bathroom, as well as the kitchen, dining room, pantry, and living room. The basement was for the men. I wasn't allowed down there unless accompanying my father to feed the fire monster. The men and women lived in separate quarters to maintain religious propriety. How Mother, at twenty-two years old, faced the duties of people often many years older than her, I'll never know.

My parents were responsible for the men and women living with us. They were to lead by example, provide meals, and conduct daily worship and Bible study.

There was a great stone hearth on the main floor in the living room. We used to sit there by the roaring fire on cool evenings. I have fond memories of playing at that hearth. I'd melt candles and make wax pools, making fingerprints and building other formations.

I remember finding ten dollars in an envelope in the garbage at the town's post office. I told my father and held my breath as I asked if I could keep it. Since it was in the trash, it was determined I could keep it. You can guess what I bought with it—candles. Colourful birthday candles were my favourite for melting.

I also had to pay a tithe, or payment to the Lord, out of the ten-dollar find. Everyone had to pay ten percent of their earnings to God. Even as a young child, I knew the tithe didn't actually go to God. How would He, who is invisible and asks for us to have faith, even as small as a mustard seed, come to collect money that wouldn't be needed in Heaven? I knew it went to someone, and that someone was the preacher and the church.

At the church service, when the plate went around, everyone was expected to put in an offering. As I got older, I wondered if people ever took back instead of giving when the plate went by them. I didn't ask questions during the service. A stern look was enough to silence me. My freedom from sitting through the long hours during service blew any questions I might have to the wind as I raced about the field outside the church.

* * *

There was a number I was terrified of when I was a child: 144,000. I didn't want to be a part of it, but it was a number my father strived to be a part of. The book of Revelations and Ellen G White's (EGW) writings gave details on the signs of the end and Christ's second coming.

They taught us that when the signs of the second coming, such as false prophets, earthquakes, famine, plagues, and wars, are finished, Christ would return. We would see a cloud in the sky shaped like the palm of our hand. Upon it would be The Lord our Saviour. We will know He's not a false prophet, for His feet will not touch the ground.

The 144,000 were said to be those who didn't die the first death, the living saints. They would know and understand the Lord's voice, while the wicked would only hear thunderous storms. The dead would rise up and be judged, and their fate determined. It was then God would decide if they die the second death of eternity or rise up to the Heavens.

Stories like this terrified me as a child. My father, like

many others, believed we saw the signs of the end already. He was prepared to take us as far from civilization as needed to live out the last days until Christ's return. He did it to avoid wars and persecution and to eliminate the chance of friends and family turning against us and turning us into the authorities for our faith.

* * *

Natural holistic living was a great fad when I was little. It tied in perfectly with the writings of Ellen G White (EGW) that we lived by. Eat healthily, live off the land, and feed your body, mind, and soul. It was blended into the religious beliefs so much I didn't know where ideals ended, and religious belief began. The community was made up of believers and those who wanted to change their lives. Everyone worked together—be it for health reasons, drug problems, legal issues, or to learn the Christian way of life.

The basis of our commune lifestyle was the Seventh Day Adventist (SDA) Church. We worshipped on Saturday, or Sabbath as we called it, which is the seventh day of the week. The SDA church based its lifestyle foundation on the writings of EGW. We followed her writings and the Bible. The basis of our daily lifestyle was determined by the interpretation of EGW's books and her written interpretation of what her visions from God meant. She was God's messenger. Her writing covered all the how-to-live items in our life. Things like social relationships, nutrition, agriculture, evangelism, education, health, diet, theology, and creationism were addressed in her numerous books. The community was built on the ideals of her writings.

I recall a story from one of her books used in a sermon. It was based on the time of the end and the trials we needed to prepare to face prior to the Second Coming of Christ. Here is how I understood it.

A group of persecuted Christians packed and fled in their wagons. The road became steep and narrow, and they had to lighten their load to keep going. The farther they went, the narrower and more difficult the path became. The wagons were left behind, then the horses, then what little they carried. The path was perilously narrow: a goat path along a steep mountainside. Thin-knotted ropes appeared. They hung along the path for the travellers to hang on to. As the path got even narrower, the ropes got larger to hold their weight. Finally, the path was completely gone, and the ropes had to hold them to swing toward the light. It sounded almost fun to me, aside from the alarming fact they could fall to their death.

Many things about the time of the end scared me. We could be turned in to the authorities for torture and death for attending church on Sabbath. The government would decide our religion was wrong, and they would hunt us down and kill us. Keeping the faith was scary. The ideas I had in my head were those of being racked, put on the wheel, hot molten metals poured into various parts, burned alive, or drowned if you were lucky. I knew those were things that happened in medieval times. I didn't know what to imagine for current times. So many terrifying ways to slowly die for your faith. I hoped the signs of the end wouldn't happen. I hoped the calendar wasn't going to be changed to make Sunday the seventh day as was predicted. I feared our identities would be put in one place so the government could track our every move. I grew up fearing more than believing.

The children's books I grew up with weren't Dr. Seuss or nursery rhymes. There were Bible stories for children and adolescents, and then the EGW series for when I was a young adult.

The children's books I grew up with were those like Jonah,

swallowed by a whale and three days later spit out. It was to save Jonah from God's wrath over his disbelief. There was Job and his suffering as a test of his love and devotion to God. And the usual stories of loaves and fishes, Mary of Bethlehem, and the birth of Jesus in the manger.

All information was heavily censored. My approved storybooks had sections blacked out with new words written above. Our beliefs were so far off the beaten path even Christian books were not close enough to our faith. I learned if you don't believe or like what is there, you can change it. Make up what you want in your reality. A gift, in a way, for nothing is worse than thinking you have to be someone's idea of normal and judging yourself by another's code.

One fact about EGW that got me questioning her teachings was her visions. Her horrible childhood could be the cause of those visions. I grew up hearing how she'd been bullied and horribly teased by a few classmates. Some girls threw rocks at her as she walked home from school. One hit her in the head hard enough to knock her senseless and leave her in a coma for weeks. This injury caused lifelong disfigurement and left her unable to attend school for long periods of time. Some years after her injury, she found Jesus and was converted. Then, she began to have visions.

I read an article, not many years after coming to the outside world about how Ellen suffered from a type of seizure due to her head injury. The symptoms displayed in her visions could be explained by a medical illness resulting from a brain injury. I had no trouble believing that. If we changed words in books, decided what food was sinful, and then redefined that it wasn't, why wouldn't someone create a religious following based on what they wanted you to believe? It fell on deaf ears with my mother, though, as the teachings warn of others trying to disprove and test the believers' faith. I let it go, for it was apparent where Mother's loyalty was.

I didn't like my paternal grandmother when I was a child. I only met her a handful of times and found her gruff and difficult. She was from a German immigrant family that farmed the land. Many years later, I came across a photo where my great aunts were posing in an ostrich pen. One woman was astride the ostrich. I loved that photo as it showed the endurance, strength, and character of those women. That's a proud lineage to me. Working hard, no matter what you were doing, was a fact of life.

It was said my grandmother was institutionalized a few times for insanity. There was no diagnosis, only a story told like a joke. She met her third husband at the institution and fell in love. They took turns breaking each other out. I laughed but didn't understand how that worked. I pictured a barren war-torn building housed with metal cots for beds with bars on the windows. I could see them sneaking each other out of a janitor's window while the other stood guard. Sacrificing themselves, left to be forcibly restrained and given a sedative while being strapped to a bed.

Mom's family was different from Dad's. She grew up the youngest in a middle-class family. She got a post-secondary certificate to work in a medical office and then became a housewife. Mom had a guitar she kept in the closet. I never heard her play even though I asked. The instrument fascinated me. I'd sometimes sit in the closet playing with its strings when no one was looking. I was left with a pit of sadness that Mom wouldn't play for me. Just because she didn't know Godly music seemed a terrible waste. Her guitar grew old and dusty in the closet and eventually disappeared.

Mom had an infectious laugh and a playful attitude. Her sense of spirit was captivating. I know she loved my father more than anything. You could see it in her face, the way it glowed.

Maybe it was her newfound belief that helped her leave all she knew. She lost all common ties with her family and accepted a drastic lifestyle change. Maybe some of the changes were subtle and, therefore, unnoticeable. Perhaps it was like being in an abusive, destructive relationship, not knowing how bad it was until you leave. The thing about joining a segregated community is that any tradition or culture is also cut off. Family is forsaken for God. Holidays like Christmas turned into a lesson about how Jesus' birth was celebrated on a pagan day instead of spring like it should be.

Mom had the biggest smile. Her brother used to say, "Ann, close your mouth so we can see your face." We would have contests to see who could fit the most in their mouth. Be it plums, popcorn, or serving spoons, Mom and I always won.

Those first few years must have been dreadful for my mother. The diet was foreign, seventy percent raw, all homegrown, and homemade. Sometimes I'd hear her as she sat on the couch crying when she got a letter from her family. The loneliness was overwhelming for her. She, at the age of twenty-two, was the head of a full household of adult men and women. She cared for, cooked for, and had to be a Christian example to a group of people, many of whom were years older than she was. In those first years, she was discouraged from going to town with my father. They were, in fact, separated and taken in different vehicles when a trip to town was required. They worked, ate, and worshipped separately the first while until proven devout followers of the Lord.

Mother used to laugh when she told the story of the night my father came home late and scared the bejeezus out of her. She punched him right in the face when she woke to a clean-shaven stranger in her bed. Dad had a big full beard and was told the Lord wanted clean-shaven disciples. Unbeknownst to my mother, he shaved it. She missed his beard, but who can argue with God?

It wasn't until recently, when I was watching CNN's History of the 1960s and 70s, that I understood my dad's reasons for his deep devotion to this lifestyle. Back in the US, there were suicide bombings to protest the war in Vietnam. People who refused to fight were imprisoned. Then there was the army opening fire on unarmed university students at Kent State and Jackson State in May of 1970.

I understand why my father wanted to build a better life away from all that. The communities I lived in weren't extreme. The leaders didn't plan for the purple drink to be passed around. There were no leaders like David Koresh, who was excommunicated from the Seventh Day Adventist Church. However, bad seeds came to root in the utopian life that was being built.

There were three closely knit fledgling communities in the province tied together by marriages and faith. They all had the same religion, SDA, and all lived their life by the writings of EGW. They all had different goals. When Dad first joined the church, he moved to their far north community. Mom and Dad married there but left shortly after to live down south near the Kootenays in the health retreat commune I was born into.

I remember one vesper (vespers is a Friday and Saturday evening group meeting to worship the Lord), there was a slide show on how our commune was built. The families lived in tents while building the homes they now lived in. Soon there were over a dozen homes and outbuildings.

Over time they added a wood workshop, mechanic shop, office/church meeting room, cafeteria, dunnage mill, huge cold room, and produce processing rooms.

Chapter Two: Growing up in a Commune

By the age of thirteen, I'd lived in three different communes. They were all linked by religion, marriage, and a common goal: to live a self-sustaining lifestyle away from the mainstream world. Each different site had different sources of income. It was always something they excelled at and had an outside market for.

The people in these communes created a reality they believed to be the true way. To me, it was a life of double standards and dominance. It worked for most families. Unfortunately, it was also a haven for predators and troubled souls. I wasn't the only one who was left with lifelong scars from my time in these communities.

There was one man who came to live with us that stuck out. I'm not sure, but I had the distinct impression he was a recovering heroin addict. This young man took a jug of bleach and poured it over his head, creating the oddest-looking hair. White hair on top dripping down, orangey tinted beneath with dark brown roots and underlying hair. I was deeply intrigued and full of questions. My parents probably cringed inside, waiting to see how he'd answer my candid questions without giving me information they didn't want me to know. One time he walked all the way to town, over forty kilometres away. My parents said he broke into someone's house to eat their ice cream. Then he stole a rifle. He was picked up by the police walking down the street, waving the gun at nothing and everything. I don't think he did those things because he was hooked on ice cream.

I still remember going to get him at the courthouse. It was well over an hour's drive from our beautiful valley. All the signs, lights, buildings, and people had my eyes glued to the car window, staring. It was a rare thing to see a city and all that comes with it.

As we pulled up to the courthouse, I felt a frisson of fear even though I was with my father. It felt serious just knowing the police took people there to see the judge. A judge to me was like seeing Father when in trouble or God when being judged at the gates of Heaven. The building was stone-grey with wide steps leading up the front of the courthouse. The courtroom itself was a fancy version of a church with hard wooden pews separated by aisles down the middle. Instead of a pulpit at the front, there was a huge desk high above the pews overlooking the room. I sat very still and silent as I watched and listened to what was going on. I didn't dare bring any attention to myself in such a place. Soon enough, the bleached head of our man was brought through a door. I have no idea what my father said, but the judge agreed to hand the man over to us.

* * *

Our single-room schoolhouse turned church was in the middle of a pasture. We dodged cow pies to get into the building. The outhouse was out back for when we couldn't hold it until we got home. The hard, wooden pews were made from planks of rough wood. My imagination ran rampant when I learned about a child who fell into the outhouse and was stuck there for ages until someone else needed the facilities. Truth or myth, that thought kept my mind occupied during the long, dry sermons.

Church, morning and evening worship, vespers, and the choir were a big part of my life growing up. It was our social event of the week—our day of rest, dressing up, and visiting friends.

The church was a close-knit community with ties across the province, country, and neighbouring states. The news flowed frequently and was embellished via phone calls from one family to another who would share with the community they were in. Often prayers were a great way to learn who was having troubles of various kinds. Those troubled souls were mentioned by name. As a child, I learned to listen to conversations a little more when someone's name came up during prayer time at church.

I took the wrong kind of lessons from that growing up. These God-loving disciples were good Christians by praying for their fellow brothers and sisters. I witnessed judgement through prayer. We never took helpful action toward those struggling. I learned to judge people's actions, for it was done daily through prayer. It was judgement through those of God-like intent who talked about what you ate, wore, said, did, and didn't do.

* * *

I was almost five years old in 1982 when the phone lines were installed. We had a party line, so multiple homes shared the same phone line.

I sat and bounced in place, waiting and watching as each telephone pole came closer and closer up the mountainside. Imagine my excitement to lift the receiver and put my chubby little finger in the dial, turning it round all the way to the number I needed. I loved the clickity click sound as it returned to the start, ready for me to spin the next number. It was exciting to be able to call my best friend, who lived at the bottom of the mountain. Sometimes, I'd carefully lift the phone to see if someone else was on the party line. It was a great way to listen in on conversations that were none of my business.

Around the same time as we got phones, I had the fright of my little life. Autumn had coloured the valley in vibrant yellows and oranges. There were cool chilly nights where darkness enveloped the world by dinner time.

One day we were working in the barn when a thunderstorm rolled in. A lightning bolt hit the mountain across the valley and started a fire. The hillside was bone dry from the hot summer. It burst into flames spreading as only fire can. My father and the other men in the car needed to go investigate. Apparently, that could only be done by leaving me in the hay barn, alone at the end of the fields beside the dirt airstrip.

I watched the fire spread and was positive Dad wasn't returning. The fire monster surely had eaten him. The only logical thing for me to do was to get help. I decided to walk to the nearest home to find an adult. It was dark by then, and I didn't have a flashlight. There was barely a sliver of moonlight to guide my little feet along the lane toward the road. I passed various footpaths and tracks that led to fields or sheds. My eyes adjusted enough to see the large shapes looming out of the darkness. I was terrified a cougar or other creature would jump out to eat me or, worse, treat me like a toy.

I walked along with the fingers of fear wrapped around me. I had expressly disobeyed an order from my father.

That became scarier than being alone in the dark. I knew I shouldn't question my parents' knowledge or authority. They loved me and only wanted what was best for me. There I was, a disobedient child far from the barn, far from home, and too scared to knock on anyone's door.

Then I saw a golden light inviting me through the darkness. It was my friend's house. How could I explain why I was there? I couldn't very well say I had disobeyed. I didn't know what to do. I was too scared to walk back to the barn and to frightened to walk out of the darkness to the warmth beckoning from the porch.

I was too embarrassed to knock on their door, so I turned around. I headed back into the darkness and walked down their long, long driveway. I was cold, scared, unsure of myself, and worried about facing my father. I had no idea what to do or where to go. It was my first taste of insecurity, fear, and embarrassment. I was at a loss. As I walked in the darkness, my feet turned toward the mile-long walk home.

Finally, a car pulled up along beside me. It was my dad. He'd found me. I have no memory of the repercussions of my disobedience, only of my absolute joy at being found. Dad had determined the fire wasn't a threat to our home and came to find me. It felt like forever when it was probably only an hour at the most.

* * *

As a child, I loved snow. I loved everything about it. I loved falling backward to make an angel and the careful, gentle reverse crab moves to try to get up without leaving a mark. I loved getting on my knees and rolling my snowball into a giant chair or snowman. I'd lie back and watch the beautiful flakes swirl around me, landing on my nose, eyelashes, and tongue. As a child, every year, I'd beg, pray, and barter with God in hopes of having a big snowfall for my birthday.

It was such a thrill to jump off our roof into the big pile of snow left from clearing the snow off the roof and driveway. It seemed high but not too high. Dad was there to make sure I was fine and didn't mind me jumping from the roof. He made it fun, not scary. Until the time I landed on the side that was frozen solid.

It knocked the wind out of me. I still remember the slam of my weight as I came to an abrupt halt, the lack of oxygen in my lungs, and the dizzying far away feel until I got my breath back. After that, I stopped jumping off the roof.

Once, someone dug an igloo into a giant pile of snow. If you were stuck in a situation in the snow, you could burrow into the snow, make a seat to sleep on, and a ledge for a candle that should keep you warm enough not to freeze to death until the blizzard or situation passed. It was a neat hideaway, but none of us kids were allowed to play in it, just in case it collapsed.

The best thing about winter, of course, was the sledding. It was over a mile from our house to the bottom of the hill. Quite a sledding hill for a little girl. I could sled almost to the bottom of the mountain we lived on. Dad would wax the bobsled runners, and we'd be off. It was always a discussion on which way was best for speed and control. To lay down facing forward or sit up. I liked sitting so I could see better, as the snow didn't blow into my face and blind me. The setback was that steering with my feet was difficult. Part of the trouble may have been I was six and dressed as the abominable snowman in all my gear.

Once I got to the first corner, where our road began to slope downhill, I'd give a little run and flop down on my belly. The trick was to go fast enough that I didn't slow to a stop when the road flattened out. But not so fast that I'd slide off the road into the ditch on the corners. There were steep twists and turns followed by a couple of long straight stretches that flattened out before declining again into sharp corners. The speed needed to make it through most of the flat area was terrifying on the corners. I usually had to walk two spots no matter how bravely I sped around the corners.

One time Dad and I went together on the bobsled and tried to make it all the way to the bottom of the mountain. The last corner at the end before the nice long lazy stretch was a killer, no matter what mode of transportation was used. We wiped out badly, and I lost a good bit of facial skin that day. The bobsleds disappeared after that, and we used our toboggan for sledding.

Mom was working with some of the ladies at a house where the road met the main road through the valley. They were carding sheep's wool for quilting. Mom wasn't impressed to find me crying with Dad, my face dripping blood from a terrible ice rash due to wiping out on the suicide corner.

That winter, I got a particularly bad cold. My parents decided it was best to treat all of us with a hot and cold treatment, also known as hydrotherapy. Hot and cold treatments were our way to combat illness and other various maladies using a natural method. It forced your body to sweat out your germs. Doing hydrotherapy at home in the shower could be tricky. The shock of the change from hot to cold could cause you to faint, especially if lying in a bath and then standing for the cold shower. The water hits like pins and needles, slashing into your skin.

Our big metal tub was hauled into the house and placed next to our bathtub. The two tubs made an L shape. How they made the two fit was quite a feat. It would be a damn tight fit in any bathroom nowadays. The indoor bathtub was filled with water hot enough to turn your skin dark pink. The tin tub was filled with a mixture of snow and cold water, making a slush. The expectation was I'd soak in hot water before jumping into the cold tub of slush. Mom and Dad tried to coax me to do this.

They would sing: "Papa bear does it, Mama bear does it, now baby bear does it."

It didn't work. I had to be dragged, kicking and screaming, from the tub. They held me down in the slush for thirty seconds. There was no willing participation in this therapy. It must have been equally upsetting for them, as I wasn't forced to do it again.

* * *

I cringe when I recall a homemade Echinacea brew. Mom kept a mason jar in the fridge with the tea. The bottom half was sludge, not tea, and that's, of course, where she'd scoop from. I can still feel the wet grainy glop as I gagged it down. Echinacea was used to boost our immune system. Another favourite was goldenseal. The root was ground up and used in a poultice to treat infections. They both tasted horrible!

The common favourite natural remedy was charcoal. We used it to brush our teeth, for indigestion issues, and a host of other reasons. Our charcoal was a homemade crushed powder from burned birch trees. Dad would make batches of it in our fireplace. He would take a round canning pot filled with kindling cut from birch in our mountainside backyard. Then he would place the canner upside down in the hearth on a set of hot birch coals. It would smolder for ages until done, and then Dad would painstakingly collect all the coal and grind it up.

The son of one of the founding families of the commune was always thinking up new entrepreneurial ways to make money. The charcoal tablets were amongst his many ventures. I remember them because they were sweet. We didn't have candy, gum, or refined sugar in any form. His tablets were tasty to my young taste buds. Sadly, his charcoal pills didn't take off, and I was stuck still using charcoal in its raw state mixed with water.

* * *

One afternoon, I was so angry that my whole body shook with indignant rage. That was it. I was running away. I packed my little hard-shell suitcase with the necessities: underwear, extra wool socks, my doll Sally, and her extra outfit. We were set. I was going to walk to Grandma's house.

I walked down the dirt road pulling my suitcase in my little red wagon. I knew Grandma lived far away, and I'd have to make it to town. Once I found the town, I had to remember to only cross at a green light. I didn't know how many lights there were and what direction I should go in once I got to town. In fact, I couldn't remember how to get to town, but I knew it was a long way away. It finally dawned on me. I couldn't run away as I was too far away from everywhere.

I snuck back into our yard and under the front porch. I sat with my back against the wall and contemplated my next move. I couldn't very well just walk back in like I wasn't leaving anymore. I would never, even as a child, admit defeat.

I was a stubborn, proud, insecure little girl. So, there I sat in the dirt, hidden by the porch waiting for my parents to miss me. My tummy rumbled, and I was cold and bored. Obviously, my parents didn't love me, or they would have come looking for me. I crept back into my room, put away my warm wool socks, placed Sally back in her bed, and resumed my afternoon as though I had never had a tantrum and run away. I still have Sally, a little dirtier maybe, with a few scuffs and smudges, but not loved any less.

* * *

Our diet was the weirdest when I was a young child. It was somewhere between all the health hype going on at the time and the transition out of the hippy movement. I was always hungry, trying to sneak a taste of anything. Honey and salt were about the only thing I could get at that was edible between meals.

We ate a primarily raw diet. We made our own tofu from soybeans. I'd help make tofu by squeezing the pulp of soybeans in the cheesecloth, doing my best to get all the liquid out. Once that was done, we would place the pulp wrapped in cheesecloth in between bricks. The bricks helped shape the pulp into a square shape that would turn it into tofu in our fermenting container in the cold room. It was quite a process to make each block of tofu. The food we ate was aimed at giving us what we needed. Energy, protein, and the nutrients our bodies required. Juice fasting was common. One young man that lived with us did a long carrot juice diet and then added whole carrots. He ate so many the whites of his eyes and skin took on an orange-yellow tinge. He wanted to see in the dark because he believed carrots would promote better eyesight at night. I still giggle when I think of him.

One day, one of the new female residents came to Mom in tears. She was beside herself and believed she was poisoned and was dying. Mom tried to calm her and asked why she thought this. The woman sobbed that she was bleeding internally. When she went to the washroom, she filled the bowl with a blood-red colour.

Mom started laughing. We had eaten beets with our meals all week, and apparently, this woman had never eaten beets. When you eat that many beets, your poop turns a vibrant purple or blood-red colour, depending on how many you eat. We laughed over that story for years to come.

At first, our diet was yeast-free, therefore, unleavened bread. It was more like rocks. On one of our hikes, we stopped for lunch on a rocky outcropping ledge. I smashed and banged my biscuit against a rock repeatedly, trying to get a morsel loose enough to eat. It was impossible. I had to suck on the biscuit to try and eat it. Yeast was added to our diet not long after those fateful biscuits.

We made substitutes for food like steak and burgers. Our veggie burgers were good but nothing like today's. Back then, a burger was a seasoned oatmeal patty. A common meal replacement was gluten steaks. A dough made from gluten flour and whole wheat flour is then cut and shaped into steaks and baked in a pan of gravy and onions. The feel of the dough was great fun for my little hands to pull and shape into steaks. It was much more fun than playdough. It had an elastic texture, like pulling a fat worm for as long as it could go before breaking. The flavour was nothing like steak or gravy, but I didn't know better.

Our gravy was flour based with water, with no oil or grease to start a roué when making it. The seasoning came from Maggi, a dark brown liquid that was an approved flavour substitute.

We ate two meals a day: one at seven a.m. and one at one p.m. During our one-hour meal, we ate as much as we could possibly fit, and then we ate some more. Mom loved popcorn and would eat it for breakfast. If I asked for a glass of juice, I was told to wait as we didn't eat between meals. Having juice would be like having a piece of fruit. When I asked for a glass of juice with lunch, I was told I shouldn't drink juice with my meal as it would dilute my digestive juices. I was frustrated and confused. No matter the timing, I wasn't allowed a glass of juice.

Pepper and cayenne were deemed inappropriate spices to eat as they were seen as stimulants. Dad loved spicy food, so we had cayenne in our house anyway. A valuable lesson growing up: when it doesn't make sense, stay silent, smile, and do what you want anyway.

There were a host of items deemed unhealthy. Many I didn't realize were missing or substituted. We used flour or flax seeds as a thickening agent. Lemon juice instead of vinegar. No coffee or substitution for coffee. Tea was always herbal. Chocolate was replaced with carob. The issue with eating chocolate is that it has caffeine.

Then there was ice cream, especially orange ice cream. It wasn't real ice cream, but I was young and didn't know any better. To make it, we took peeled frozen bananas and put them through our juicer. The juicer made me think of an elephant. It had a large body with a snout that sent out the pulverized items we fed through the top opening. For a treat, Mom would add frozen orange juice concentrate making the orange flavour. It is one of the few things I still mildly enjoy today. However, I prefer it more like a smoothie for breakfast.

Homemade cheese sauce was okay, but once I met dairy cheese, I fell in love and never went back. The cheese I grew up on was a nut-based cream blended with peeled frozen red peppers for colour and flavour. Cashews were the preferred nut, but almonds were a cheaper version. Mayonnaise wasn't much different. Blended nut or tofu base with lemon juice and a hint of garlic.

A favourite treat of mine was blueberry cheesecake. It was my main birthday request growing up. Mom would thicken the blueberries with cornstarch. The tofu was blended and chilled to solidify on the granola-style bottom crust. It was a delicious favourite and a cherished treat.

The ladies decided to make some money with cooking classes and a cookbook. All the women combined their best recipes and created a cookbook of healthy natural food. They printed off the cover and the pages and got their hands on a spiral binding machine. Even my maternal grandma came to help. We had that cookbook for years. They didn't make them a second year, so they must not have had a huge customer base.

Crazy, right? I mean, who wouldn't want to make hamburgers out of porridge and steaks out of gluten flour?

Chapter Three: Living Off the Land

A big part of the lifestyle my parents were trying to live was to be self-sustaining or off-grid. We had gardens, fruit trees, beehives, kerosene lamps, and of course, wood heat. Mom and Dad built a greenhouse just before I turned four. I remember it clearly because I hurt myself and felt no one cared. I was so darn angry because my dad didn't stop what he was doing to worry and baby me immediately.

I was playing around the building as Dad and the others finished putting together the frame to attach the polycarbonate plastic. As I walked backwards, I stumbled over the stacked frames and sat back onto one with a heavy thud. I fell onto a large protruding nail that pierced my bottom, going rather deeply into my butt cheek. I cried and hollered as loudly as any hurt child could.

The reaction wasn't as I felt it should be. I wasn't grabbed, hugged, kissed better, and taken up to Mother at the house.

No, instead, I was forced to walk up the hill carrying the heavy utility ratchet jack. Crying and sobbing, I carried that fifteen-pound jack all the way back to the house. With each step, my anger and resentment mounted and formed this childhood memory.

For a week, I had to lie on the bathroom counter twice a

day while Mom washed the puncture wound with saltwater. It stung, it was embarrassing, and for a few years, I had a scar. Over time the scar faded, but the memory didn't.

* * *

I started helping in the garden at a young age. I have a photo of me as a toddler that I love. I was holding a giant potato I had helped plant that spring. Mom taught me how to plant potatoes. My feet were so tiny I'd take two, toe to heel steps, then plant a potato. Rows upon rows of them. That was my version of one potato, two potatoes.

We grew giant fields of corn, delicious, sweet, juicy corn. On the way back up the mountain for lunch, the others in the car would be husking the corn and tossing the husks out the window as we drove. The pot of water would be boiling and ready for the husked cobs when we arrived. I loved corn on the cob picked fresh from the garden.

Producing and preserving food was a very big part of our life. We grew and preserved enough fruits, vegetables, legumes, and grain to keep us through the winter with lots to spare. Most of it was grown in our orchards, vineyards, and huge personal gardens larger than most suburban yards. We froze, canned, and dried fruits and vegetables in four-digit numbers.

Our dehydrator was the size of a refrigerator. It had sliding screens, much like horizontal window screens layered as shelves from top to bottom. We even made fruit leather with it. We had two deep freezers, large army containers filled with beans we had grown, and a cold room filled top to bottom with single and double-quart mason jars of preserved food.

Our canner was something else entirely. It was a huge square metal tub on legs in the yard. A fire would burn beneath it for days on end during the canning season. It had wooden racks on the bottom to keep the glass jars from touching the bottom, thereby possibly shattering from the heat. It held forty double quart jars at a time.

When we moved north, we couldn't grow our fruit and had to order produce from our southern neighbours. We ordered and canned approximately ten thousand pounds of pears and apricots each and twenty thousand peaches, apples, and tomatoes. We even made our own applesauce. We didn't use vinegar, so to preserve the pickles, we used lemon juice, grape leaves, garlic, and dill. They tasted amazing to me then, as I knew no different.

We planted beans, corn, broccoli, Brussels sprouts, cabbage, carrots, and melons. You name it; we grew it. No sprays or pesticides were used. One particularly gross thing Mom used was cannibalism. Or at least that's what I called it. There were fat worms eating the Brussels sprouts, so Mom took a few cups of them and blended them with garlic and a few other ingredients. Then she poured them around each plant. Apparently, the worms wouldn't eat their own kind. Every time I used a blender, I thought of that. It wasn't until recently, when I got a margarita maker, that I began to have a slightly better feeling when I use a blender.

* * *

One taste I remember clearly once coming to the outside world was the taste of tin. I'd never eaten processed or canned food from a grocery store.

The first time I tried peaches from a can, I was so disappointed that I never bought them again. They didn't taste sweet like a peach. They were hard, almost with a crunch. When the sugary sweet taste of the glucose began to fade, the tang of tin long remained on my tongue.

When I had my children, I canned peaches to use for baby food as I didn't want to use the baby food sold in the local markets.

Chapter Four: Guns and Bears

My dad was a hands-on, make-it-himself, fix-it-himself kind of man. He made our bookshelf, knife handles, wooden utensils, kitchen table, and benches. He even made an A-frame feeder for our food scraps to feed the deer. You name it; he made it. Maybe it was because he had parents who grew up in the depression. Or maybe because he grew up in a group home or he put himself through university, earning two Bachelor of Arts degrees while eating potatoes to survive. Potatoes were the Ramen noodles of his era. Obviously, he was handy and thrifty. Mom was, too. Maybe a generational thing. It was often said that if my maternal grandfather couldn't fix it, then it was really broken.

Dad made the bed frame for their bed. It was a box that fit the mattress perfectly, situated on top of a smaller square base that doubled as a gun safe. He would lift the box to reveal the rifles below. He kept them in cases or wrapped them in woolen blankets. The ammunition was stored separately in army ammunition cases.

Dad loved guns. Over the years, his collection included a 30-30, a 30-aught-6, a semi-automatic 16 mm with clips, and various .22s. He finally added his prize piece, a 10 mm handgun. We didn't hunt, but target practice was acceptable. Dad owned guns as a gun lover and for safety.

I grew up with guns, and target practice was a fun family

occasion. When Dad's friends came to visit, they would pull out his newest toy and try it out in the backyard, a.k.a. forest. My favourite gun to spray bullets out of was the Mini 14. It was a semi-automatic with a clip of bullets that could be emptied in short order. Naturally, it wasn't for me to play with. After my turn, under close supervision, it was time for the men to talk and shoot, while I was sent off to sit on the swing.

I grew bored with pumping my legs on the rough-hewn board Dad had strung from the tree with a rough, itchy rope, and I hopped off. I began to twist the swing round and round until it raised itself as high as my little arms could reach.

Clinging to the seat, I folded my legs up beneath me to spin faster and faster as the ropes unwound themselves. My knees almost scraped the ground as the swing fully unspun and began to twist up the opposite way until it slowed to a stop. It didn't take many times until I was dizzy and sick to my stomach. Even though I was told not to, I spun the swing up as tight as I could and let it go to spin freely.

Without my weight on it, the swing began to haphazardly twist about, arching out this way and that. Next thing I knew, the corner of the swing seat caught me in my mouth, tearing out a chunk of my inner cheek.

I had interrupted Dad's visit over guns, disobeyed a direct order, and gotten myself hurt. Sympathy was limited. I was treated with a twice-daily compress of bread soaked in goldenseal, wrapped in cheesecloth, and stuffed into my cheek. Days of gagging on a morning and evening compress were the best punishment I could ever have had.

Goldenseal has many wonderful healing properties, including being a natural antibiotic. The taste, however, is difficult to describe other than absolutely horrible. The yellow powder looked harmless enough, but the lingering bitter taste stayed with me long after I healed.

At night I carefully cradled my cheek in my hand as I lay on my side. It was the only way to best avoid choking and swallowing the build-up of goldenseal saliva from the compress.

* * *

Guns were not just for collecting or target practice. We lived deep in the wilderness, putting ourselves in the animals' habitat. On occasion, they had to be shot for our protection. Our orchards, gardens, and natural compost methods tended to attract bears and deer. The deer weren't a problem. We had a feeder out by the garage for them, and they would regularly come to eat. When I was four years old, I held a carrot in my hand for a doe. But I just couldn't stay still. She got close a few times. It drove my parents nuts that I couldn't sit still for that last foot the deer had to come to take the carrot from my hand.

Bears were a different story altogether. One bear went so far as to sit in our cherry tree in front of the porch and make a feast of the ripe treats. They were attracted by the delicious smells of our fruit trees and rotting compost. Out of sheer laziness, some wouldn't leave and kept hanging around the community, which caused a safety concern.

When that happened, Dad would kill it. One time, when I was but a toddler, someone else took on that duty. They didn't wait to get a clean shot and only wounded the bear. They came to Dad to track it with them so they could put the bear out of its misery. They went to where the bear was shot. They found the trail and began to track it. They found its den empty, but the bear's trail didn't end there. In fact, it went up and back along the original trail. They found the bear dead against a tree a yard or so above the trail they'd come in on. The bear had circled back to attack them but bled out. Never underestimate an animal's intelligence. Especially a desperately wounded one.

Over the years, a good number of bears had to be shot. At first, Dad would try to tan the hides, but it was one of the few things he wasn't good at. He paid to have a few turned into pelts. He kept the claws and teeth. They would sit on the bookshelf in front of all the Ellen G White books. After we got dogs, we froze the haunches in the deep freeze for them.

There was one lady who opened the door of her A-frame house to a bear on its hind legs knocking at her door. Fortunately, she was able to slam the door shut in time to keep the bear out. She missed church that day as she couldn't safely leave. She couldn't call for help as our telephones weren't installed yet. She asked God for help, and, as she told it, he sent the bear away. Or so the story went at church.

I remember the year we shot our last bear. There were so many of them coming around that we ran out of room in the freezer. We had to discard the entire animal. I was almost thirteen at the time, and it sticks in my memory better than any other bear that we shot.

Dad had recently traded a bearskin for a new 30-06 rifle. It was a powerful rifle, and he was excited to own it. I was told it apparently had quite a kick. This bear came up through our gardens and climbed up into my treehouse. There wasn't anything for him to do but leave the supper table and shoot the bear. It died less than four hundred metres from our front door. A few of the boys and my father went to skin it. I went too, of course. I was adept at skinning by then. The exit wound was impressive. I was able to stick my hand in it almost all the way up to my elbow. This made one of the boys vomit, which I loved. Since the freezer was full, we hooked a chain from the back of the Land Rover to the skinned carcass to drag it to the river at the edge of the acreage.

There the wild animals could feed on it so the meat wouldn't go to waste.

The images of that animal being dragged behind the Rover will always be with me. The flesh, tendons, and veins filled with gravel and dirt as the carcass twisted and rolled. Watching it was disturbing, to say the least. I turned my head and closed my eyes. I didn't want to see it or show any weakness.

* * *

I grew up to be prepared for anything. My first practical gift was the Swiss army knife that Dad gave me when I was five.

He got an engraving machine, and soon everything was engraved, including my knife. I learned to whittle sticks into sharp pointy spears for roasting tofu hot dogs.

I got a hatchet for cutting down little trees or limbs to whittle with my handy knife when I was about six. I received the bow and arrow set Dad made for me about the same year as the hatchet.

Then when I was eight, I was given the ultimate gift. A wood stock single shot .22 rifle. I practised and practised getting my aim sure, my hand steady. My brother still has that rifle. For all we have been through over the decades, somehow, my beloved rifle is still in the family.

It is funny to me how much is deemed unsafe for children now compared to what was acceptable back then. Survival of the fittest, I suppose. Maybe it was those with common sense, the quickest, that made it.

All the same, we didn't grow up to be softies. We didn't grow up to be whiners because we didn't have the job or outfit or boyfriend or app that we wanted. We worked and played and got hurt and kept going, laughing about it later.

Chapter Five: Our Holidays

We camped during the holidays for as long as I can remember. Whether it was the middle of winter or the peak of the summer, it didn't matter the season or reason: we camped. In the early years, Dad set up a canvas tent and heated it with a wood stove he made. As the years went by, he preferred building large teepees to live in. I have photos of Mom and me in front of various shelters we camped in over the years. It's like I was born camping. My parents had a funny story that probably never felt entirely funny to them.

I was a winter baby, and by the time my first winter came around, they were ready for a big camping trip. Dad had Macgyvered a backpack frame to have ropes attached to pull a sled. Dad strapped on the frame and pulled the sled with me nestled in with the gear. The sled was loaded, snowshoes were strapped on, and they set off.

When they arrived at the destination, I wasn't in the sled. I can only imagine the panic they felt. I'd slipped off the sled half an hour back. The slide off the sled didn't wake me. I never made a peep. I was still sound asleep when they found me lying in the snow.

Fear imprints a memory like nothing else. There was one canoe camping trip that stuck in my mind even though I was but a toddler. We lived near a beautiful lake with emerald-green water.

The lake wasn't filled with speed boats or tourists. There weren't loud, raucous groups filling the campground.

On this camping trip, my parents loaded up the canoe with our supplies and paddled across the lake to camp. It was completely remote and away from everyone. The perfect spot to camp for a weekend together.

On our way back, heavy storm clouds appeared. A wind whipped up the lake, creating large waves. The canoe sat heavy in the lake, loaded with all our gear. I was in the middle of the canoe, with panic building up inside of me. I was afraid of drowning, of the canoe tipping us all into the water. Fear of dying, of my beloved parents dying, frightened me to tears. I was told not to move. They told me to stay still, stop fussing, and not tip the canoe.

I can still hear Dad hollering at Mom, "Paddle, paddle harder." I didn't know how to swim yet. How would I survive if we capsized? My mind raced, trying to deal with the terrifying situation.

We made it across. We didn't flip. I didn't drown or lose a parent that day. My fear of deep water was created on that trip. But I also learned things will work out even if you don't know it yet. That no matter the situation, stay calm and keep paddling, for you never know when the waves will cease, and tranquillity will return.

That fall, Dad wanted to go back there. I flat-out refused. No bribery or force of will could make me go unless they picked up my rigid terrified body and forced me. There was no way I was facing death to cross that lake.

I won out, and it became a guy's trip with Dad and some friends. He wanted to harvest branches from the yew trees that grew in abundance there, as it was great for making quality, lasting bows. The wood is denser, storing energy better, and is pliable for narrow bows. I had a wonderful bow and arrow set made from the coveted yew wood across that lake. I loved that bow and arrow set. I took it everywhere with me. I shot at all sorts of targets, from rusted-out cars to bales of hay. Until I got a rifle, then the bow and arrow were for play. I was forced to leave that bow and arrow when we moved the second time. I was angry and heartbroken that I couldn't take it. I hid it in an old, abandoned car with all the other wrecks. I vowed to return for it. Years later, when I did, it was long gone.

* * *

Dad built a camper for the back of the International pickup. It was a log camper, much like a log cabin. It wasn't as heavy as that, or it would have cost an arm and a leg to travel with. I remember that camper because of two scary memories.

The first time was when I woke to it rocking and bouncing down the road with me alone in the back. It was dark. So dark I could feel it. There weren't any windows to provide even a sliver of light. I banged on the walls. I screamed and cried to no avail.

When they finally stopped to check on me, I was a bundle of angry, traumatized nerves. I never wanted to be alone in the camper again after that.

The second time, I was in that same camper with my parents. We were all awakened by a rocking, scratching racket coming from beneath the carriage.

We were parked in the base parking lot of a national park. We were set to head out early in the morning. There were no windows, and even through the door of the camper, we couldn't see if it was a bear, wolverine, raccoon, or porcupine attacking the truck.

Dad grabbed his light and axe and went to investigate before the truck was destroyed, or eaten, from the sounds of it. As luck would have it, it was only a naughty porcupine trying to eat the wiring.

* * *

When I was five, we went to Yellowstone Park for a week-long hike. On the truck dash, we had one full roll of toilet paper and half a roll. I mentioned to Dad we should bring the full roll of TP on our hike. Dad said no. The half a roll would suffice for our weeklong hike, and that was that. The full roll was left in the truck.

It quickly became obvious the TP wasn't going to last the week. We were rationed to two pieces for the women and three for Dad. And that was only for number two. I remember being so angry I only got two squares. I made do with moss and leaves and complained about fairness. Dad made of point of reminding me that life wasn't fair. I took it as a lesson for mothers: women put themselves after others' needs. It was the Christian way, a mother's way. You give the shirt off your back to those in need. It was around then that I learned the harmful habit of putting myself second to men.

We took two days to hike in, sleeping at a campsite along the river the first night. On the second day, we arrived at the cabin where we would stay for the week. The cabin was a multi-room building to be shared by those staying. It had basic bed frames, bunk-bed style, and a wood stove for heat and cooking. A long table with benches was in the main common room. From there, we took day hikes from the cabin, coming back every night for supper. It was beautiful beyond words, the thick, lush forest with moss throughout and wildflowers in various stages of bloom. The late spring weather was already showing changes for summer. The mountains were coming alive with colour as the leaves, tiny buds, and wildflowers added to the incredible landscape. Only a nature lover can understand the beauty of being surrounded by wild nature.

One day, we headed out for a day hike. Our daypacks were filled with water bottles and trail mix. Mom and Dad were armed with whistles around their necks. The map was in Dad's back pocket. Somewhere along the way, it became apparent we were lost. Dad said we weren't lost. He just didn't know where we were on the map. The trail turned into a goat path. I turned into a whiny kid, done with the day's adventure. Mom was frustrated that we were truly lost in the middle of nowhere. Dad remained silent and strong, leading the way, refusing to admit to being lost. We followed the narrow goat path along the side of the rocky mountain, high above the treeline. Suddenly, we come to a dead stop. Below us, maybe five hundred metres, was a grizzly digging up roots to eat.

Now a grizzly isn't a cuddly stuffed bear or a cute, playful pet. They are massive and weigh between seven and seventeen hundred pounds depending on sex and age. They are marked by humped shoulders, with an elevated forehead and short round ears. I have always found bears to be adorable. But not that day. That day I was terrified. The unspoken knowledge was we had to be careful, or there would be horrible consequences.

Where we were on the map didn't matter anymore. We were way too close to a predator with no means to protect ourselves. Mom set to blowing her whistle at frequent intervals. Dad led a brisk pace around the mountain so we could get ahead and hopefully down before the grizzly. Dad suddenly went down on his knee. The toe of his boot caught on a sharp rock and ripped from the inside centre all the way around to the outer side. It was hanging on by a thin strip of leather. He tied it with a cord the best he could, and we set off with care.

We made it around the mountainside and started our descent toward a creek. Dad spotted a trail to lead us back to the cabin. We just had to make it down the side of the mountain and across the creek to the trail before the grizzly decided it was tired of roots and wanted to eat us. As we picked our way down the steep rocky incline, we saw large holes dug into the ground by the bear. To me, they were ginormous, bigger than Mom's huge stainless steel mixing bowls. We were in the middle of his territory. It was terrifying.

I felt like I had to pee every ten minutes, but I couldn't go when I tried. As I was squatting, trying to pee yet again, I asked how come I had to go but couldn't. Dad explained fear made me feel like I had to pee. After that, I didn't ask for potty breaks. I kept moving toward safety.

We didn't see the bear when we went around the side of the mountain, but our urgency didn't lessen. We got down to the valley floor and found a fallen tree that we used as a bridge across the stream. Once across, we found a trail, a real path used by hikers, not the animal trails we were following.

When we made it across the stream, we saw fresh wolverine tracks in the snow. Wolverines were even more dangerous than bears, according to Dad. There was no chance that playing dead would save you. There are few documented attacks of wolverines on people; however, their razor-sharp teeth, their agility, and their ability to run twenty-four kilometres an hour were a concern. They could cause serious damage, more than any other predator.

Thankfully, aside from the fresh tracks, there was no sign of the creature.

After a few miles, we came to a clearing with a large boulder in the centre. It was there we finally stopped. We sat back-to-back, keeping watch on the forest. Even though we hadn't been followed by either animal, it was best to keep constant watch instead of being unsuspecting meals.

We ate our lunch of dried nuts and berries before heading

the rest of the way back to our home base.

The following day the ranger came to check on all of us. A few more outdoor enthusiasts had arrived as well. The ranger wanted to make sure we all knew the dangers and precautions to be adhered to while staying at the park. We told him about the harrowing hike we'd had the day before.

He was glad we made it out without harm and advised more care in future adventures. The ranger explained that grizzly bears could charge and attack you before you have time to cock your rifle. The severity of his tone and admonitions stayed with me for life.

Chapter Six: A Baby Brother

Mom couldn't conceive after me. She had a couple of miscarriages which I believe was because of the diet or lack thereof. Two meals a day, seventy percent raw diet, one hundred percent vegan is not conducive to a healthy weight.

In the first eight years or so, the diet was legumes, homegrown produce, preserved fruits, nuts, and imitation meat meals. A typical breakfast would be toast, homemade granola with home-canned fruit, and porridge or cream of wheat on occasion. Lunch would be beans and rice, gluten steaks in gravy with potatoes and onions, hearty vegetable chilli with homemade whole wheat bread, or baked vegetables and squash with a sprinkle of brown sugar.

At lunch, we would eat as much as we could fit and then sit awhile to see if we could fit any more in, for there wouldn't be another meal until the following morning. If they had added another meal to the day, it might have helped. Hours of physical labour in the outdoors on a daily basis burns more calories than you can consume in two meals a day on that kind of diet. Photos of my mother before joining the commune and a few years after show a dramatic change in her appearance. Fast forward twenty years, and it gives healthy living an entirely different twist.

My parents investigated adoption and placed their names

on the waiting list. One day they got the call they'd been waiting for. It wasn't from the adoption agency, though. It was from Dad's brother.

They had neighbours going through a bitter divorce, and the wife was pregnant. She was only willing to keep the baby if it was a girl. Otherwise, she was giving it up for adoption. Now that made no sense.

Wouldn't the father have something to say about that? I didn't understand how she could be so cold. Mom and Dad didn't have an answer for me other than she didn't have God in her heart. I had a strong dislike for a woman who would dare treat her unborn child in that way. It gave me a fierce feeling of love and protection for this unborn child. I wanted to take away the hurt that I felt for this potential new sibling of mine.

My parents were excited and nervous about the process of being approved. They practised with me what to say or not to say to the lady that came to do home visits. It was all very serious and nerve-wracking, sitting like a proper young lady with a straight back, not fidgeting on the couch while she asked questions. I couldn't get the answers wrong, or I might not get a baby brother. I had to carefully listen and answer clearly with what she wanted to hear. I must have done it correctly, for a few months later, Mom and Dad left to bring home my baby brother, Daniel.

Grandma, Dad's mom, was staying with me to babysit while they were gone. I was surprised that Mom and Dad chose to have her stay and watch me since she hadn't raised her own children for various reasons.

To Mom and Dad, her past was water under the bridge. They believed in forgive and forget and that people could change.

I hated her. Mom would say I shouldn't even think the word hate, for it's too strong to use. I couldn't help it; she was awful. I don't know why I thought she was awful. I only met her a handful of times. I felt a strong dislike, the feeling of wanting to be anywhere but near her, the wish that she'd disappear.

I was excited when they left to get my baby brother. This was way better than having any kind of pet. I wanted a little brother or sister to play with. Aside from Bible class before church, the kids of the community didn't get to spend much time together. There wasn't preschool, playdates, or playing in the streets. We lived too far apart, and our parents were busy scraping a living off the land. Sometimes parents took turns hosting other kids. A baby brother or sister, though, was the best thing ever.

Mom and Dad came home with a swaddled bundle. Daniel had white skin, white hair, and big blue eyes. At seven pounds, this baby brother wasn't quite what I had in mind. He cried, slept, pooped, and ate. That was it. There was no playing because he was so small. The glow wore off as the reality of an infant became clear.

Mom nursed him as though he was her own. She used an IV bag with a tiny tube so that while he nursed, he got milk. She had heard that nursing might bring on real breastmilk. She wanted a strong bond between them and believed the first things babies could see were a mother's face while nursing. Apparently, it's the perfect distance for infants to be able to focus.

We knew we had to wait a full year before the adoption would be permanent. I watched my mom care for baby Daniel every day. She was so dedicated and diligent with his care. She was a great role model for me in caring for others as I grew older. I lost interest in him as the reality of a baby's needs became apparent, and I spent more time with Dad.

A year after they brought my baby brother home, we got the phone call. The call that would change our lives forever with whatever decision was made. It was the call that told us he would be able to stay. The sense of relief was euphoric. The joy was unlike any other I had witnessed or experienced. The adoption process was final. The biological parents hadn't changed their minds and didn't want him back. With a collective sigh of relief, we let the joyful moment envelop us.

Chapter Seven: Life in a New Community

In the summer of 1985, when I was seven years old and a few months after we got Daniel, Mom and Dad sat me down to share some big news. We were moving to a different community. I took that as well as any child would. I cried over leaving my friends and expressed my fear that I didn't have anyone to play with. I let my anger spill out in a torrent of worries.

Then I let my curiosity out with a tirade of questions. Where would we live? Were there any kids my age there? I had a baby brother now, but with Daniel only a few months old, it was still much like being an only child. I'd be starting over not knowing anyone or having any friends. I was heartbroken to leave my best friend, a little girl who lived farther down the hill. Whenever we were together, we shared our thoughts and dreams. Friends weren't a dime a dozen when you lived so far off the beaten path and didn't attend school.

We had to leave our dog, Kitimat, but she and I weren't that close. She wasn't a cuddly blue heeler. Dad said we couldn't take her because she tended to snap and potentially bite people, thanks to being teased as a pup by some of the adults. I was promised a new puppy, and that made me feel better.

We moved to the hottest part of our province to a commune based on helping and teaching teenagers. It was a self-supporting

Christian boarding school. This was more Dad's calling than the health retreat I had spent the last seven years in. Instead of saying the health-conscious community wasn't what Dad had a passion for, it was said that the Lord told him to go and use his skills elsewhere. It's all in how you portray it.

I remember the day we arrived. We crested the rise in the highway, and I saw fields laid out on either side. Ginseng and desert farmland to the left and orchards to the right. There were two roads to access the main part of the farm that lay between the highway and the river. Houses were scattered across the sloping hill a least a half kilometre apart.

Orchards of peach, apricot, plum, and apple trees were interspersed between the houses. Large fields spanned out below with a drop to yet another set of fields. The gravel roads were like a bumpy washboard year-round unless it was the short rainy season, at which point, it was mud.

The farms' outlay haunted my dreams for years. The man-made pond below the mechanic shop. The different fields stretched out with corn, melons, tomatoes, and ginseng. The ginseng was a fun crop for me. It was a fabulous investment for the community. The black tarp material with sprinklers interspersed in a square pattern had to be regularly checked.

I'd occasionally hitch a ride with the field foreman on the three-wheeler to check the fields. He would let me run on the top canvas bouncing and rolling while he checked the grounds. I loved it. On occasion, the sprinklers would come on, and I'd squeal with delight. It was the closest thing to a trampoline I ever had.

Our new home was a large three-storey with a view that spanned most of the valley on either side. Beautiful mountains rose high above us across the river.

We had several female teenagers living upstairs. Two to five teenage girls to a room shared between four bedrooms. The teenagers were students. The new community we moved to was a Christian boarding school for grades nine to twelve.

The basement suite was home to another family who had just moved from the other side of the country. The parents and their two teen daughters were a great fit with the community. They shared the same religious beliefs and wished to live off the land, creating a life and a community away from the corrupt world.

Most of the houses were large to enable the host family's lifestyle. Quite often, the basement was for a new or small family. Generally, it functioned like a separate home. The main floor was for the host family, with the upper floor for students. Some families took the girls, others the boys. They ate with us, shared rooms, had a shared bathroom, and overall were treated as a part of the family.

That move marked many changes. Before we moved, the overall focus was health and geared toward adults. A healthy lifestyle through meals, treatments, vitamins, exercise, and daily habits.

This new place was an academic boarding school for high school students from across the continent and as far away as Japan and the Northwest Territories. The draw to the school varied depending on the family. Some families were of the same religious faith and zeal. The school was the perfect place to send their children, and the children wanted to attend. For other families, it was a place to send their problem kids. They had given them an ultimatum. Attend the Christian boarding school, join the army, or be on the streets. They used the school as a last resort with the threat of abandonment if they didn't attend.

There were less than two dozen students, plus staff members and their children, when we arrived. Within two years of our arrival, the number of students doubled. Dad's charismatic personality drew attendance like no other staff member could.

This was good news as there were bills to be paid for the land, electricity, and all the other amenities of daily life. This wasn't an off-the-grid farm without power, heat, or telephones.

There were about a dozen homes on the land. Almost half of them were large enough to house students living with the family as family members. We called this *home heading*. The parents of the family were the head of the home, and the students were welcomed into the family home. The world maybe would describe it as host families. I called it *the world*, as the commune ensured there was an invisible wall preventing me from knowing of worldly things. Students went to homes based on gender. There was an annual fee, tuition of a sort, of four thousand dollars to attend the academy, broken down to a monthly bill. The tuition was partially worked off by labour, and labour wasn't optional.

The industries required employees to process the saleable products, the student labour was essential to run them. The students provided the needed labour and income to keep the farm running. If some students couldn't or wouldn't go home during the summer, Christmas, or spring break, they could stay with their host family. They could work off even more of their tuition that way. Staying over the holiday season was optional. It was taken only by a select few.

There was a hierarchy within the community with a democratic ideal behind it. There was a president, a principal, and board members. My dad held the position of principal, which is why we moved there. The lifestyle rules set out for the commune, like our past home, were based upon the interpretation of Ellen G. White's book and the board's vote for implementing it into everyday life. What staff did behind closed doors and when off the campus was very much like the Las Vegas slogan: what happens outside the commune stays outside the commune.

Dad's role in the new community was as principal and as

a teacher. He taught chemistry, physics, and algebra. There was an extra course that was added to the roster—survival camping.

Dad created his own curriculum for the class and included three camping trips to go with the course. He taught the students about edible plants, various shelters to build, and how to survive camping in the winter with only ten items to help you. As a survival enthusiast and nature lover, Dad was in his element teaching this class.

During the day, I'd explore the handful of outbuildings, looking for entertainment. The mechanic shop situated above the pond held little interest for me. A small woodwork shop, more of a hobby shop, was useful for making picture frames. There was a musty run-down granary filled with mice that I liked to try and catch. I liked playing hide and seek in the barn. It was usually filled with hay bales which would be sold to nearby farmers. Tunnelling between the bales was great fun, although the subsequent red, itchy rash I got afterward became a strong deterrent.

There was a building for cleaning and packaging produce that was grown and sold. It had a large cold room, too. I knew to stay away from there as I didn't like how cold my hands got when I helped sort the freshly washed carrots.

The main produce grown were tomatoes, watermelons, carrots, and corn. The orchards were more for the families' winter preserves, as was the small vineyard. Each family had a large section of land to plant and tend as their personal garden for their food. Mom would always say that we may be living like paupers, but we ate like kings and queens.

Once settled into our new community, I wandered the new farm looking for things to do. I'd run like a gazelle through the orchards, grabbing an apple to munch as I went. I'd lie under the grapevines rolling the velvet-feeling leaves in my fingers. I wished the grapes were juicy and sweet instead of sour green balls teasing me. I explored the fields, climbed trees, dug holes, and did whatever I could to ease my boredom.

A little five-year-old boy, Michael, lived down the lane. He was my sole playmate, my one friend. His mother trusted me to look after him and let us play in the yard, sometimes even going farther down the lane toward my house. We played in the dirt, dug holes that we pretended were forts and drove the mini semi and trailer with the space station rocket I was given. I dragged Michael up and down the lane in the wagon. We talked and laughed and climbed trees as youngsters do. Michael's mother's faith in me was a priceless gift. There was another family with two children, a boy and a girl, around my age, but they wouldn't let me play with them. I didn't understand how a family could judge me as unworthy of being friends with their children when they didn't know me. I didn't know they kept their children separate from everyone, young or old.

Michael and I dug a cave in the clay hillside. We made little progress before it was deemed not safe in case the hill gave away. We were told the sand could bury us alive. We had plenty of other things to do. We played with matchbox cars in the dirt, but they were too small, and the dirt just wrecked them.

Then I was given a giant innertube from some large piece of farm equipment. I loved it! You could fit up to four kids jumping on it at once. It was like a giant donut-shaped rubber balloon. It provided hours of fun to bounce and jump. The numerous slips, falls, and failed landings were half the fun until some lasting injuries, a cracked tailbone and sprained wrists, deterred me from having more fun on the innertube.

* * *

True to Dad's word, he got me a puppy when we moved.

She was a beautiful grey wolf-coloured malamute husky. We named her Kitimat, the same as our first dog. To supplement the small stipend Dad earned, he decided to breed husky pups and sell them. He found Panda, a stud dog, for sale. He had never been anywhere but his kennel until we got him. It was beautiful watching a kenneled dog realize he has a home and a family. He had a yard to live in, a companion with four legs, and a chubby little girl who just wanted to hug and squeeze and love him. You could feel his joy and see it in his expression.

The dog would have a litter once a year. They were papered pedigree malamute huskies. I loved to snuggle with the puppies. I was the only one Kitimat would allow to touch and hold her pups. I could lie with them, and they would crawl all over me, licking and nibbling my ears, hair, and face as I squealed with laughter. When I fed them porridge mixed with seasoning, I'd sneak some, too, because it tasted so good. We never kept a pup even though we loved them so much. I knew this and knew better than to fuss when they left for their new homes.

On particularly lonely days, I'd lie with the dogs in their barrels that doubled as dog houses. I talked to them while I ran my fingers through their thick fur.

When I was ten, we traded one set of pups for two mountain bikes. One for Dad and one for me. I was overjoyed. It marked a new kind of freedom for me. I'd fly down the road, hair streaming behind me. I learned how to navigate the washboard roads, only tumbling head over handlebars a time or two. I tucked my skirt into my waistband so that it wouldn't catch in the chain.

With the newfound income from the pups, we went to the dentist. I'm not sure what brought on that initial visit. I had never been before and was terrified. The dental exam showed my teeth were full of cavities. My terror was well-earned. I had so many cavities that I had to go see the dentist every second Friday for months. Needles upon needles in my gums and the roof of my mouth. Pulling, prodding, and grinding away at my teeth while my mouth was locked open with an evil metal clamp and plastic barrier. As it turned out, charcoal and unmonitored teeth brushing wasn't the best way to go.

I loved animals of all kinds but had to be content with having dogs and a cat. I went through over half a dozen cats that first year living at the new commune. One kitten fell asleep on the car tire and was run over. Another was deaf. The plough disks ran her over, and she became fertilizer for the fields.

I had a hard time believing that's how she died. Wouldn't a deaf cat feel the ground vibrate as the tractor neared? The president's wife, Ella, claimed our cat was getting into the main market garden building, contaminating the carrots. She made Dad put down three more cats because she said they sprayed in her house.

When Ella's own cat was caught doing exactly what she had claimed Snowball, Boots, and TomTom had done, I was ecstatic with vengeful joy. Now her cat would be put down. Dad said I could be the one to put a bullet in its head.

I swung the cat by the slip knot around its neck over the edge of a cliff. Then, I hardened my heart as my finger pulled the trigger on my little twenty-two. Its limp body rolled down the hillside. It left a cold spot in my belly. I no longer felt joy, only sadness over the act of revenge. Unable to acknowledge how sad I felt, I locked those emotions away.

* * *

Our communities had access to small airstrips. In 1987, I was enamoured with flights in small planes. One memory of flying was for a funeral. I begged and pleaded with my parents to let me go to the service. They made me promise to behave and be very good. I was vibrating with excitement at seeing my old home and friends. We took a small plane back to our old commune. The awe and surprise at all the small lakes scattered below during our short flight made me love being up high looking at our amazing world. It took less than an hour to fly to the cool mountain range I had first lived in.

One moment in time stands out above all else. The reason behind our visit in the first place. Someone had died. It was a lost battle with tongue and throat cancer. She was resting in a home that was halfway between my old house at the highest end of the lane and the valley below.

I knew to walk quietly, not making a sound as I tiptoed up the stairs. I crept down the hall to her room. The pilot and the lady of the house were there, talking about the deceased. I stayed unseen outside the door. I peeked in through the narrow slit between the door and the wall. I listened as her body and death were discussed. Her burial wouldn't be for a couple of days. He was concerned she'd suffer from lockjaw in rigor mortis. The lady of the house took a pair of pantyhose and tied them around her head and jaw to prevent lockjaw. Thus, ensuring a proper facial expression for the open casket. I'll never forget the elderly woman lying there, her paper-white skin, and the pantyhose tied in a bow on her head.

The feeling of loss was tempered by my joy of seeing my friend again. I missed her terribly and wished she'd written to me. Being able to visit was a short but sweet reprieve from my loneliness at our new home. All too soon, the trip was over, and we were flying home.

* * *

After the first year at the new commune, we were moved to a smaller home close to the main office building. With that move came a change in the gender and number of teenagers living in our home. The house only had two small rooms for students, so our limit would be four. My parents decided to take boys instead of girls.

Dad had a passion for helping the downtrodden boys. I'm sure they reminded him of his younger self. He gave them the guidance he wished he'd received. The more energetic, troublesome boys ended up in our home.

Dad always liked to give a second chance to those who were misunderstood or mislabeled. He took the angry ones, the hurt ones, the ones others would write off. He knew what it was to have a hard life. To have the feelings they did. He wanted to help. He always rooted for the underdog and stuck up for the runts of the pack. Those boys, the young men living in our home as a part of our family, were my brothers. They came and went, changing from year to year, but they were my brothers. I was the annoying principal's daughter they had to put up with.

Another reason we moved to a smaller home was that mom was pregnant. Her health had improved with the move to the new community. Maybe it was because we now ate a better diet or because she had Daniel. There's an old wives' tale that women often conceive after adopting a baby. So, after years of failed attempts and two miscarriages, Mom had a baby girl. I had less excitement about Damara's birth now that I knew what having a baby brother or sister entailed. There was diaper duty for two now.

I'd constantly pop into the office to check the mail and visit with the ladies working there. One time a man was in the office. He didn't live in our commune. He was part of the family that had investments and relations at all three. He was quite taken with my full smile and twinkling eyes. He handed me a one-hundred-dollar bill "for my smile," he said.

At first, my parents were confused about how I got a hundred-dollar bill. They called me a liar. They let me keep it after they talked to the man. I also had to pay tithe and split it equally with my two siblings. I didn't care that I had to share. I had a hundred-dollar smile.

The following year, I got better at running wild with the other kids in the youth church group. I wasn't allowed to go on sleepovers. My parents didn't believe sleepovers were acceptable, and no reason was given to me. I just wasn't allowed. Over time, I began to really love this one family. They lived farther down the river on a large property that had originally been the home of the commune I was being raised in. Differences in religious interpretation and lifestyle caused the change of location. Thankfully for me, it didn't stop them from attending our church. They had two girls, and I fit right in the middle.

* * *

Our days were divided in half by two grades. Half the students worked in the morning while the other half studied in the classroom. After lunch, the groups traded places. It was a brilliant idea, really. It kept the farm running. The labour went toward their fees, and it saved the school from paying out wages. The students gained a diploma and hours of work experience in many different fields.

The aspect of working half the day and only sitting in a classroom the other half is one thing I still strongly agree with. It's one of the things I wish more schools would adopt. It would be easy to medicate kids, labelling energy as an issue. Sometimes what would be helpful would be to run about and burn off all that excess steam. Once that is gone, it's much easier to sit and dissect a sentence searching for the nouns, verbs, and adjectives. Math is easier to concentrate on when your wiggles are long gone.

One year was particularly memorable for playing practical jokes. We were told it was unchristian to be silly and frivolous. We should be serious and solemn for the Lord all the time.

Dad wasn't of that personality, and it leaked through the year we had students enrolled from Japan. They were young teens and spoke a little English. One student was asked to mow the orchard. He was the youngest, only fourteen. His broken English was good enough for communication. He took the push mower and began mowing the orchard. Four hours later, when we all were seated at the table for lunch, he commented that it would grow back by the time he finished. We laughed and laughed, for he didn't realize he was to use the tractor and trailer mower, not the hand mower. Dad had let him use that push mower all morning.

One student's father taught my dad how to make gunpowder. He would make little batches of it in the basement. Dad would set up little triggered explosions using the gunpowder. He would fill a film container with the explosive and hide it in the driveway. Then he would tie the trigger string across the path and when an unsuspecting student walked up the path to our door— BANG! The sound of a gunshot terrified the living daylights out of the poor bastard.

Dad was admonished for his fun by another commune member, so those pranks didn't last long. Pranks and fun are not the solemn Christian way. It was a constant battle as we were normally the outgoing, infectious, laughter-loving type.

Friday and Saturday afternoons were for family walks. In the summer, we would go on family walks down the gully to the Fraser River. It's the longest river in British Columbia and starts at the western side of the Rocky Mountains and ends near

Vancouver, BC.

I loved going to the river. The dogs would run and splash. I'd take off my socks and shoes to feel the sand. I love the cool, soft squish of the fine granules between my toes and the imprint of my feet filling with water. I loved the sound of the water rushing by and the cool air bathing my hot skin.

Walking back from the river, we often explored the old run-down log homes, trails, caves, and all the nooks and crannies we could find. The roofs on many of the abandoned log cabins were caved in. Some still had newspapers tacked to the walls. There was little to scavenge as the cabins were picked clean over the years. One time we lit a fire and roasted a cactus to eat. It was of a texture like a kiwi, soft wet, and flavourless. It was good enough if one was thirsty or hungry.

We had such a good laugh on one of our walks. Panda was running up ahead, playing with Kitimat, when suddenly Kitimat stopped and dropped back between him and us.

The dogs had startled a young black bear. We watched as Panda ran alongside it. He was all excited about making a new friend as he wasn't used to meeting wild animals. He didn't realize this new friend was the enemy.

I don't know if it was the scent or because of Kitimat's reaction, but he clued in rather quickly, and later, it was one of our favourite tales. How he suddenly jerked and swung off the dirt road into the ditch, dropping back to join Kitimat. Once Kitimat and Panda were in sync about the bear, they gave chase. The bear quickly scrambled up a tree with the dogs barking at the base. Dad called the dogs off, and we walked back home, shortening our walk to give the bear his space.

Chapter Eight:
The Winter the Ceiling Burst

Our first winter at our new home broke many record lows. Our first and coldest survival camping trip started with an innocent hike up behind the farm to camp along the ridge. After we'd settled in at the camp, we were caught in a terrible blizzard. Half the students and an adult decided to head back the second day while the rest of the die-hard campers stayed for a second night. Cold isn't nearly the word to describe the bone-freezing chill we felt as we huddled in our lean-tos. Our windbreak walls did little beyond keeping our fires from blowing out. I remember some frozen feet slid a little too close to the fire, and the boots melted beyond recognition. One young woman got frostbite on her toe, and it turned into a terrible, frightening black oozing example of why you wear the proper gear when heading out. Needless to say, her misfortune was the lesson for years to come as to why proper gear is so important. Thankfully she didn't lose her toe. She also didn't fall in love with nature.

The homes and facilities weren't prepared for such cold. This was supposed to be one of the hottest places in the province. That winter, the weather was bone-chilling, pipe-freezing, water-stopping, and cold.

The cold wouldn't have been a big deal if it wasn't for

ruining my birthday lunch. As was our tradition, I got to choose my birthday meal. For my eighth birthday, I chose pizza bread with blueberry cheesecake for dessert.

Pizza bread is slices of bread with our pimento paste for cheese baked in the oven. You could add olives, onions, peppers, or any toppings you wanted. I liked just plain cheese. Even commune-raised vegan children love cheese pizza. As we all sat around the table with our eyes closed in prayer to bless the food, Heaven opened. Actually, it was the roof. The pipes burst and poured water and ceiling debris all over the table. The meal was soggy and ruined except for one lone pan in the oven. Everyone was so shocked by the deluge that we sat and laughed for a few minutes. I never fully closed my eyes during prayer again.

* * *

Our water came from the mountain above. It flowed down through man-made canals to our home. That winter, it was so cold it froze the water solid in the canals. The entire community was up there with axes, chainsaws, picks, whatever we could get our hands on to try and break it up.

The length of the canals and the depth of the ice were more than daunting. It was too big of a job in some places, regardless of the students and staff working on it. For a long time, our drinking water came in large pails that we filled from a source we didn't normally use. In my mind's eye, we went to a dark cave and filled them with slow dripping water. The cold forced the water to flow underground and out to a new source.

After much hacking with axes and picks, it was decided the canals needed to be redone in a few areas. Once summer arrived, a crew began the task. Dad and I were in charge. Actually, Dad was, and I, his faithful shadow, was there to assist. Dad decided to acquire his blasting license and use dynamite to widen certain areas. I can see now where my brothers and I get our ideas from.

Off Dad and I went down the bumpy washboard road to a local neighbour who had old dynamite in his shed. Dad talked him into letting us have it and loaded a few old wooden crates into the back of the Land Rover.

Picture those old wooden crates that you see in historic towns. We had three or more of those filled with yellow-crusted dynamite. It was so old the compound makeup of the dynamite had leaked out, crystalized, and made solid crates of dynamite.

It was my job to sit in the back and keep an eye on the dynamite. The dynamite was very unstable due to age and the obvious changes in the chemical compounds. Though the crystallization and colour change was neat, it was a sign of danger.

There I was, eight years old, sitting in the back of our Land Rover, watching the dynamite. Dad carefully maneuvered the bumpy gravel road. He tried to avoid the worst bumps and ruts. I was terrified yet at peace with the fear. It was an odd combination, I know. I had no idea what to watch for. I figured we would be particles the size of pea gravel should anything bad happen. I kept my mouth shut and studiously watched the boxes. Stress sweat-soaked my shirt. I didn't dare question or complain. I'd be dying with my father and not dying from the religious torture said to come before the time of the end. So really, this wasn't as bad as what was to come prior to Christ's second coming.

We arrived back at the main meeting area with our cargo. Dad rigged various spots with dynamite, fuses, and blasting caps. We were all directed to stay far away across the road in a small turnaround area, mainly to ensure no falling debris could harm us. The explosion was unlike anything I had heard or seen. The boom was deafening. There wasn't any explosion to see as I had my eyes screwed shut. The trees absorbed most of the falling rocks and debris. The slightly sweet smell that lingered in the air after the rain of debris ended was almost a sickly scent. I thought it would smell more like the sulfuric scent of a gunshot, but it turned out there was no similarity in smell or sound.

We had all huddled at the far side close to the trees, except for one student. And as sometimes happens, she did get a small sharp rock right on the top of her head. It was hard enough to cut the scalp, and it reminded all of us that head wounds bleed rather well. I wanted to tell her, "I told you so," but I stayed quiet. I mean, we are told stuff for a reason; she should've listened.

* * *

We didn't put much ado into celebrating Christmas. Mom said Santa was from a satanic holiday added to Christmas as a compromise between heathens and Christians hundreds of years ago. Mom said a lot of holidays were changed to make heathens happy when Christianity was brought to them. I never had a Christmas tree. Instead, we decorated the house plants on a stand. We strung popcorn on a thread to decorate the window frame.

That first Christmas at the new commune, we all got a little silly. Dad found the biggest stocking he could and hung it on the wall since we had no mantle. That year we all had socks for stockings, and Dad had a stocking larger than I was!

Now the joke was if you were naughty, you got coal in your stocking. Of course, Dad was going to put coal into everyone's stocking. We decided to get him back for being so greedy with his stocking.

We started with the biggest box we could fit into the stocking. Then we filled that box with another gift-wrapped box, and so on. We used as many boxes as possible that would fit into each other. Finally, once he unwrapped and opened the last one, it was the size of a small jewellery box. Inside the tiny box, we had placed a little black piece of coal. There was such fun and laughter shared over those cardboard boxes. After they were all opened, I tried climbing into them.

That same year, Mom decided to make pinecone wreaths. We collected baskets of pinecones for the task. We must have used a gallon of glue to make them. The glue looked like the runny top of homemade peanut butter.

Let me assure you that in no way was the taste similar. It was horrible. No matter how much water I drank or salt I licked afterward, I couldn't get that awful taste out of my mouth. In the past, I had tried many things I shouldn't have eaten, partly from curiosity and largely from hunger. However, the peanut butter-looking glue was at the top for bad things tried. It was terrible and awfully bad tasting.

Mom and I made a dozen wreaths to hang on doors and give to other families. Each time I placed a cone on the peanut butter-looking glue, I felt a little like throwing up.

* * *

Worshipping the Lord was a weekend-long event. We had vespers at seven p.m. every Friday and Saturday evening. Church service was always from nine a.m. until noon on Saturday. If the pastor was long-winded, he could drone on past noon.

Vespers were less formal than church. Those gatherings were a time to socialize and celebrate the end of the workweek. Families that didn't live on the community farm attended the Sabbath service. That was a formal occasion where everyone dressed up in their best attire.

Some of the families had children for me to play with. Saturday church had a youth service separate for the kids before the sermon. I tried attending, but my anxiety was terrible when I was around that many children, so I didn't go. Dad kept pushing me to attend the youth service with the other kids. I was terribly shy and didn't know how to interact with them. For most of my life, I was an only child in a home filled with a dozen adults. I only knew a handful of other children, and I only had limited interaction with them.

Being with other children I didn't know was a terrifying concept. What if I did something wrong and they didn't like me? What if they laughed at me? Instead of attending the children's Bible classes on Saturday mornings, I chose to stay with my mother and sit with the adults while they reviewed their Bible lessons. Even the board stories made of felt and songs for children couldn't entice me away that first year.

* * *

One time, as Mom and I cut out paper dolls, she asked, "What do you want to do when you get to Heaven?"

That question bothered me something fierce. My mind scrambled and raced like a doped-up mouse running a maze, trying desperately to get to the cheese. My mind slipped and slid as I tried to grasp at an idea.

"I want to slide down an elephant's trunk," I blurted out. That was a big fat lie. As false as Grandpa's dentures. I didn't want anything more than what I had, what I knew.

I played alone, mostly outdoors, ate homegrown, homemade food, and had dogs to cuddle. I had parents who loved me, read to me, and taught me how to do things on my own. I didn't know about sitting in school all day. I didn't know how to connect with my peers, or about bullying. I didn't know cruelty yet. I didn't know about trying to fit in, trying to look the same, or trying to colour inside the lines. I didn't know how to make friends, keep friends, or worry about losing friends. I just knew I was happy, and that would have been the wrong answer to what I wanted to do when I got to Heaven.

For us, every action taken, planned thought, and lived moment was to get us toward the time of the end. The end goal was Heaven. The cherry on top would be to be in the 144,000. They were the select few that lived through persecution and torture to see Christ's second coming. This was the coming of the one true Christ, not one of the false prophets sent by Satan. His second coming would be known to us as a cloud in the sky shaped like the palm of your hand. The cloud would come down with Jesus standing on it to bring us back to Heaven. He wouldn't touch the ground. Only imposters claiming to be Jesus would be on Earth. Jesus standing on the cloud shaped like the palm of your hand coming toward us was how to tell if it was really him.

When he came, the dead would rise, and all those deemed worthy would go to Heaven. Those who had overcome the devil's temptations and were the chosen holy ones would not die the second death. All those who had succumbed to the seductions and the temptations of the world would die the second permanent death. The eternal death in Hell.

Chapter Nine: My ABCs

Our diet evolved with our move, yet I was still always a little hungry. Unleavened bread and the primarily raw diet were abandoned for softer homemade wholewheat bread. We baked our own homemade granola. Before we moved, we ate muesli which was an uncooked mixture of oats and seeds ground up to be a soft raw cereal. I was able to occasionally sneak a few nuts from the pantry, but rarely was the kitchen empty to allow me to sneak a snack.

Margarine was added to our diet instead of using cornmeal. Cornmeal as a margarine replacement, yes, that's right. Super easy and normal, I swear. You make cornmeal in a pot following the recipe. You place said cornmeal in a Tupperware container, square if you want the shape of a block of butter. Refrigerate said cornmeal and bring it out at mealtimes to spread on your toast with a knife, just like butter. It's the yellow colour, not the taste. It's all in the eye of the beholder.

Mom's siblings and parents came for a visit a year after our move. There was a family reunion of sorts at our home. Grandpa and Grandma had an RV that they stayed in in our driveway. The rest crammed into the bedrooms, the kids on the floor on makeshift beds.

Mom's brother and his wife had two children a couple of

years younger than me. I didn't know my cousins very well, but I was excited for the kids to play with. They had never seen a country lifestyle like ours. Growing up in the city, they had no idea corn came from a plant in the field. We laughed as we ran through the rows of vegetables, sneaking a pea off the vine or a carrot from the earth and eating it.

Even our dog loved the garden. She'd occasionally get loose there. We always knew when the peas were ready, as she was great at slitting the shell open and taking out the sweet morsels. Her talent made us laugh.

Mom's sister, Auntie Mildred, and her husband, also came for a couple of days. They were both career-orientated with good government jobs and pensions. They had chosen not to have children and instead to enjoy a child-free lifestyle. Curiosity about the farm and seeing the different lifestyles may have prompted the visit.

I'm sure they tried not to judge and to have an open mind. However, Auntie had lost her baby sister, my mom, to this different lifestyle, she was full of well-meant advice and opinions.

Aunt Mildred tucked me into bed one night and asked me if I wanted to say the Lord's prayer. She was shocked when she learned I didn't know it. I grew up talking to God, not reciting prayers. Mildred grew up in the Catholic church, where memorizing and reciting prayers was a huge part of her religion. In hindsight, she was probably trying to bond with me while upholding my parent's rigid Christian lifestyle. I can imagine how that conversation went with my parents afterward.

Aunt Mildred was shocked over a few things, such as I wasn't taught the proper way to hold my utensils and that I wasn't in school. She felt that needed to be rectified.

Mildred noticed I had a growth under my tongue and insisted I be taken to the doctor. That was nerve-wracking for me as I had no experience with doctors. When he pulled out what looked like a giant pair of scissors, my mouth closed with a snap. It took many questions and explanations before I was willing to accept that he was just going to gently snip the skin on a blocked gland.

Sure enough, I survived and made sure to massage the lump under my tongue regularly to help it unblock. There was no way I wanted to go back for any more lumps. I hoped I didn't have any more blocked glands because I never wanted to go to the doctor again.

To the educated middle class, it was shocking that I ran around wild and free, playing in the mud. I was a regular tomboy ruffian instead of a young lady. There was no school to attend. I think it may have been after that visit that Mom's family started raising a stink about what I was lacking—specifically, my lack of education.

It took my uncle and aunt threatening my parents with reporting them to child services before they got me started with homeschooling. Why they had to go that far is beyond me. Both my parents were post-secondary graduates. My father had two Bachelor of Arts degrees, and my mother had her medical administration diploma. So why neither one of them thought to educate me defies logic.

Mom started homeschooling as we didn't have preschool or elementary school of any kind where I lived. Homeschool was the only option. I took to reading like a duck to water. It opened the door to exploration and adventure far beyond the acreage that I roamed like a wild pony.

As I learned to read and write, my door to freedom swung open. This was my escape from boredom, loneliness, and scripture. Honestly, how many times do we need to discuss the time of the end? "Daily," I was told. "It needs to be discussed and planned for daily."

The gaps in my education are hard to explain. When I was home-schooled, I skipped grade three. I got a spelling tutor in grade four and loved spending time with her. She'd give me Tums as a treat. It was the closest thing to candy I had.

I loved numbers. Simple bits like addition, subtraction, and even division weren't hard to do. By grade five, I was diagramming sentences.

Science was simple but fun. I loved to colour, cut and paste the human anatomy onto a life-size cut-out. I was halfway through grade six when Mom stopped teaching me.

When I was twelve, I went to school. I skipped grades seven and eight and went straight into grade nine. I only completed half of it. That was the extent of the education I had by age thirteen.

The following year I completed the second half of grade nine and all of grade ten. Those were done at a government-recognized school.

By eighteen, I just fibbed about where I graduated. I crossed my fingers and hoped no one would need a copy of my diploma. It was impossible to explain to someone without raising many more questions.

It still doesn't make sense to me as to why my parents didn't push me to learn from an early age.

Homeschool had its benefits, to be sure. I loved how it only took a few hours each day to complete my work. Then I was free to run and play outdoors.

Mom and I got so frustrated trying to communicate the lessons. We didn't speak the same language and would become brittle with frustration at our inability to say it the way it would make sense.

Being homeschooled accentuated my seclusion from peers. I didn't learn how to interact with them.

I was ecstatic to be able to read. Previously I had to bribe people with back rubs to get them to read to me. My escape route from the boredom and the seriousness of life was found.

Chapter Ten: Survival Camping

Dad's survival class included hands-on camping trips. Generally, three class trips a year. I never attended a class, and I never missed a campout. We started out with a lean-to on the first trip. We had sleeping bags, pots, utensils, and everything else we needed. By the third trip, we were sleeping in teepees without sleeping bags. For the last trip of the year, an axe, a spare pair of wool socks, and three matches were all we were given. I didn't mind, as I always stayed with Dad in his shelter.

Survival camping trips were usually within an hour or two hike from home. Once we arrived at the chosen site in the forest, we would build our shelter. The shelter would be per class curriculum.

We had to make a meal for my dad, the teacher, from the surrounding edibles. Main edibles were the cambium layer from trees. They were best when fried with seasoning. Pine needle tea was a staple, although never a favourite of mine.

Old Man's beard (a long, lacy, greenish lichen that grows from tree trunks and is also known as black tree lichen) was cooked like spinach. The Lillooet and Salish were known to use it to weave clothing and footwear though it wasn't durable or lasting. Bella Coola people were known to use the lichen as false hair and beards for dances and masquerading. We ate it, but only to get a passing grade in a survival class.

One winter, we found a nest of large-winged frozen ants. Whoever ate one got an automatic A. I didn't eat one. I didn't need to because I wasn't a student. I was Dad's daughter, his tag-along shadow.

The next summer Dad and I hiked up that same ridge. We stopped at a cute old hunter's shack and had a lunch of noodles with chicken seasoning and a little salt. We had these tiny thin egg noodles for our soup. I thought the salt must have gone bad, as the soup was quite sweet. The more salt Dad added, the sweeter our soup got. We had a good laugh when we realized that Dad brought the film container of sugar, not salt. The sweetest fake chicken soup I have ever had!

* * *

Our style of camping evolved over the years. At first, it was shelters like teepees and lean-tos. Dad found a teepee was much warmer, and he didn't have to pack as much as when they used a canvas tent for winter camping. Later a mummy bag tent for camping atop mountain peaks was bought. There was a large six-person tent for the weeks of summer camping with puppies and my siblings. Students were occasionally included, although Mom preferred it to be just family. When I was almost double digits, we spent a couple of summer holidays camping as a family.

Turning ten was a big deal to me, a grown-up age. I counted down for almost two years waiting for that birthday. I was busy with my two and half year-old brother and an infant sister. I'd help Mom by changing diapers, playing with them, and rocking them to sleep. A cargo trailer was fully loaded with gear for all our needs. We left with a new set of puppies, enough food to last for a week longer than our planned trip, the canoe, and a tent. It was late when we arrived and pitch dark with heavy rain. We kids stayed in the car while Mom and Dad set up the six-person dome tent by headlights and feel. It was a daunting task. Like anything else, Mom and Dad went about the task regardless of difficulty. Our first day was spent hiding from the rain in the damp tent. There were only so many naps and I Spy games kids could play before becoming wiggly with compressed energy.

After the first twenty-four hours of our trip, the weather was gorgeous. Walks, wading, and canoeing were just some of the things we did. I even got to canoe across the lake alone. I was almost double digits and able to earn my independence a little more. I remember the pride of being deemed responsible enough to paddle out alone. It was a fun yet slightly boring trip. I paddled the circumference of the lake, passed the island, then went up and around toward where the water flowed in via a creek. I started to paddle up the small creek, then realized what trouble I could get into going that far. The possibility of capsizing, being unable to turn around, or getting high-centred on a fallen tree all rushed through my mind. The little voice in my head warned me not to take my freedom too far, as I could lose it. I paddled back to the camp.

I had a life jacket to keep me safe, but losing the canoe would have been horrible. We didn't swim, as the river we lived on was much too dangerous to do more than toe-dipping at the edge. I had never heard of a public pool.

We practised shelter-building techniques and our rock-repelling skills. You had to harness yourself up in a full skirt over pants if you were a woman. Then you hooked up the rope with your gear. You had to remember to stay horizontal, keep your rope hand below your hip to brake as you walked or jumped out, and then slide down the cliff. It was fun, although a tad tricky in a skirt. We would lay jackets, blankets, and other items on the rocks to try and eliminate any rope rub and subsequent tearing from the sharp rocks. Over time we switched from cliffs to large trees. We'd climb up one tree, traverse across to another, and repel down.

Everyday fun camping trips were usually a few hours' drive before a good half-day or more of hiking. One particularly beautiful trip, we hiked into a large watershed area through thick clouds of mosquitoes. We made the mistake of taking a shortcut. Instead of an old-growth forest, we ended up bushwhacking through Devil's Club, which made me feel like this was a precursor to Hell. These giant plants were thick as an untended garden. They were taller than the average person, with long stems that were evilly equipped with sharp thorns hidden beneath their harmless-looking leaves. Even having my skirt over my pants didn't save me from the thorns. I never saw rhubarb or burdock again without remembering the time I waded through that valley of Devil's Club.

The trip was incredible, nonetheless. We found an ice-cold lake, fed by a glacier, that fell down a waterfall into another lake. The water was cold, crisp, and sweet to the taste. I have always loved the taste of water, but that was by far the best-tasting water I've ever drank in my life.

* * *

Playing outside was how I grew up. Whether playing in the fields, tunnelling through the hay bales in the barn, or pretending no one could see me in the tall grass. I was outside and always wearing a full skirt. I'd hide in my forts beneath huge sagebrush bushes, ride my bike, and run wild until I was put to work.

My full long skirt over my jeans felt like a second appendage, and I thought little of it. Then one day, when I was climbing trees, it caught tight when I swung up to the next branch. The skirt held fast and yanked me down. I fell, barely missing the branch I had originally been on. Then my skirt caught on another branch. This time it kept me from falling farther. I was able to right myself and unhook my skirt from the offending branch.

The irony wasn't lost on me as I recounted my story at the dinner table. It was then Dad decided no skirts were to be worn when climbing trees. We also stopped wearing skirts when repelling. I think it was after that incident that Dad started to question things. It was the rules of Ellen G. White versus wise decisions.

I grew up being taught to be self-sufficient, independent, and able to think for myself. It was a bit of a contradiction, living in a religious community where faith was key, no questions asked when it's God's will. It was definitely a problem trying to mold me into that lifestyle, and a gift watching Dad question things and change things.

* * *

Winter camping over the Christmas holidays changed over time. Now we had two huskies that could pull the sled of gear. Mom, Dad, and I all had packs loaded with gear, appropriately weighted to our size. Dad could carry up to seventy pounds, Mom forty pounds, and I, not more than twenty pounds. The dogs even had packs to carry their food.

Our Christmas holidays were spent in a teepee that Dad would build before bringing Mom and I with the dogs and kids. Mom and Dad would pack a toboggan with gear, hook the dogs to it and head out to camp for a week or so in the bush. The toboggan was loaded with sleeping bags, spare clothing, and food.

Dad would have already been to the site and built a shelter before taking all the gear and us kids in. Dad led the way, carrying a backpack and leading the dog-pulled sled. Mom followed behind him. I was last, slowly plodding along, my twenty-pound bag feeling heavier with each step.

After a couple of hours of hiking through the snow, we arrived at our destination. Once we arrived and settled into the large teepee, we just relaxed. We explored the woods, sat around the fire, ate, and napped. We had warm goose-down army mummy sleeping bags that kept us toasty warm at night. A large fire pit, complete with small trees as firewood sticking out of the fire, was outside our teepee to sit around. A tree that had fallen a little way from our fire and teepee acted as the toilet seat for us kids. The tree was large enough that our bums didn't touch the snow as we slung them over the side. We all lined up on the tree to do our business together. I remember being so affronted when my parents laughed and took a photo of us.

Dad let me bring my rifle, and I spent our winter camping trip target practising on squirrels. I'd pick a quiet secluded spot to lie in wait, whether on a log or in a tree branch. I'd wait quietly, patiently, for a squirrel to stop long enough so that I could get it in my sights and shoot it. It took patience to lie there. By the end of the week, after many missed shots, I managed to shoot a few.

I tried not to feel bad when I grabbed the squirrel and took it back to camp, where I lopped off its tail with my hatchet. I fed the body to the dogs and kept the tail as a bookmark. As I later learned, the hair falls off the tail and leaves a skinny stick-like shape that isn't nearly as neat a bookmark as a freshly dried tail. By the end of the following summer, I was all out of squirrel bookmarks.

During the day, we snowshoed, explored, and climbed trees. My favourite thing to do was to play tag with my Dad from the treetops. The snow was only a couple of feet deep, and the old logging road was lined with slender young trees less than twenty feet tall. As I climbed them, my weight would pull the tops down, swinging me toward the ground and the next tree. If I leaned correctly, I could leap to the next tree and the next while Dad chased me on foot from the road. He may have been letting me win, but I chose to believe I was faster and getting away using the treetops. It was great fun that filled my heart with such joy I can still feel it years later.

Our last summer camping trip as a family, we didn't have a litter of puppies which made it easier. It's not that we knew it was our last; it just turned out that way. We went for the usual two weeks, hours down a bumpy logging road to a little spot next to a creek.

Between our tent and the creek, Dad set up our very own playground. He placed a plank of wood over a stump for a teeter-totter for us. Dad tied one end of a rope over a thick branch, and the other end hanging down was knotted around a large stick to make a seat. Not unlike the T-bar lifts you see at a ski hill. We now had plenty to play on or with for our time camping. Within hours, my brother Daniel was covered in mosquito bites. Red welts covered his back and his entire body. We, kids, didn't care about mosquitos, and we ran about half-naked in our underpants.

We practised the earth oven way of steaming the vegetation we harvested for lunch. We dug a two-foot-deep hole about four feet in diameter and lined it with rocks. Then we built up a good hot fire to burn down inside the hole. While the fire was burning down, we then foraged the hillside and meadow for various greens and bulbs like Blue Camas bulbs, Tiger Lilly bulbs, Lamb's quarter leaves, and Nettle leaves. After it burned down, the hot coals were covered with dirt. The now hot rocks were pulled from the sides to place on top of the food we had foraged and wrapped in leaves. The hot rocks were then covered with dirt. A natural earth oven was built to steam the roots and bulbs we foraged.

On one of our daily long walks down the logging lane,

we spotted a black bear up the mountainside wandering along, eating berries. The bear wasn't a big concern, for he never came toward our camp. The dogs would have let up such a ruckus long before it got near us. That summer was laid back and relaxing. No students, no stress, no reason for our parents to be unhappy and arguing. This was how Mom and Dad had courted one another. It was how they were most happy.

Chapter Eleven: Delivering Produce

Our community had large market gardens. Two primary fruits grown were tomatoes and watermelon. These were sold to local clients and delivered to non-local clients who were often introduced to us through church ties.

Dad delivered a five-ton truckload of produce up to northern BC once a summer. We would stay with his brother and family while we were there. It was a nice respite after a long drive and a great two-for-one trip—working and visiting.

I got to go with Dad for the drive and loved our one-on-one time. I got to try real bubble gum, and he taught me how to blow bubbles. I must say bubble gum is much tastier than pitch. I was never able to pick the right ball of tree sap to turn into gum. The other kids had great collections on their bedposts of all the sap they found, chewed, turned into gum, and saved for repeated use. Whenever I grabbed a clump and chewed it, it filled my mouth with a horrid taste. The sap disintegrating into flavourless bits in my mouth. Never gum. So, when Dad let me pick out a package of gum from the gas station and taught me how to blow bubbles, I was in seventh heaven.

We stopped at a rest stop for lunch, and Dad cut open a watermelon for us to eat. We ended up eating three watermelons. The rest of the drive, we stopped at every rest stop and pulled out to pee. I always remember that with a smile when I drive that highway.

We spent a couple of nights at my uncle's while delivering all the fruit orders. Dad and his brother would visit and catch up as they hardly ever saw each other.

One time I got to attend elementary school with my cousins. That was a traumatizing experience and not well thought out by the adults. I went in my long full skirt over my jeans belted up to keep them from falling off. All different colours and patterns mixed together, making up my hand-me-down outfit. I had never seen a school or classroom setting. Never mind a playground full of kids. It was overwhelming and terrifying. To mask my fear and anxiety, I put on a tough, don't care attitude and smiled a brittle stiff smile while I tried to ignore the questions.

Why do you wear clothes like that?

Why do you have that skirt on over your pants?

What do you mean you don't go to school?

You don't know how to play dodgeball?

You've never played on monkey bars?

You mean you have never heard of red rover red rover come on over?

I'm sure it wasn't meant cruelly. But it hurt and embarrassed me. I was ashamed of my clothes, my lack of understanding, and the inability to fit it. The worst part was that I didn't know how to fit in, and no one was going to teach me.

* * *

Something we always looked forward to on those visits was my auntie's cooking. She was originally from Mexico and made a mean flour tortilla from scratch and a great enchilada sauce. It was so hard to pick which meal we wanted as she always gave us a choice. We always wanted both, and she was so sweet she'd make them both during the two nights we were there.

We didn't have television, radio, newspaper, or anything that connected us with the outside world. Movies were not something we watched. When we visited my aunt and uncle, Dad would have a movie or series he just had to see.

They watched *Star Wars*, swearing it was a must-see, life-changing film. I didn't quite understand the difference between reality and make-believe. Largely in part to the fact I was growing up in a solemn literal lifestyle that didn't joke or allow fictitious thinking. Funny, considering the life that we created was based on belief, not fact.

So here I was, a little girl watching *Star Wars*, not really clear on what was and wasn't real in the big, strange world we visited. There was one part of the movie that scared the bejeezus out of me. When Princess Leia's message was beamed out from R2D2. I thought a vacuum had sucked her in and that she needed help to get out. Her wavering image, as she called out, stuck with me for decades.

When we were at Dad's brothers, they watched all the *Rambo* movies. They hid down in the basement half the night watching them. They were both into the outdoors and guns, making *Rambo* a perfect movie to bond over. My cousin and I would sneak down the stairs and take turns watching the movie through a little hole in the wall.

My cousin was close to my age, and both of us were curious, energetic outdoor kids. We loved to explore and question. So, when our fathers hid themselves in the basement, and we weren't allowed to join, of course, off we went to spy. I was terrified of the violence. It was gripping yet shocking. For someone to be that hurt, to never give up. It was a beautifully odd lesson of strength and resilience at a young age.

Chapter Twelve: Baking Bread

When I was ten, at the second commune, I came up with a great idea to make some spending money. I'd bake bread and sell it to the other families that lived in the community.

Mom and I painstakingly compared the cost of the individual ingredients to the number of loaves of bread made per batch. Mom then added in the cost of electricity. Those figures, plus a small amount of labour, created the price of the loaf.

Every week I paid my mom her portion of the cost of the bread and got to keep the rest of the money. I baked a dozen loaves each Friday and delivered them to local families. The first week Mom made sure I was measuring and letting the dough rise correctly. First, let it rise in the bowl and then again in the pan before placing it into the oven. That way the loaves of bread shaped nicely without bursting, causing tears in the beautiful crust.

After that, I was on my own. I'd stand at the counter with the big metal mixing bowl adding the sugar, yeast, and oil. I'd look around and make sure no one was nearby. Then I'd add a few extra spoonsful of sugar. Another shoulder check to be sure I wasn't being watched, and then I'd pour a generous amount of oil into the bowl.

Once the yeast started to rise, you couldn't tell how much sugar and oil had originally been added to the recipe. While I let the yeast rise, I mixed the dry ingredients: whole wheat flour, salt, and a touch of white flour. Again, I looked around to make sure no one was coming and added a much larger amount of white flour than whole wheat. Not so much that it didn't look like whole-wheat bread, just enough to cut the ratio in half.

The community was hooked. They loved my bread and kept raving about how good it was. Some of the ladies asked what I did to make it so light, fluffy, and tasty. I just smiled and said I didn't know. I hugged my secret to myself, reveling in the forbidden delicious food.

I loved baking bread. It gave me something to look forward to each Friday. The smell of freshly baked bread still makes my mouth water. I loved the smell of the crusty brown loaves cooling on the counter before being bagged for delivery. My little heart filled with pride at my weekly accomplishment.

The monetary value held little meaning to me. I was making twenty-five cents a loaf, but I didn't get to feel the money. It was just a number in a little book wrapped in a knapsack in my parent's closet. I'd do the math each week, and the number would change. The baking, the smell, the accomplishment, now that was something that felt amazing.

My parents used my income to begin teaching me about finances. I had a little notebook to keep track of the costs incurred and paid to mother as well as the income from the bread. There was a section for my earnings which were added to my bank account list. My parents didn't believe in or trust banks, and they didn't believe in having debt. They had a little backpack with a small accordion folder inside that held statements and monies being saved. It was folded up and hidden in the sweater closet for safekeeping.

I learned at a young age that money wasn't something to speak of in public. It wasn't something to admit you have or don't have. Living frugally and believing you were living like kings was something to be proud of. Most importantly, money caused fighting. If my parents were in the bathroom with the water running, they were fighting. The arguments I overheard were about money.

Mom taught me to cook, clean, use the Singer sewing machine, care for the children, and wash cloth diapers. I was being groomed to be a submissive housewife and mother. I can hear my friends reading this and snorting aloud at how that turned out.

Chapter Thirteen:
Staking Out a Claim of Land

We camped in many places over the years. We would drive a few hours down logging roads, getting as close as possible to the trailhead. Sometimes we travelled in the back of a dark cube truck. The sunlight would blind us when the back door was raised up. From there, we would do our stretches, gear up, and hit the trail.

Well, there really wasn't a trail, more like a faint deer path that we followed until we blazed our own path. The hike took us through the forest, past the tree line. The mountain ridge narrowed as we hiked higher and higher. (Note to future mountain hikers: when peeing off the side of a mountain, pick the side the wind isn't blowing upwards on.)

We took short breaks and stopped to eat lunch, replenishing our energy levels. We would finally reach the summit close to nightfall. We set up a quick camp so we could sleep atop the mountain ridge.

Everyone ate a hot meal thanks to portable camping stoves. The following day we hit the trail down the mountain into the basin. There we would set up camp at the edge of a beautiful lake. Untouched nature is difficult to describe. It's easy to love and hard to forget when raised in it.

On one of those hikes, I sunburned my eyes. I was gifted

sunglasses with protective side shields after that.

Dad decided to stake a claim on land next to the lake. Once the year was up, we would move there. He said we were going to build a small log cabin and live there. My mother must have been a saint to support all his off-grid lifestyle ideas while raising little ones.

We hiked in with Mom and the kids so she could see where he wanted to claim land and live. We stuck to valley hiking as we were travelling with two toddlers. We had enough gear to camp out for a week. Hiking with a three-year-old and an infant made the trip take a little longer. Mom had just suffered another miscarriage, and unbeknownst to them, she got pregnant that trip. It shocked the heck out of Mom when she found out.

Dad had already talked to the government about the process to stake off crown land and claim it. You had to stake it off for a year and wait to see if anyone else laid claim. If no one did, then you needed to live on it another year to make it your own. We began to prepare to move there once the year was up.

There was a budget for the helicopter to get the stove and supplies that would be too difficult to bring in by foot or with a donkey. We began to stockpile more food than usual. We had an extra deep freeze filled with fresh and dried fruit and vegetables. Dad compiled a collection of large army containers filled with beans and rice. There were also architectural plans for making the essential materials for building a log cabin with a small loft. We would carve out basic furniture from logs. We had dogs, guns, and a volunteer student for labour.

I often wonder if Dad had become disenchanted with the ideals of the commune which he was helping lead. I know my mother was quite unhappy with the lifestyle they were living. To search out a remote area away from everyone seemed a bit extreme. I'll never know what motivated him. I can't imagine how

Mother felt to live cut off and alone in the forest with a young family.

* * *

Between adopting Daniel in 1985 to having a baby sister and then a baby brother by 1988, the cloth diapers and potty training seemed endless. There was always another seatbelt, car seat, or highchair needed.

Cloth diapers are burned into my memory. I remember a beautiful *Precious Moments Bible* in a case hidden under the cloth diapers as a treasure hunt gift. I have a photo of Dad holding me while having an afternoon nap. A cloth diaper over his face to block the bright, beautiful sunshine so he could sleep. I remember the dirty diapers almost getting sucked down the toilet as I washed the poop out of them. The stench of urine burned my nose as we washed them by hand. I will never forget that toxic smell.

When Mom was pregnant, she suffered from low iron. Instead of taking supplements, she went natural and blended a raw egg into a shot of an iron-boosting breakfast smoothie. So gross. Mom would joke that when she could finally have an egg, it couldn't be sunny side up or anything tasty but instead raw and slimy. I never ever wanted to try an egg after watching her gag back that drink every day for months.

Chapter Fourteen: Unhappy Mom

Somewhere between my baby sister and baby brother being born, Mom hit a wall of unhappiness. I don't know if it was the exhaustion from another difficult childbirth or a deficient diet, or both that made her so unhappy.

There was also the continued segregation between her family and the world, which inevitably drove a wedge between her and her siblings. Her family saw how I was being raised and couldn't fathom why she didn't prepare me for anything beyond the small world they lived in. All I was being prepared for was to be a good wife, mother, and the time of the end.

Mom was tired, burned out, exhausted, and done. She was done with being broke, done with having a house full of pubescent boys, done with a life of giving to the Lord's work that Dad was called to. I remember she was frighteningly underweight, and her hair stopped growing. Her eczema flared up so bad she had cracked, bleeding hands. Then the eczema spread to her face.

Just before my baby brother Matthias was born, Dad acquiesced to Mom's stress, and we did not have students stay with us. It was just me, Mom, Dad, my brothers, and my sister. Mom had a student come in a few times a week to help.

Can you imagine two toddlers, cloth diapers, a garden to supply a year's worth of produce, cook vegan from scratch, and homeschool? It's exhausting to think about.

How Mom felt began to affect everything in our family. I don't know to what extent she shared it with my father.

We started the long process of preparing to live deep in the mountains, building a cabin, and being completely off the grid. We had stored large quantities of dried beans in army pods and dried numerous types and quantities of fruit. We always did this as we didn't buy prepared food.

This time, however, it was being taken to a whole new level. Mom was making large batches of chili, beans, and sauces, then freezing them into meal portions. I didn't realize why Mom was doing that at first.

I was still being homeschooled at the time, and it was difficult. I hated the change from Imperial to Metric measurements. I couldn't seem to grasp the metric system, even though it was a much easier way to convert and calculate. I still baked bread once a week to sell. I sang in the choir and went on choir performances with the other choir members. I tried my best to be and act like a little grown-up. I tried to fit in and be allowed to join in with the older teens.

In all honesty, I was bored and lonely. I had no friends, no classmates, no one to talk to, giggle with, and share my life journey of growing up. I tried with the other teen girls that came and went, but either they didn't stay at the commune, or we were separated to discourage the friendship. I followed the teenagers around and particularly adored one girl. I felt like she was my best friend.

I learned how to cook for the family and care for the younger children. I changed, washed, and hung cloth diapers on the line. I did laundry and cleaned the house. I learned how to cut the children's hair. Thankfully there are no photos of those haircuts, as it wasn't my strong suit. I had a hard time thawing and heating the frozen chili as I'd get sidetracked and forget about it until a thick black crust coated the bottom of the pot.

While I did chores, Mom spoke to me as her confidant, her sounding board. She was unhappy and didn't feel the zealot fire as my father did. She grew up in another world, and this wasn't what she'd signed up for. She loved my father, but not the life he brought her into. Those conversations are hard to write about. I've never discussed them with anyone, not even my therapist.

At the time, my mother's main objective was to leave. How to leave was a problem as she had four children from a few months to a preteen. She hadn't worked in years, had no money, and would be at the mercy of her family in a world she hadn't navigated in over a decade. To me, being in that situation and having a family to go to would have been amazing.

Mom tried to make a plan but didn't know how to act on it. For months she'd run her ideas past me, trying out different scenarios in the hopes of finding one that fit, one that would work. She desperately wanted to escape the life she was trapped in. Mom would sway back and forth, trying to decide how to leave my father. She spent numerous afternoons talking it out.

She'd leave and take all three young children and go to her sister's. Or she'd leave the two toddlers for me to care for and take only the baby. Or she could take only the two youngest and leave me with my four-year-old brother. No matter what the options, I was always left behind to care for my father and possibly a sibling or two. This went on for months. I wasn't to tell father. I had no one else to discuss it with, even if I dared share my worry and my pain.

It fucked me right up.

She was like a broken record, constantly reviewing her plans. She reviewed them time and time again. She had plans to set herself free. Each time, I was left behind. It made me wonder if she ever really wanted me. I didn't understand why I was always left behind with all that she hated.

The rejection my preteen self felt was unfathomable. The pain was too great to find appropriate words. When she'd leave to visit her parents, leaving me with my father, I'd beg to sleep with him. I'd wrap my legs tight around him to keep him from leaving me. I always woke to an empty bed as he rose early to pray and read the scripture. He had no idea of the fear and pain I was suffering. The fear of not knowing when I'd be left to care for him—left by the woman I loved as only a child loves a mother. This went on for months.

Then one morning, it happened. I realized with a start that Mom had packed up the Land Rover with bags and the little kids. She was leaving. She hadn't told me she was going, and I wasn't allowed to go. I started to cry. I asked when she'd be back. She said she didn't know. I asked her if she was leaving for good. She told me to ask my father. I was heartbroken, shattered into a million pieces. Mom was really leaving me. I knew she might not ever come back. I ran inside and called for Dad. He calmly brought me to the living room to sit and talk.

I remember sitting on the scratchy yellow and green striped couch beside my father. I looked out the window and kept my eyes fixed on the highest branch I could see of the giant pine tree to which my rope swing was attached to. I stared as hard as I could and tried not to vomit, not to cry. I sat very still and waited to hear what Dad had to say. His words blended. It was all I could do to sit still and wait for the story. I didn't dare get angry or cry or say a word.

He'd made a mistake. His indiscretion was found out and shared across the community. He had an affair with one of the students. The principal, my father, had made the ultimate mistake.

Who was she? Even as I asked, I knew the answer. Staring at

that branch, my stomach in my throat, I feared the answer. It was her, the one I thought was my friend. The girl who had time for me, who would come and stay with me and sleep in my parents' bed when they went away. My mother had abandoned me, my father had broken our family, and my friend wasn't actually my friend. I was a means to an end.

This marked the beginning of the end of my childhood. I was now an angry pubescent with a grudge against my father and our so-called Christian lifestyle.

Chapter Fifteen: Moving North

Mom came back after a week, acting like nothing had happened on the outside. We had to move. The commune couldn't keep a middle-aged man who accepted the advances of a besotted teenage girl.

No matter what may or may not have happened, the mere idea of his indiscretion was unforgivable to the president's wife, Ella. She had butted heads with my father from day one and could now banish him from the commune, the church, in any and every way that she could.

We had to leave and leave fast, for we weren't welcome any longer. The move would need to include employment for my father. It was decided by the current commune's church and leadership board he couldn't hold a position of leadership, teaching, or preach sermons. They wanted to excommunicate him.

News travels as fast on the church grapevine as it does in a small town. Leaders from the northern community reached out to Dad and asked him to come back. They offered him the same position he had just lost. Principal, teacher, home head leader for boys, and, of course, his own survival class. There would be no living off the grid on the land Dad had staked off.

Mom and Dad had lived in all three of the communities in the province. When Dad first joined the church, he and Mom had lived in a far north community. Mom and Dad married there but left shortly after to live in the health retreat commune I was born into. Dad wasn't a fit with the health retreat. But, his love of rugged mountain life and charismatic personality that drew all walks of life to the church made him a shoo-in for the north.

During the preparation for our move to our new home, I was sent to stay with family friends. They had a huge farm and a couple of girls my age. I was allowed to spend most of the summer with them. I was twelve years old at the time, and the three of us girls milked cows. The cats were crazy about it when we squirted the nipple their way. One mouthful straight from the cow and I almost threw up. Never again would I want to drink milk.

We explored the fields and hills and splashed and played in the mud when we chanced upon such prized coolness. We took long baths in the giant old clawfoot tub, giggling and talking as only girls do.

We all weeded long rows of onions, garlic, and carrots. We got five or ten cents a row, depending on the type of produce. It was a great incentive to do a good job and get those long rows weeded.

We would splash in the stream as we wandered the property looking for wild asparagus for dinner. We would sit in the black cherry trees in abandoned yards, snacking away. We ate so many cherries our fingers were stained purple. We put mud on our inevitable bee stings and then ended up tossing handfuls of mud at one another in the best mud fight ever.

We tied thick cotton sheets to trees to make hammocks and lay there swinging back and forth in the breeze, making up stories. We spun tall tales about things we knew nothing of. We dared to dream of things outside of the Bible, labour, and the end of time. It was a beautiful way to spend summer as a child. I almost forgot that Mom had abandoned me just like she said she might. I even forgot, for a little while, that Dad had fooled around with a girl and that everyone whispered about it wherever we went.

It was then my obsession with sex began. It was a taboo subject and an action to be done only when married. I was concerned about this. What if it didn't work with the man you were married to? My father's sexual indiscretion had ripped apart my family and home. The opposite sexes were separated in church seating, seating in the cafeteria, and housing. When working together, students were constantly monitored. This only fueled my newfound obsession. That summer, as the girls and I swung from our hammocks, I made up tall tales about sex. I had more imagination than a young girl ought to in that department. And I was full of questions with no one to ask.

Chapter Sixteen: Another New Home

The move was done with pre-air-conditioned vehicles in the heat of the summer. The two days it took to drive two dogs, five puppies, three toddlers, and one pissed-off tween must have seemed like a never-ending trip through Hell. As scared and angry as I was to have to move, I was also excited for the adventure that awaited.

Our new house was at the very end of the community's property on the last patch of cleared land. It was a large three-storey home with five bedrooms on the top floor that would be for the students. We would have seven male students again.

The main floor had three bedrooms, one for the three little ones, one for me, and one for Mom and Dad. The basement had another family with two little children and a student. We were a few hundred metres from railway tracks, and there was a train that went by nightly. It didn't take me long to sleep through that ruckus. There was a pond next to our garage that was perfect for paddling the canoe about. It was also perfect for dumping unsuspecting teenagers into it.

My parents reconnected with some old friends they hadn't seen since they moved away more than a decade earlier. One set of friends was a family that lived at the very end of the long winding washboard road past the commune's property. The ferry had long since stopped running, so to get to the highway, they had to drive miles upon miles to the Alaska connector to meet up with the main highway to anything civilized.

Our families met at the river for a walk. They came with their two boys. Flynn, the youngest, and Finn. Finn was two years older than me. It was love before I even said hello. We walked along the riverbank, hopping from rock to rock and chatting.

Finn was a beautiful Irish boy with pale skin dotted with freckles and topped off with dark red hair. It was my lucky year, for he started attending the school at the commune we moved to. He attended as a day student and occasionally stayed overnight in our home. We would be in and out of each other's lives for most of our teen years after that fateful visit by the river.

We met up with another family on that same road. We had met them a time or two before when living down south. She had always lived on the outskirts of the community. She was one of the families that were often prayed for. She had a blended family that ended up accounting for five kids or so with a few dads in the mix. I vowed then and there that if I ever had children, they would be with one man.

The fallout with Dad's affair had halted my completion of being homeschooled for grade five. That fall, I started grade six as though nothing had happened. I spent a few hours a morning doing schoolwork and then wandered the backyard, which was basically a forest.

There was a small fort built on stilts fifteen feet above the ground. Dad clambered up the stilts and hung a knotted rope for me to climb to gain access to it. I spent hours in my tree fort. I'd light my wood stove and toss about in boredom. I nibbled on dried fruit and nuts I managed to sneak in. Much to my dismay, a few months after our move, Dad installed a ladder so the little kids could come and play in the fort, too.

With the move to our new home came another happy

addition to our diet. We got to have supper. Mr. Noodle was introduced to our diet and was allowed for supper once a week. Supper was usually a light meal of cereal, fruit, or popcorn. Nothing heavy like meat and potatoes meals. Our big meal was breakfast, as it was deemed the most important meal of the day. Breakfast was to prepare you for a full day of labour and study.

One of the students in our home had a hollow leg and was always hungry. He would want four packets of Mr. Noodle for supper after working in fields all day. Mom said he had to pay twenty-five cents for the extra packets as only one was needed for a meal. He didn't care and was happy to pay up. A Japanese student liked to add lettuce to his noodles. He would have added eggs had that been allowed in our diet. It was a simple Pho bowl before I even knew what that was.

When we moved, I wasn't allowed to make bread anymore because it was competition with the bakery the commune already had. Even though I was a kid and only wanted to sell to the community families, it was expressly forbidden. I wasn't even allowed to work at the bakery. I was back to having nothing to do and no job to earn spending money.

I was shy and unsure of myself in our new environment. That winter, my twelfth birthday came and went with little notice. The places my parents had enjoyed hiking before I was born were of little interest. I had no ties to the area they had left before I was born.

I was terribly angry with my father and wasn't hesitant about showing it. I wrote endless stories that mother burned. I wrote in my journal, but no matter where I hid it, she found it and destroyed it. I wrote my stories on the backs of letters that I saved from friends who wrote me, and she found those, too. I wrote to anyone who would write me back. I was lonely and wanted a friend desperately. My writing was burned as anything else contraband, unchristian, or in general wrong was.

Her anger at my writing came to a head when she found my notebook hidden in between my saved letters. How dare I write the truth. Or a story that might have some shred of the truth. My stories were about what happened. I was trying to vent my pain and anger and work through my confusion.

Instead, I was treated to regular room searches, loss of belongings, and lectures on the wrongs of writing or admitting the truth. When we moved, Dad was re-baptised, giving him a shiny new clean slate. It was forgive and forget for his indiscretion. The irony of that version of Christianity is not lost on me all these years later.

Like the community before, some families had children that were not allowed to play or associate with other families' children, and some were. I met a few kids from a large family. They were a little younger than I and had a plan for me. I was allowed to play with them and be their friend if I played house, as they had learned from their dad and sister.

The things they wanted me to do left a terrible feeling in my stomach. I couldn't bring myself to say no. I wanted friends so badly. Once the pants being removed were a part of the play. I ran away. I just couldn't bring myself to participate in these games, friendship or not. Not long after that, word got out about these so-called games. I was grateful, in a way, for now, we wouldn't be allowed to play, and I didn't have to keep saying no. That summer friendship haunted me for years.

I have no idea what happened with the other kids. My parents were confused and heartsick. It didn't matter what I said. I was the oldest and culpable. I was to blame regardless of where the idea or knowledge for these games came from. It was my fault from the moment the story was told.

The only thing they really wanted to know was if anything

or anyone had penetrated me. I didn't understand what they meant. They tried to explain how a penis gets hard and then can go somewhere in my privates. I didn't understand how a penis could get hard and certainly wasn't aware of any spot I had to put things. I just knew I didn't like being looked at or touched because it felt weird in a bad way. It made me not want to be there anymore. Looking back, I don't understand why no one thought to question where young kids got these inappropriate ideas from in such a sheltered environment.

How I was treated changed after that. The sin they believed I committed was never forgotten. I was never a victim in anyone's eyes.

I got a roommate. Rhena was a nice young Christian lady who would help guide me toward a Christian life. I'd be like a little sister to her, and she'd shield and guide me as I passed through puberty in our home full of troubled adolescent teenage boys. Rhena was trusted enough not to fall prey to the young men or be a temptation to them.

Lonely and bored, I tried using washable markers to put on makeup. The absolute terror of being unable to fully wash it off prevented me from doing that again. I tried to pierce my ears with thumbtacks. After numerous attempts, I looked at the tip and realized they were ball pointed at the end, not actually sharp as a needle. I began to make forts and shelters in the forest and build little fires.

That was the end of my freedom. Survival skills or not, you don't build fires in the forest. After that, I was put to work for the second half of my days. I was sent to work in the dunnage mill in full skirts over pants. Quite a job considering I wasn't even five foot and was only eighty pounds soaking wet.

The dunnage mill produced 2x4x48 pieces of wood with a groove in the centre. The purpose of dunnage is to protect and secure shipments. Metal or plastic banding is used in the groove of the dunnage to wrap around a load securing it without causing damage. They put me on the loading dock that fed the lumber to the man who fed the saw. I wasn't strong enough to get the lever pressed down to lift a load of lumber to slide on over in line for the saw. A piece of wood was used as a secondary lever to give me the extra oomph I needed. If I jumped on it, I was able to get the belt up high enough so the long two-by-fours would slide into line for the saw.

I liked working at the mill. It was fast-paced enough, so I didn't get terribly bored. I was sometimes allowed to feed the cut pieces into the machine that cut the dunnage groove through the centre of the two-by-four. Sometimes, I was able to pair up with the person at the end and catch the dunnage flying out the end. We would race to stack them so as not to get behind. My skirt ripped right through in the centre from the constant pressure of using my torso and thighs as leverage to press the pieces into place on the trolley. The mill was momentarily turned off, and I was sent home for the day. It was immodest to have my body dressed in pants exposed through my torn skirt.

A few months after starting at the mill, I was given a different job. I was sent to cook lunches for thirty-plus students and staff. Five days a week, I made vegan meals from scratch. After lunch, I cleaned up and washed all the cookware, cafeteria trays, and silverware. One meal I made that I need never make again was perogies. I made perogy dough and filling. I cut the shapes from the dough, filled them, folded the top over, and pressed the seam closed. I made enough for forty hungry people. To this day, I have never had the urge to make perogies again.

I learned quite a lot at that job. I learned that if I left a pot of water with a few drops of oil on the stove, the water would evaporate, and the oil would start on fire. I learned about salt—put salt on the flames if you start an oil fire. I learned that if you use dish soap on the floor to make a slide, you will spend hours upon hours trying to wash up all that soap. It wasn't quite worth the fun of sliding from one end to the other of the linoleum-covered floor.

Working in various industries enabled me to talk with Finn occasionally without being caught. We wrote each other long letters, folded up and hidden in an unfinished door frame. He was the centre of my daydreams, thoughts, and conversations with girlfriends.

I gained newfound freedom that summer. I was twelve going on twenty. Mom and Dad let me spend time with Celine, the girl from across the river. Her family attended our church. We were almost the same age, and she had older brothers with driver's licenses. This meant we could ask them for rides to hang out as our parents were too busy.

Celine sometimes attended class as a day student. The older siblings interacted with our commune's events and outings from time to time. Saturdays after church, I'd often go with them for lunch, then off-roading up old logging and mining roads. Other times they would pick me up, and we would go splash and sunbathe at the river.

I spent the summer petitioning Mom and Dad to stop homeschooling me and let me attend the academy. That fall, I started grade nine in the academy with the other students. A classmate offered to keep an eye on me and help me adjust. I went from grade six to nine and got to be with the older kids and learn with them in a classroom setting.

We had Bible class, math, science, and English. The Bible was the same old same old. Math was hard, as they were throwing in algebra and geometry. I didn't speak that language. I couldn't get ninety percent to save my life. Ninety percent was required to pass in all academic areas. After many attempts, I cheated my way past one chapter.

Science was fun. We dissected a frog and learned about grafting a pear branch into an apple tree. Our science textbooks had chapters blacked out with markers, much like the children's Bible storybooks I read as a child. Those chapters didn't follow our religious beliefs, so we needn't learn or be able to read such things.

As I neared my very exciting long-awaited first teen birthday, I began to run a little wild. I picked on some of the kids. I spent my money ordering fake nails, magic hair growth formulas, books, and whatever else the back of magazines offered in their little ads.

Everyone had their little stash of hidden items that were deemed contraband. My favourites were magazines and books. I devoured every word. I had my orders shipped to the older girls who didn't live in our home. I managed to get my hands on romance novels and hid them beneath my pillow, between my sheet and mattress. It was too obvious to hide them in between the mattress and box spring.

* * *

Our house was always lively and full of noise. Ever since our move to the new commune, we had anywhere from four to eight teenage boys living with us. Their ages ranged from fourteen to twenty. A couple of them were from Japan, others from the Northwest Territories. Most were from various states. All were in the throes of puberty and unaccustomed to the lifestyle.

I was also in full-on puberty with a curiosity for the opposite gender that confused me. They were like brothers to me, they were handsome bad boys, and they were annoying boys suffering from acne. They all had to put up with a moody little sister following them around.

I got chickenpox that fall. It made me the most popular girl around for a week. I was so sick with fever and discomfort that I floated in and out of semi-consciousness. I was either sleeping, delirious with itching, or lying in a bath of oatmeal water.

The oatmeal wasn't directly in the bathwater. We filled a cut-off leg from a pair of nylons to use as a filter. I tried not to scratch as I didn't want to be covered in lifelong pockmark scars. My skin was covered in red itchy bumps that drove me mad. I had socks on my hands so I couldn't scratch in my sleep.

Everyone who hadn't had chickenpox yet was brought to visit me. Sitting as close to me as they could, holding my hand, touching my forehead, trying to catch the disease. That's how the children were immunized at the commune.

That year was the first time I played a board game. We got Monopoly and UNO. A couple of the boys and I sat on the living room floor. It was exciting to have something to play together. I read the instructions and learned what the rules were. It was such fun trying to buy everything and not go broke. I always wanted to be the shoe or hat for some reason, never anything else. The boys and I got so competitive trying to win that the game was deemed sinful and taken away. Any competition was unchristian.

Being better than someone, beating them, was ungodly. The game was burned like everything else over the years, deemed unchristian.

They burned my Walkman from my aunt and the short stories that I wrote. They even burned the cross necklace I got from my uncle because, according to them, the Saviour still lived. Wearing the cross meant I was wearing a symbol of his death. Everything I cherished was burned, gone forever.

* * *

I got my first real birthday cake when I turned thirteen. I got to invite my friend Celine for lunch. I was so excited to have a friend over for my birthday meal. She made me a giant bunny rabbit cake from real cake batter with real icing made from sugar, with coconut flakes for fur. I had never ever had a real cake before. I was so excited, and her gesture meant so much to me. She also gave me the doll house her grandfather had made her when she was a little girl. It was a huge two-storey multibedroom building on wheels. The miniature furniture was complete with hand-sewn coverlets. That evening my parents pulled me aside and gave me a choice. I could return it, or they would burn it, for I wasn't allowed to play with doll houses. I chose to return it because I knew how much it meant to her. Yet another gift that was discarded for God.

I evolved quickly, and my parents tried to rein me back in. Once, in a fit of anger, I ran for the phone to call the authorities. I was going to turn them in because it was wrong how we were living. Original, I know.

I thumbed through the phone, looking for the right number. Before I could find the correct number, I was sent to my room. My parents proceeded to put a hook and eye lock on the outside of my door. I was on room arrest with a bread and water diet and three bathroom breaks a day until I was contrite. Once contrite, I had to submit a thousand-word essay expressing my belief and understanding of the doctrines we were living before I was released from my confinement.

I hit my teen years with an axe to grind. I had grown up learning to think for myself and to make the right choices. I'd also been taught my choices were a hoax, a test. There was no real choice, as I had to do what was right in the eyes of the leaders and the communal rules. I knew there was an entire world we weren't allowed to be a part of, to know about. The students who came and went each school year were living, talking proof of that.

I saw my father change rules he didn't agree with. Something as simple as cayenne was bad, yet we ate it at home and didn't speak of it. Something like choosing safety over dress code, not wearing long dresses or skirts when I was in the treetops. Dad was losing his rose-tinted glasses when it came to the stringent religious commune and its endless rules and judgements.

One of the best things Dad shared with me was during winter break. We watched VHS videos in the empty church. The office had a TV and VCR as they had made a video to share with others, their version of a commercial. I'm not sure where Dad got the videos for us to watch that December. He had quite a collection about mind control, brainwashing, religious trances, and of people being placed into trances for us to watch.

Images from those videos stuck in my head. The dirt roads, cornfields, and bell-bottom jeans were not so different from the community we lived in. There were families searching for their missing loved ones. It was as though they had disappeared. I watched the sadness the loved ones felt as they were shunned and ignored as worldly by the family members who chose to live in a commune.

I recall two slender women dressed in seventies-style clothing. They had long, unadorned hair and wore a blouse or shirt and jeans. These women were paired up. One was a proven long-term believer, the other a recent recruit.

The trick was to not let the newbie have too much time to think, to be alone with her thoughts. Keep her working hard, sleeping little, bombarded with the beliefs. She couldn't even get away to the old wooden washrooms for peace and quiet to think. Dad and I didn't talk much about the videos. We both were silent. Each lost to our own thoughts and feelings, the comparisons to our own community that came to mind were never voiced.

Other videos showed big revivals at tents and large

gatherings in churches where the devil needed to be cast out of people. Other times the Lord would be brought in, speaking in tongues through his vessels, the people in the audience.

These videos were generally very high-energy and exciting. They got your heart and pulse racing. Then the preacher would take the disciple or volunteer into their hands. They would speak with strong, loud words and then press their hand forcefully upon the forehead of the volunteer. After that, the person would be changed.

I had never seen anything like it. Full-grown adults made into zombies swaying about in a trance, speaking in tongues, sobbing upon the floor, gyrating to an unseen master. This was the product of a cult, of brainwashing at its finest.

I have no idea what my father thought of it. That isn't something we discussed. I'm not sure if he was comparing the lifestyle he chose to live to those in the videos. The lifestyle we lived wasn't nearly as obvious or drastic with control; however, there were key similarities to a lesser degree.

I know that those videos were a gift to me that would last the rest of my life. Use your noggin, as Dad would say. Don't be a follower. Be an individual. The irony doesn't escape me in this.

Chapter Seventeen:
Losing My Religion and Dad

The winter I turned thirteen, the weather was mild considering our northern location. The students petitioned for an extra survival camping trip to be added to the class in the spring. It was an easy sell. Camping was a favourite pastime. On the last survival trip, the type of shelter was optional. Teepees were always recommended when camping without a sleeping bag.

Shelter from the wind and close proximity to the fire was ideal in a teepee. A few boys, of course, opted for something a little more daring. They chose to make a tree fort. I never saw how that turned out. They were camping across the invisible line that separated the genders. Absolutely no intermingling allowed.

I built my very own teepee not far from Dad's to sleep in. It was the first time I camped alone in my own shelter. I had the proper ventilation from three spots on the ground. My bed was a comfy two-foot-deep bed of bows. My fire burned well, considering the damp wood.

There was a massive flaw in my shelter. I sat in my little teepee with my eyes burning and tears rolling down my cheeks from the thick, choking smoke that filled my shelter.

Something wasn't working right, and the middle of the night wasn't a time to figure it out. I finally caved and crawled onto the foot of Dad's bed during the night.

The next day was Sabbath, the seventh day of the week, our day of rest. We packed light fanny packs with our trail mix, canteens, and Bibles. We set off to enjoy a nice hike before stopping for lunch and our usual hour of prayer and meditation.

Dad had his usual hour of rest, which I said was a nap. He always said he was just checking for holes in his eyelids. After the spiritual rest, there was some free time. Some would take photos; others would collect little treasures from nature.

On this trip, the location of rest was on one of the many rocky outlooks jutting out from the mountain. We had a wonderful view of the river below. It snaked through the valley as far as we could see. It was a beautiful place to stop for our midday break. A few students enjoyed a little refresher lesson from Dad on how to use a compass. I wasn't as interested in the lesson so much as one of the young men there. Amid this, Dhillon came to ask Dad to help them with a particularly large boulder they couldn't quite budge to roll over the edge of the cliff.

Dad asked if I wanted to come, as this wasn't an uncommon pastime for us. We loved to push giant rocks and boulders down cliffs and ravines to hear the loud crashing sounds and see how far they would go. I was more interested in the boy than crashing boulders, so I declined. Dad went off with Dillon. They found the perfect boulder to push.

Then I heard a deafening noise. It was much louder than any one boulder crashing down a cliff. I stood up and ran to the ledge to see better. Rocks of all sizes were bouncing and rolling away into the forest below. A tree shot out like an arrow from the cliff. Something was terribly wrong. I thought I saw someone falling. This couldn't be happening. The boy I had previously been so interested in was now forgotten.

I neared a jagged slide area between two parts of the cliff.

I stood on one side and looked to the other side, where Dad and Dillon were. Before I could clamber across, I saw a student running toward me. I couldn't understand her words, but her skin said it all to me. Her beautiful golden skin was now closer to yellow. I'd never seen such a yellow hue on anyone's skin before. Almost all the colour was gone from her face. Deep inside, I knew what had happened.

I remember her shouting she had to get help because Mr. C was down there. I didn't need to ask where down there was. I knew he was at the bottom of the cliff. I changed my direction and began to make my way down it to see if there was a viable way to the bottom. Within minutes a couple of the chaperones hollered at me that I couldn't go that way. I was told in no uncertain terms I was to not go to my father and to go back. I didn't know where back was. I had to go somewhere, so I blundered along in a blind stagger away from the cliffs.

I felt lost. Not lost as in didn't know where I was; I was lost in myself. I couldn't see clearly, and my sense of direction was gone. Essentially, I was a bumbling fool. I walked off a large boulder and fell a few feet below to the mossy ground. I walked into tree limbs and scraped my face and arms. I wasn't crying or hysterical. I was more like a zombie searching for a reason or a place that would make this all better.

Thankfully my friend, Rhena, found me. We didn't head back to camp and instead walked back to the commune. On our way, we saw my mother being brought in by a snowmobile. We passed some very exhausted ambulance attendants hiking in with their first aid equipment. We kept walking.

I never saw my father again, except in my dreams.

Life changed drastically overnight. That day all the boys were moved out of our home. I had lost my father, the full household I grew up in, and the sense of family all in one fell swoop. The weeks and months afterwards were a blur of sorrow, grief, anger, depression, fear, and a deep abiding belief the entire world should stop and acknowledge who was lost.

That first night after Mom came back from the mountain, we sat in the hallway of our very empty home, in stunned shock. There was a strange feeling that permeated every part of the atmosphere. Mom held Matthias on her lap. Daniel and Damaris sat on either side of me.

How she found the strength to say the words, I'll never know. My siblings sat there waiting to hear where Dad was and why we were crying. She struggled to find a way to tell them Dad was never coming home.

At six, Daniel understood we would never again set eyes on our father. The grief emanating from Mom and me was like a black pool of suffocating pain. The children couldn't help but burst into tears which broke our fragile hold on our emotions. We all sat there sobbing. What else could we do?

They were so little, so innocent, and young. The depth of that loss was beyond their years. We sat there crying and hugging each other. My heart broke all over again to know these beautiful babies would never know their father. My baby brother Matthias was barely two years old, the same age as Dad was when he lost his own father.

Sometime later, the pastor knocked at our door. He stood there in the entryway and offered his condolences and the Lord's spiritual support.

"It was God's will to take him. We must trust in His will," he said.

"Fuck God!" I shouted and stormed upstairs. I had watched my father fall from a cliff. Trees shot out like flimsy arrows. Rocks rolled and crashed down. I could only imagine how his body was pummeled by debris as he fell.

That was in God's great plan? I couldn't bear to hear that—to think that. What kind of God planned this? What kind of God would want this for our family?

I was livid that the pastor would dare comfort us in that way. Over time I'd hear how Dad would have hated to have been in a wheelchair, so it was better this way. Or that he couldn't have lived with himself if it was a student instead of him. People kept saying how sorry they were. They were empty, useless words that did nothing to ease the black hole my life had become.

My aunts, uncles, cousins, and grandparents all came to support Mom in all the planning that happens when someone passes away. The memorial and subsequent months are jagged shards of memories, incoherent moments tangible as thin gossamer threads of a spiderweb.

I choked out words at the open mic at Dad's service. To this day, I've never watched the recording of it. It's the only recording I have of my mother. I had an audio tape that had a recording of my parents singing at Vespers. The sound of their voices has been both comforting and painful over the years.

Mom and I were unable to function normally, even though we tried. I moved upstairs to the top floor where the boys had lived. We now had five empty bedrooms that used to house seven teenage boys. I moved from room to room like someone changing clothes. Nothing fit right anymore. Mom began to attend meetings for surviving spouses in town. We couldn't sleep. We could be found in the middle of the night doing the oddest things.

Mom and I would say good night at bedtime and go our separate ways. I'd begin to move my things to yet another room. The action of doing something, anything, sidetracked me from my desolation. I'd hear Mom outside hauling wagon loads of firewood even though it didn't need to be done. We would end up meeting in the kitchen to have toast with avocado, sprouts, and brewer's yeast at midnight, laughing that we were both up doing the craziest things even though we were meant to be going to bed. Mom and I ate at odd times, never really hungry. There was no need to prepare meals anymore. Only the little ones needed to eat now.

Mom and I had lost our purpose. The needle of our compass was gone now that Dad was dead. We had no reason or direction.

There was no one calling out at six a.m., "Rise and shine and let the Glory of the Lord be upon you." There was no reason to hold morning and evening worship in the living room anymore. Now it was just Mom and me with the toddlers.

Life went on as though Dad was just away, not gone. The fields were worked, the bakery baked bread, the greenhouse produced cucumbers, and classes continued. Still, I couldn't move forward. I felt as though the world would forget him. I'd see him walking down the lane, and my heart would jump for joy. As I'd draw near, I'd see it was someone else wearing my father's clothing.

Mom sold almost everything she could of his. Everywhere I looked, I saw pieces of his life being used by other men. I cried so much that my eyes were swollen. My eyelashes started falling out. I cried so often that I threw up walking down the dirt road to class. I don't even know how I went to class, although I must have. I was despondent, inconsolable.

I remember someone told me that as he was scrambling away from the ledge and walking backwards, he called out, "Everything will be fine!"

Fine, my ass, I thought when I heard those words. Nothing was fine. I was adrift with no reason to move forward. Adrift in the middle of a religious community where it was God's will that took my father away from me. This God who dictated our every action.

I couldn't bring myself to care about anything outside my

own pain. Why those who were with him didn't fall to their death haunted me. Why would unseen hands pull others back from falling to their death but not my dad? I embraced anger as I tried to mask my grief.

I was too afraid to close my eyes at night. I became obsessed with knowing what happened when Dad lay at the bottom of the cliff. I hadn't been allowed to go to him for my own good. My nightmares conjured up a worse reality of his injuries.

I bullied and pushed one of the students that was with him when he died until he told me how Dad looked. He said his eyes were bulging, and he spat up blood when they gave him mouth-to-mouth. He was unconscious from the moment they found him until he died.

I read the autopsy report, and it supported the story and fueled my nightmares. A rock had bounced off his chest. It smashed his ribs into sharp razors that shredded his insides. The back of his head was damaged so badly that his eye bulged out.

The report said he was dead by the time he hit the valley floor. His body was in the throes of dying. I imagined it was the same as the gophers we shot. They twitched away until, finally, they were still forever.

I was haunted by this gruesome ending to a man I loved more than anything. I felt that I needed him the most as I entered my teen years. My father, who I was angry with until his death, now gone forever.

I spent many an evening sitting in my parents' room on the floor, talking to Finn. He was going to a different school, no longer welcome at the commune's academy.

When Mom was busy with the kids at bedtime, I'd take the phone and stretch the long cord as far as I could. I'd sit next to Dad's bedside table on the floor, wrapping the coils around my finger as we talked. Finn's family was a war zone, thanks to his mom's deep faith in God.

His father, patient as he was, would never be able to appease his wife's faith unless he joined. Finn and I shared our worries, our dreams, and our feelings of being helpless. If either of our mothers came, we had to hang up because they didn't want us talking.

Chapter Eighteen: Life Without Father

One thing that really stuck in my mind for years was Mom repeatedly saying she didn't know how to do anything. Mom wished she'd have learned instead of just letting Dad do it. She regretted she hadn't been more self-sufficient and independent.

She didn't do any of the paperwork, banking, taxes, etc. She didn't know how to change a tire or the oil. She was the perfect stay-at-home wife and mother. Now she had to be both mother and father. She had to be able to do everything herself. That really stuck in my mind for years and strongly influenced the woman I became.

Our life drastically changed, and so had Mom. She wasn't the same after he died. She pushed us to heal and move on. She sold most of his belongings, in part, to survive financially. I don't know how she handled that. The need for money must have been worth the pain. There was no life insurance. Things like that weren't needed as they believed God would take care of us. Later in life, I really wanted to point out to these idealists that "God helps those that help themselves."

Mom didn't qualify for government assistance for a variety of reasons. One large one was that she had over a thousand dollars left in savings after paying for Dad's cremation. The logic defied her as they would only help her once she had spent all her money. Donations had come in with bereavement cards totalling over a couple of grand. By the time the cremation was paid for, she had very little left and no income coming in. The Canadian government refused to pay a survivor's benefit to her as Dad hadn't paid into it long enough. He had only been in Canada a few years prior to joining the community. The United States offered to take the hours he had in the USA and Canada combined and pay out a monthly survivor's benefit for each of the four children until they turned eighteen. The kindness of a country Dad had left stuck with me for the rest of my life. The community offered to pay half of Dad's salary to Mother as a survivor's benefit as well. She felt terrible taking money she didn't earn but was left with little choice. A stubborn pride runs in my genes from both sides.

Not long after Dad passed, a couple of packages arrived. Mail was always exciting, particularly as we were so cut off from outside contact of any form. One package came on Mom's birthday. They were slippers that Dad had specially ordered. They were made by someone in the Northwest Territories. It was a bittersweet moment for Mom on her birthday.

The other package wasn't so sweet. I came home to Mom and Dhillon, one of the boys that used to live with us, sitting at the table with a small box between them. I was so excited that I ran up to them and asked what it was and if I could open it. I was given permission and eagerly ripped into the box. Inside was a bag of ashes. I was terribly confused and turned to Mom and asked what it was. It was Dad. I screamed and dropped the box. Mom and Dhillon chuckled at my reaction as I ran away sobbing.

As weeks turned into months, I began to realize I never knew what I'd find Mom up to. I worried I'd find her, and possibly the children, dead. She'd walk and talk like she was fine, but if you observed her, the truth could be seen. Except I don't think anyone really looked.

I never knew what kind of situation I'd come home to after a day of work. Sometimes she'd be folding laundry and looking after the kids. Other times she'd be locked in her bedroom. She'd be in her closet surrounded by Dad's torn and bloodied clothes that he died in. Other times she'd be gone. The kids, the guns, Mom, all gone. I didn't know if she was coming back or killing the children and herself out where I wouldn't be the first to find them.

Mom was having discussions with me again at an adult level. This time instead of leaving Dad and me, she talked of suicide. She'd say to herself, and to me, that it might be the day to end herself and the little ones. She told me it would be easier. Coming home after work was always a long walk of fear and uncertainty. I was in so much pain, and the only advice I kept getting was to deal with it. They wanted me to act as if nothing was wrong, as though I hadn't lost my father. I was supposed to act as if my home life wasn't an emotional rollercoaster ride. I couldn't even comprehend, much less put into words, the turmoil of my night terrors and dubious home life.

I was torn. I thought the world should stop and acknowledge my father was gone. I was angry that he was gone. I worried about my mother and siblings day and night. I didn't know what to do and knew little besides what I was taught. Be a good Christian, and you will go to Heaven and be reunited with your loved ones for eternity. Or you could live life as you choose and burn forever in Hell.

I wanted to be with my father again. To say sorry for how angry and mean I had become to him after his affair. I wanted to help Mom come back from the abyss of grief she was drowning in. The only way I knew how to do that was to embrace the Lord.

Chapter Nineteen: Leaving

My heart felt lighter than it had in months. This was the right decision for my future. I stood beside the fire barrel tossing in the last of my writings, fiction books, and other contraband paraphernalia into the flames. Tears streamed down my cheeks as I watched my handwritten stories go up in smoke. Fear squeezed at my heart as I watched my escape from life curl at the edges as flames caught on the book's edges. I was determined to accept God into my life and live according to his wishes. I'd be a devoted servant to the Lord as my father was. To prove this, I was willing to give up the things that were precious to me to pledge my heart, soul, and life to God's will.

At that moment, Jimmy, a leader in the commune, came up behind me, demanding to know what I was doing. Why wasn't I at his home working with the rest of the crew? I opened my mouth to answer, but he was too busy loudly ranting at me to hear anything I said. He was standing too close to me. He was inside my personal space. I could see his mustache quivering with anger. I was mesmerized by the hideous caterpillar sitting upon his top lip that was shaking with rage.

Jimmy was technically the president there. I was assigned work detail for his wife for the week and hadn't gone back after lunch like I was supposed to. I'd spent the morning pulling weeds from the family's large garden. While my body mindlessly worked the field, my mind was busy. I was deeply concerned about Mom and about seeing Dad again in Heaven. I had a plan to be one with God and was mid fiery burn to getting there when Jimmy showed up.

While he vigorously admonished my horrible behaviour, I mentally stepped back and watched him. I wondered what the heck was the point of all this. Then, as I watched the spittle fly from his mouth, something in me snapped. This wasn't my future. Jimmy was clear he had had enough of me and was done. He told me I'd better get my act together or else. Or else what? There was no choice in the lifestyle I was born into. We worked, ate, prayed, slept, and studied all by their schedule, their rules. So, what could possibly happen to me now?

I watched his angry tirade, unable to break through his rant to speak on my behalf. Something inside me stepped up. It was obvious he had no intention of listening to me. He didn't care. None of them cared if I became a lifelong vessel for the Lord. And if they didn't care, why should I?

I turned and walked into the house. I told Mother I was leaving and hugged her goodbye. She didn't even bat an eye. I hopped onto my mountain bike and pedalled away. I didn't stop to say goodbye to those I passed in the fields. Fury and determination fueled my actions. I set out on a new path. The path of freedom.

I was thirteen years old, in runners, pants, and a full dress, bawling my eyes out. I pedalled my bike toward parts unknown from the only life I had ever known. It was a journey that would begin much like my parents, down a dead-end dirt road. I was leaving. Going where, I didn't know. I wasn't running away; I was running to a new life. I had no money, no plan, and no place to go, but I was going. It took everyone by surprise, but no one came after me. Perhaps they underestimated my level of done with their *ask no questions and do as you're told lifestyle*, or maybe it was a relief I left.

Gone was my epiphany of how to be with Dad and save Mom. It was replaced with a deep-seated resentment for the life I was born into. I was filled with anger at the duplicitous behaviour of these God-fearing people who hid behind religion. They controlled as much as they could while allowing bad things to happen behind closed doors. I was leaving all I'd ever known and going into a world I knew little of. I could count on one hand how many times a year I'd been outside the commune in my short life.

As I pedalled down the bumpy washboard road, I thought about the people I might be able to stay with. As the kilometres rolled away under my tires, I ran out of tears, and my crying ceased. I could think a bit clearer. I needed a plan. I'd stay with one of the young men who had come around to the youth services we had held in the neighbouring reserves during the summer. I still remembered some of their phone numbers. Once I got to a gas station, I went to the payphone and realized I didn't even have a quarter to make a call. Thankfully, the waitress at the diner let me borrow the telephone.

The young man who answered the phone said I could stay with him if I could get myself there. Thank God that was his answer. My life could have gone so much worse if he'd been willing to come to get me. There was no way I was adding another thirty kilometres to my ride. It would be dark long before I arrived at a destination I'd never been to. Fear kicked in, and my gut said to make another call. Who could I call, though? I called Maria, Rhena's mom. She was a mother. She'd understand. Her children were students at the farm. Maybe she'd come and get me.

I must have broken Maria's heart with that phone call. She came and got me, then drove me home so I could pack a suitcase. My Mom didn't stop me—didn't talk to me. She just stood there and let me go. She never asked me to stay. She never asked me to change my mind. Maybe she'd been counselled to let me go. Maybe she wanted me to go. I sobbed about the unfairness of life. I sobbed for all I'd lost. I sobbed for a life I wanted but didn't know how to get and wouldn't be able to get. Maria was so distraught she left her wallet on the roof of the car. We pulled over to retrieve it partway on the drive to her home. She laughed and thanked God she had the mind to remember she left it there and got it before it fell. I hollowly laughed with her.

I didn't have much stock in this God everyone thought so highly of. I knew better than to say a word. Dad's fall from grace and then the cliff, coupled with Mom's adult ways of conversing with me, had changed something deep inside me. As the shock wore off, I realized my stomach was hurting. Finally, we arrived at Maria's house.

I was given supper, and we had a long talk over the supper table about my future and how they would try and intervene with my mother on my behalf. Maria was kind and patient with me, and no judgement for my actions was verbalized. I knew Maria and her husband were going to discuss and plan my future with my mother after I was put to bed. As far as I was concerned, living with my mother wasn't an option.

The next morning, I was shipped to a nearby town where an uncle and aunt lived. I slept on the floor in their guest room while I waited for my fate to be decided. It wasn't that they didn't have a bed for me to sleep in, I just couldn't sleep, and the floor somehow comforted me. I was tormented with sleeplessness. I had nightmares. There was a weight upon my chest so heavy that I couldn't breathe. The pain consumed me day and night. Even though I was done with God, or at least the God of the commune, I slept with my Bible open upon my chest. Reading the Song of Solomon soothed me enough to sleep when I woke in the middle of the night from nightmares.

I was unable to bear the visions when I closed my eyes. It was my father I saw. My dad lying broken and bleeding at the bottom of the cliff. He was splayed out over the rocks like in a bad horror film. My dreams were strange. I had one where Dad had a girlfriend, and he was hiding from me. Maybe it was all a farce so he could escape with his lover. That did little to appease the pain that blocked my ability to function.

I ate, laughed, talked, and worked, but deep inside, I wanted to die. I wrote angry, hurtful, suicidal letters to the boys who'd been like my brothers. I blamed some and wished upon them the fate my father suffered. I cried out for strength from others. No one could provide a salve for my wounds.

After a short time, it was decided I'd go south, far south, to live in the first home I had lived in. I'd live in the house with the beautiful stone fireplace where I used to melt birthday candles. The house with the view of the entire Thompson Valley spread out below. I just wouldn't have my family anymore. The family living there now were experienced foster parents and happy to take me in. Their own children were grown with families of their own. My grandparents came to visit Mom and drove me there. It was neat to ride in their smooth K-car. I stretched out and napped. The sunshine streamed through the window and lulled me into a warm cozy zone of happiness. It was probably the best sleep I'd had in months.

I was given my old childhood room and a list of daily household chores. My bedroom was a haven for stink bugs. I'd wake to a bed filled with dead ones from me rolling on them. Live ones stared at me from atop the blankets. Bugs all over the bed, floor, windows, and walls. I was reprimanded for being upset and for crying out. I soon learned to carefully step out of bed to vacuum them all up. I did this morning and night until the cold came and killed off the bugs.

I wasn't sent to school with the other children. The school didn't go past grade eight. No one thought that a thirteen-year-old, having missed half the grades, including grades seven and eight, might benefit from any classes available. No one thought to let me attend and redo a grade. No one bothered to check where I was academically. My mental and social well-being were addressed by keeping me busy. I was given a job at the bakery. I started work at three a.m. and finished at noon. I was home alone until the end of the day. I knocked about this big, empty house filled with the ghosts of my parents from a happier time.

I was terrified on my walk to work. The bakery was a mile down the mountain. This was the same mountain I had watched the telephone lines be put in years before with such excitement. There were no streetlights. I had no flashlight. I took the shortcut, which was a goat path, by memory only. At times the moon shone through the trees, lighting the path. I'd sing the few lines I remembered to "This Little Light of Mine," "Jesus Loves Me," and "Joy to the World." I hoped that my voice would warn and scare away the wild animals that might think me a tasty snack.

One day, while walking back from work along the road instead of the trail, I ran into a mountain lion. I wasn't really watching my surroundings. The meadow to the right had a path to the lookout. There was a little cave out there that always caught my eye. I loved that spot and remembered going there as a girl with my mother and father. I decided to go see it again.

Just then, a movement caught my eye. There at the treeline stood a mountain lion. It just looked at me for a moment and then sauntered into the forest without a backward glance. I still had a good half a kilometre before I was home. I made that distance in record time. I was white as a ghost by the time I walked in the door.

The home I grew up in had changed. It was modernized with things like an electric stove and a built-in vacuum. It had changed, yet it was the same. The logic behind moving me there defies me as my pain intensified with all the memories of my family. It was still hard for me to fall asleep and stay asleep. My dreams were filled with grief and loss. I wanted to die and thought of the ways I could end it, but I was too afraid of pain to hurt myself. My social skills were atrocious. All I talked about was my father, my loss, my pain, and my wish to die. I had one friend, but she was too young to help someone in the depths of emotional turmoil.

One afternoon after work, I came home to find the house mother lying in wait for me. She had done a thorough search of my room. I shouldn't have been surprised because that's what they did. She had a couple of books on the table beside her that I was required to prove I had purchased.

Mom was sending me twenty dollars a month to pay for personal hygiene and feminine products. She'd determined I couldn't afford to buy books. Therefore, I must have stolen them on my last trip to town. It didn't matter what I said unless I could provide a receipt. I hadn't kept it. I gave up my protests of innocence, my words fell on deaf ears. I saw the judgement on her face. I was taken back to town to the local bookshop and forced to apologize for stealing the books. My photograph was taken and placed on their banned shopper's board. I was blacklisted from entering their bookstore chain anywhere in the country for ten years. There was no way to prove I had bought the books.

I don't know what was worse. The refusal to believe me or the mortification of being taught a lesson at my favourite store. The irony wasn't lost on me that I'd stolen the blue eyeliner I hid in the heating vent. I always paid for my books, but I couldn't afford eyeliner. I couldn't afford anything. My work at the bakery was for the privilege of having a room and meals.

I had a few highlights in my few months there. I found some newspapers lining the top shelves I was cleaning. I got to read some of the old articles. I hadn't read a newspaper before, and it was a nice reprieve from cleaning. I read an article debating the decency of a young actress who played in a movie called *The Blue Lagoon*. I was curious about what kind of movie would create such a debate. I didn't realize the world judged and talked about everything. It picked and poked, no matter the subject.

One afternoon I answered the door to some Jehovah's Witnesses. I had a lovely, animated debate with them about religion and set meetings with them a few times to debate their religious interpretations with mine. They were doggedly close-minded. They couldn't have a reasonable discussion. I loved to play devil's advocate and look at different sides to any story. I was soon tired of them. Besides, God and I were at war. I had no interest in more close-minded God enthusiasts with their life rulebooks to get to a better afterlife. This current life was enough trouble for me.

I turned fourteen in my old home. The kids from the community and a few adults all gathered to wish me a happy birthday. It was a bittersweet day for me. I was happy to have a birthday gathering. It was my first without Dad, without any family. I wasn't with my mother and the adorable babies I loved as my own. I missed my family so much. I was given a large, oversized teddy bear that I slept with for years after that. Despite their efforts, it was a shitty birthday.

Chapter Twenty: Can I Come Home?

At Christmas, I caught a ride with one of the staff members to the second commune we had lived at to meet Mother. It was the commune we had moved to when I was seven. I hadn't seen her in almost six months. It was her first Christmas without Dad, and she wanted to spend it in the bush.

Whatever mixed emotions I had about my mother, she was one tough cookie. She had three tots, six and under, and a dozen teen students. They loaded up the old Land Rover and headed a few hours up the back road into the mountains where we used to camp with Dad. We'd spent many a Christmas living in a teepee for the holidays.

Everyone was already up the mountain and set up when I arrived. The frozen snow crunched loudly as Mom and I ran to each other. I was so excited to see her after being separated for months. As she hugged me, she grabbed my boob and commented how I'd grown into a young woman. I was uncomfortable and embarrassed by her action. I wasn't ready to be that open.

During that week, we shot off Dad's rifles and handguns. Mom brought all the ones she had kept. We climbed the trees previously set up for climbing and traversed across to repel down the opposite tree. We went on day hikes and sang carols. It was an empty attempt to get through the holidays.

At the end of the week, Mom told me I'd be coming back with her and the kids. Where I was staying wasn't going to work. They, as a community, had decided I couldn't come back. I didn't understand why the family I was living with didn't have the courage to tell me that themselves.

I didn't understand why I was being moved. It wasn't that I was upset because I wasn't happy there to begin with. I was terribly homesick for my family. Yet, I wondered why I was being sent away with no warning.

Mom said it was because they weren't equipped to handle someone with my problems. I didn't understand. I was born into this life. These people, these communities with their ideals, had created me. They made me, and now they couldn't handle me.

I was angry, hurt, and frustrated with my situation. My meagre belongings would be packed for me and shipped up when someone was driving that way.

After the camping trip, I went back with Mother. We travelled north to the commune she still lived in. It was the same place where Dad died and everything changed. Now she lived in the basement of one of the larger households. The kids shared a room with a bunk bed.

I had my own room with a window overlooking the greenhouse where the cucumbers were grown. Behind that was the mountain range I loved, so tall and majestic. Dad had climbed that mountain not two years prior. Only one other group of climbers had reached the summit.

The move into the new place helped erase the ghost of our past family life. The memory wasn't as painful when walking the roads he had walked. In a way, his memory became like a pleasant brush of warm sunshine on my soul.

I liked being close to Mom again and being able to talk and cook together. I loved the warmth of the chubby arms of my siblings around my neck. Whether playing on the floor, lying in bed together, or racing through the orchards, their closeness brought peace to my spirit. I adored them and mothered them with careless abandon. They were the balm to my wounds like no other.

I wanted to come home permanently. I wanted to live with my mother and my siblings. I wanted to go to school and work the farm as I had before. Mom said we had to gain permission from the community first. It had to be taken to the board of adults that ran the school. The same board that my father had been a part of.

I approached my friend Susan, who also sat on that board, and asked her what my odds were of getting in and if she could sway them to allow me to live with Mother. I just wanted to be with Mom and the kids. She was different now. She wasn't locking herself in the closet or talking of killing herself and the children. She had a beau and seemed to have found a reason to wake up and smile.

While we waited for the commune to have their vote at their monthly meeting, I was taken with the school kids to a nearby ski hill. Few of us had ever gone skiing before.

We must have made quite a spectacle unloading from vans, all geared up for snow with long full skirts over top. After a lesson teaching us the basics of the *pizza to stop* and how to sit on the T-bar lift, we were off. It was such fun flying down the mountain. I stuck to the green runs with gentler slopes. It was rather scary going that fast, and I tended to fall.

One such fall tossed my ankles overhead in a reverse somersault. The pain left me dazed in the snow. As I sat and gathered my bearings, one of the Japanese students came skiing down. He decided to take the left-hand route instead of going straight, and he ended up taking neither. Instead, he did the splits around a tree.

My gales of laughter didn't amuse him; however, it did jar me out of my physical pain enough to ski the rest of the trail down. I never forgot my one experience of skiing, skirt and all. I felt like I'd been run over by a truck for a few days after that.

On the night the committee met, I was sick with worry and excitement. This was it. This would have me officially allowed to be a part of my family again. I'd be able to attend school and work the farm. I was nauseous with worry. I couldn't focus on my book. I couldn't sit still. Soon word would come. I didn't doubt the decision would be a yes.

Why wouldn't I be allowed to live with my mother? I thought the hearing was only a courtesy. I mean, my father had helped build the place. He sat on the right hand of the leader, providing his life and blood to building the academy. His charismatic personality had doubled their attendance in less than a year. I was his daughter. I was conceived on this land.

When Susan came through the door with a serious look on her face, I was confused. When she said the decision was no, I thought I must be hearing things. How could they choose to send me away? How could they tell me I couldn't stay? I wasn't crestfallen. Crestfallen describes not getting the doll you want. I wasn't even in shock, for all my emotions were so twisted about. I didn't know how to react. This was their final mark. These so-called Christians were telling me I couldn't leave and then expect to come back. I was allowed to visit, but there was no home for me there.

My Christian foster family had told me they weren't equipped to handle my problems. Now my community, where I lived, where my family lived, told me I couldn't live with my family. I could only visit. The depth of that emotional wound lasted for decades.

Chapter Twenty-One:
Living with Auntie & Uncle

Mom was stuck with a problem. What to do with me? My aunt and uncle offered to take me. They lived in a nearby town and were of the same faith. And so, I left to live with them.

I was excited to be with family, and it was close to Mom and the kids. I'd be around kids my age and going back to school. My aunt and uncle had a full house with kids from elementary to college age, including foster kids.

My room was a curtained-off corner of the basement with a bed and dresser inside that. There was a red patterned carpet to dress it up a bit and hide the concrete floor. Mom gave me my care card and birth certificate and told me to keep a close guard on them. I hid my wallet with them inside under a corner of the carpet for safekeeping. I forgot where they were and found them when I stepped on the bump in the carpet months later.

I enrolled in the local non-denominational Christian high school just as the first term ended. I was offered a choice between grades nine and ten. No tests were given to see where I was academically. It was assumed that I'd be fine in either grade. I'd been homeschooled and started my education at age seven. In the seven years following, I completed less than half the grades required to start high school. Passing was fifty percent, not ninety percent, at the high school I entered. It was a shock and a lifesaver.

School overwhelmed me. I felt like a complete oddball. I'd never been around that many peers in my entire life. Instead of twenty or thirty teenagers scattered throughout a farm, there were hundreds of them in one building. I got lost a few times before I learned to find my way. I didn't know how to socialize, dress, do my hair, or do anything an average kid did. Those things held little interest to me.

Conversations were difficult. I knew the Bible and its teachings, EGW, and the time of the end. I knew about survival camping. I even knew how to run a household to a degree. I didn't know how to interact with kids, to play and laugh, to not be serious. I didn't know jokes, games, music, and other everyday activities. On top of that, I was still grief-stricken from my father falling off the cliff. I was profoundly hurt over being denied living with my mother. Those feelings were locked deeply away. I had no common ground with my peers.

One fantastic thing about attending the school was Finn was a student there. We had rarely talked since the previous summer. We weren't chummy in the halls and didn't hang in the same circle. Finn hung out with the older kids while I hung back and tried to find my bearings and not embarrass myself. I sometimes went for coffee with Finn and his friends at lunch. I'd sit and listen to the chatter flow around me as I tried to make sense of it. That first cup of coffee he bought me was the worst-tasting thing I'd ever drank. Even worse than Mom's echinacea sludge. I added packets of sugar and creamer, but nothing helped.

The classrooms were not much different from the classrooms at the academy. These textbooks didn't have chapters removed or text blacked out. Gym was the hardest class for me. I'd never seen sports and didn't know what baseball, hockey, or basketball were. Everyone was kind and supportive of me. They took the time to teach me what other kids had learned years before. No one was mad when I scored a goal on my own net, as I didn't know the difference. I was mortified, though. My fear of making a spectacle of myself, of failing or getting it wrong, held me back. I spent most of my spare time in the school library or sitting in front of my locker with my nose in a book. It felt safe, and it helped me escape from life.

I made a few friends. I tried sleepovers and hanging out after school. We did homework together, went horseback riding, walked along the river, and kicked leaves. I couldn't fully connect with anything or anyone. Nothing felt real.

At one point, an intervention was held in an empty classroom. They expressed their sorrow at my loss but said I needed to get over it. I had to move on and find more in life. There was only so much a person could listen to about what I'd lost.

They were right, but I didn't know how to get over it. My counselor didn't know. My cousin, who was in university, didn't know. No one knew exactly how I was to get over it, just that I needed to. That battle lasted for years. I never found an answer. In time I learned what was needed was time. Lots and lots of time.

School came with the usual homework, pop quizzes, and tests. There were bi-annual course tests that accounted for forty percent of our grade. It was then I learned I wasn't that smart. Homework I aced. Pop quizzes were a breeze. Tests were difficult. There was some stuff I should have known because it was taught in Grades five, six, or seven, so everyone just knew it. This was something I couldn't learn from classmates' notes. I was years too late for that. No matter what I tried, I couldn't seem to do well on big tests and exams.

Classes, for the most part, were boring. Sitting still all day long, listening, copying notes, or reading texts was a painful way to spend the day. There was no reason to know why Custer's battle went as it did. It had no relevance to my life. It bored me to tears—actually to sleep.

School was either boring, non-consequential, or easy compared to my homeschooling. I didn't see what use knowing all the American presidents would have for me in the future. My brain had little ability to memorize things that were meaningless. The only class I truly enjoyed that year was math. Numbers were hard to screw up until I got into geometry. That was my Achilles' heel.

I tried to fit in and be a part of the family at home. We all had weekly chores to complete. We pitched in with supper and cleaned up afterwards. We attended church together and did the usual errands and such as a family. We watched TV in the evenings. My cousin and I sat on the floor together in front of our uncle. The boys sat on the sofa with their mother.

I soon got to have a real bedroom when a foster boy went back to his family. I tried doing my hair like my cousin did. We were only a couple of years apart, but she was light years ahead of me when it came to being a teen. We tried Oxy for our acne and hairspray for our front wave pushed forward with our clips. We spent copious amounts of time pushing and pulling to get the perfect front poof. We laughed and giggled together as girls do. We went swimming in the public pool sometimes. We girls had to wear a T-shirt over our swimsuits so as not to be immodest. It was embarrassing as no one else was dressed like that. It didn't matter though as I used to swim in a skirt and shirt for modesty.

I was full of questions and looked for explanations that made many adults uncomfortable. When I asked questions, I was told I was arguing and being rebellious. I didn't understand why some rules were to be followed to the letter, others were adjusted, some abandoned, and a few ignored. If our life was based upon

God's will, through his written word, the Bible, and EGW writings, why were only some kept or partially kept, or kept when in front of other Christians?

We watched TV shows like *Rescue 911* and *Married With Children* in the evening. After school, I watched the end of *Tailspin* and then *Goof Troop*. They were the first cartoons I really saw. I loved those funny cartoons. They were such a novelty to me. While watching the cartoons, I stuffed myself with real cheddar cheese wrapped in iceberg lettuce. I hadn't had either one growing up, and I loved it. I still do.

My aunt wondered why they were always out of cheese. I began to fill out due to lack of exercise and the new array of foods I had at my disposal. Okay, maybe filled out isn't the right term. I began to gain some serious softness to my shape. Instead of walking miles every day to navigate the farm and working a physical job five days a week, I was now confined to a bus seat and then a desk, followed by lying in front of the TV or on my bed.

By the end of grade nine, I felt incompetent and unintelligent. I was unable to get any sort of grade besides barely passing. Grade eight French was required to graduate. I did it via correspondence and was given a pity pass. As time went on, I felt more and more like I couldn't learn. My self-confidence sputtered and died out as I failed at the one-size-fits-all education system.

No help or tutors were offered. I was told to study harder. I fell further and further from building friendships as I retreated from a life I didn't belong in. The teachers felt pity for me and passed me. The stress I felt over exams caused me to lose sleep and suffer terrible nausea. I passed grade nine with a strong sense of incompetence.

Auntie, Uncle, and cousins went on annual family summer trips, and I was sent home to Mother. When I asked why I couldn't go, I was told the trips were for family.

"I'm family," I said.

She answered, "Yes, but not that kind of family."

I was family for church and chores, not a family vacation. I was family for judgement and lessons. If anything was needed outside of a roof and food, I was to get it elsewhere. As an adult, I now understand they needed a break. Some kindness and tact would have gone a long way back then.

I was sent home to stay with my mother while they all went to Mexico on their family vacation. I was hurt to be left, not understanding the need for them to get away. I wasn't allowed to live with my mother, but I could be sent there when the others didn't want me.

I didn't get to work in any of the trades while there and was discouraged from socializing with the students. I rode my bike along the fields. I played with my siblings. I cooked meals. I read piles upon piles of books. I talked to Finn on the phone when I could, but he was busy working full-time. I built LEGO® cities. I was terribly bored within a week.

Then I heard of a way to get a sure A in grade ten English. You had to write a one-hundred-page book, typed, and double spaced. Excitement set in as I went about doing just that. I'd get the jump on my next year of school.

That summer passed in a blur of madly writing and scribbling out my novel in the hot summer air. I remember lying on my stomach on the bed, knees bent, toes wiggling in the air. My sweaty hands stuck to the papers. I scratched out a fictional story twisted with the things I knew in my life. The fact that I had no real experience writing didn't deter me. I was on a mission and wrote with gusto. I spent that summer lying on my bed, pounding out a novel.

Mom had a beau courting her. Rick would come over for supper or to take her for a walk while I watched the kids a few evenings a week. He lived in a hick town down south near the border. Rick had heard of Dad's death and, after waiting almost a year, decided it was long enough. He moved north to court Mom before someone else did. I didn't pay Rick much attention. He was quiet and left me alone.

I often went for a bike ride to get some fresh air. I rode all the way to the edge of the property and enjoyed the wind in my hair, the calm of being alone. I loved to feel the air tickle my skin and cool me. One day, I saw a car parked at the edge of our outer field. Someone was setting up an overnight camp. Of course, I had to stop and say hello and see who was willing to spend the night on the edge of our commune.

That was when I met her.

She had such light-coloured hair I couldn't even describe it as blonde. Her accent was so strong I struggled to understand some words. Paula was a strong, vibrant woman driving across the country, camping along the way. She was headed back home to attend university after spending a year in the far north. I'd never met anyone like her. She was independent, confident, opinionated, and enjoying life's adventures. I was awestruck and wanted to learn more about everything she knew. I wanted to be more like her.

This was the beginning of a lifelong friendship. We exchanged addresses and became pen pals. The candidness with which she wrote and answered my questions was refreshing. She was going through her own trials and struggles, which helped take my mind off mine. I empathized with her thoughts and feelings. It was refreshing to learn and think of more than the religious bubble I couldn't seem to get out of, even as a pariah.

Chapter Twenty-Two:
My First and Only Full Year at School

When I went back to school for grade ten, I felt a bit more confident. I knew how the school worked now, how to navigate the halls and find the classrooms. I knew some of the kids and could even say a few were friends. I felt I knew what to expect from a classroom.

This was a new year, and I'd do better than the previous year. I'd managed to pass grade nine. I was sure I knew how to do the work expected. I also started at the beginning of the year, which I felt would make all the difference.

I had completed my goal that summer and wrote a one-hundred-page novel. Finn had told me how he had written a novel the year before for his English teacher. Word had it that if you wrote a one-hundred-page novel for Mr. G, he would give you an A for the first term of his English class. I had typed it out in double-spaced sentences. I was ecstatic. I'd done it.

I was so proud of myself for writing a book. I didn't proofread it, and my mother didn't ask to read it. I was fourteen, and I'd written a book. I'd created a story. I had my rough copy with basic chapters and titles. Smoothing it out and going past a rough draft didn't cross my mind. I had completed something that I'd never tried before. I felt such a sense of achievement. I was so proud of my novel that I gave it to Auntie and Uncle to read before I submitted it to my teacher. That innocent move marked the beginning of the end of my relationship with them.

My aunt's reaction, coupled with my uncle's silent agreement, stuck with me forever. Their response wasn't what I expected at all. She was livid and refused to return the book to me. She said that it was vulgar and disgusting. She said it showed what a deviant I was.

She claimed my book showed I wanted my uncle in an inappropriate manner—that I wanted to have sex with him. I was shocked. How could she say that to me? She went on to say I had to stop being inappropriate with him. She had no examples to give me except that I sat at his feet with his own daughter. I was so taken aback I didn't have a response. He was the only link I had left to my father. He was my uncle. I was a lost, hurt teenager, not even fifteen. I didn't have thoughts about anyone at that age. Except for Finn, I'd had a crush on him since I was twelve. I was still a virgin. I hadn't even French kissed.

Her reaction and his lack of support left me shocked, heartbroken, and angry. I was angry that she thought so little of me, that all my hard work was taken away from me in such a heartless manner. It didn't matter the writing might have been terrible. Or that the story was missing strong characters and a good plot. I had written a novel at fourteen. Where was the guidance, the encouragement?

That was how I started my first full year of real school, with my family thinking badly of me. My book was taken. I was now officially deemed a concern by the family I was living with.

After my aunt read my novel, the cold war began. I hated her, yet loved her and wanted her love and acceptance. At that age, I didn't understand the emotions I was feeling. I was deeply conflicted.

Depression and the deep knowledge that I didn't fit in anywhere were written in long angry letters to boys who were my brothers growing up. Those poor young men probably had no idea how to respond. I inflicted emotional scars on them as I poured out all my emotions onto pen and paper.

I was angry at everyone who survived the edge of the cliff giving way. How come it had to be my father? I understood he would have rather died than anyone else, but it didn't lessen my pain. I was disappointed in the religious world my father dedicated his life to. That world abandoned me, and he was gone. I was confused and angry with the values and treatment I received living with my relatives. I didn't understand how to maneuver through high school or build friendships with my peers. It all poured out in long letters to them.

Finn was sent to a different town half a province away to work and attend a Christian school. We wrote and talked on the phone when we could. He faced his own demons and struggles between financial stress and his crazy mother. I missed him terribly. We always seemed to be like ships passing in the night with the occasional same port.

On a drive back from church, I commented I had to "piss like a racehorse." My aunt got so upset you would have thought she was trying out for a part in *The Exorcist*. She almost got whiplash the way her head flew around.

I tried defending myself by telling her Dad used to say that. I was trying to keep his memory alive however I could. She was angry with me and with him. She told me he was a terrible example and a terrible parent. My parents obviously didn't know what they were doing. I sat very still, silently fighting back tears. My cousins were silent, too. My uncle kept driving as though it was perfectly normal to have his wife condemn his dead brother.

My aunt was full of condemnation for my father and

mother's parenting. The Sabbath clothes I had were inappropriate; the shoes were unacceptable. To be truthful, if I'd been the adult in that same situation, I'd have felt the same.

My parents let me choose two-inch spiked high heels and a beautiful blue silky dress. It was, of course, an inappropriate outfit for a young girl, but the message was lost on me due to an extreme lack of tact. The clothes and shoes were confiscated, and I was taught to dress as my cousins did. I wore proper loose-fitting dresses, baggy sweatshirts, and T-shirts over jeans. For shoes, it was only flats and runners.

I became accustomed to being in denial always before even hearing the question. *Why did you read that book? Did you eat the last of the cheese? You slammed the door too hard, be more careful. What are you wearing? Go change. Did your father teach you that? Do it this way instead.* I was always being questioned yet never allowed to ask my own.

My emotions were all over the place. Stress and anxiety weren't emotions that were acknowledged back then like they are now. I became defensive and secretive. Anything I did she thought was wrong. After a while, all my answers were denials even if I did it.

If I reached out to my cousins with general teen issues, they went to their mother, who came at me again for not communicating with her. Their favourite type of conversation became the silent one. They would sit and silently wait for me to fill in the blanks.

My aunt decided I needed counselling and signed me up with a large, single overweight lady in the basement of a church. I had nothing to talk about with her. I didn't have words for my emotions. I didn't realize the lifelong pain and ripple effect of my upbringing sprinkled with various traumas. Mother and the commune abandoning me wouldn't seem unusual to me for a long time. There was no way I could discuss my father's affair. In a way, that was at the bottom of the barrel now. I'd often forget I had appointments with her and get a lecture when my aunt arrived home. She believed I didn't want to go and purposely forgot.

She was partially right—I didn't want to go. I didn't see the point. I'd swear I'd forgotten, but she never believed me. It was an argument I always lost. I'd never really go against an adult at that stage in my life. If they wanted me to do something, I did it. I might have questions and might not agree, but I did what was asked.

There was a divide that, over time, became clear to me. For example, when we went shopping, Auntie purchased things for the other children's needs but not mine. She said that was my mother's job.

I needed jeans and a light jacket. Mom took me shopping. It was exciting shopping together. We were shopping at a brand-new store, too, not the second-hand shop, which was a first for me. I felt guilty about the expense and tried to choose carefully. She picked out cute acid-wash skin-tight jeans for me to try on. We laughed as I had to almost lie down to zip up my fly. The jacket was a beautiful, lightweight, colourful windbreaker.

When I got back to my aunt and uncle's, I was proud as punch over my cute outfit, and my aunt wasn't. She said I was dressed inappropriately, like a cheap harlot. What was once a cute outfit to wear with joy became inappropriate and an act of rebellion from me. To Auntie, it was just another example of my mother messing up. Nothing was ever up to her standard as far as what my mom or dad had done. Although Auntie wouldn't purchase anything for me when she took her children shopping for clothing, she was happy to give negative feedback on my mother's choices.

It wasn't all bad while living with my relatives. It was easy to be negative, and I was at the prime age for that. The good is harder to remember.

We went to a Steve Bell concert at the church in a nearby town. Steve Bell was my aunt and mother's current favourite Christian singer. I was able to get him to autograph a cassette as a gift for my mother.

I learned about Terry Fox that year. Auntie took me with the cousins to hear a motivational speaker on behalf of Terry Fox. Death to someone so young was a big reality check. When you are young, it's eerie to think you aren't invincible.

Our church held a youth intervention to save the younger generations from the dangers of the devil's music. The adults sat upstairs and had a book club-type meeting about some section of the Bible or passage from EGW. A group of teenagers set up in the church basement with the TV/VCR combo on a trolley set up to play us a documentary video by Eric Holmberg on the evils of AC/DC.

It was fascinating to hear the snips of music videos intermingled with the speaker's dialogue. I was terribly curious how you would play a tape backwards to hear the message from the devil. Above all, I wished the music clips were longer. The music was fascinating and made my toe tap for some reason.

* * *

Over Christmas break, I stayed with my mother. I spent most of those two weeks shut in my room. I was determined to write another novel and, this time, show only my teacher. What had taken me the entire summer to write, I did in less than two weeks.

A new story, printed and double-spaced, to hand in. It wasn't a good story. It wasn't edited and didn't have any of the requirements the teacher wanted. It was angrily and belligerently written. A rushed job completed in less than two weeks. But I had written a second one-hundred-page book and would be damned if this one was taken from me. I kept it in my backpack in the middle of my English essays and notes until I handed it in. I didn't show my mother or aunt and uncle that story. I sent a copy across the country to my friend, Paula, to keep for me. I didn't want this one taken, too. Ironically twenty-five years later, when visiting that same uncle, he returned the first book I wrote. My aunt wasn't there when that happened.

After Christmas break, as I prepared for mid-terms, I realized grade ten was going to be no better. It was the darn mid-terms. Pacing beside the wood stove, textbook in hand, I studied. I tried to remember, to learn what the dry texts were conveying. Instead, my eyes glazed over. My thoughts drifted to the mountains, to the cute boy whose attention I so badly wanted, and to my dogs I missed dearly. I'd reread the paragraph only to daydream again. The content held no real meaning for me. I drew a blank as I sat in the huge gymnasium and stared at the questions reviewing all that we'd been taught so far.

It wasn't that I didn't try. In fact, my high marks prior to the mid-term and year-end exams were what kept me from failing the classes entirely. I managed to keep a high-grade average, particularly in math and English. Numbers made sense if they didn't toss in angles and circumferences. I enjoyed English as it was mainly reading novels and writing essays. I even enjoyed Shakespeare because I could easily decipher his language. It wasn't much different from reading the old wording of the Bible.

School was a terrible struggle. The geography of Canada, our provinces, and our capitals weren't hard or even a little interesting. Learning about the presidents of the United States was slightly more difficult, and I didn't understand the need. We weren't American, so why did we have to study them? We had giant books on civil wars fought, not WWI or WWII. Instead, we learned about obliterating savages and about Americans trying to save their wagon trains. I didn't understand why we were learning it. At the time, I didn't think it pertained to our country's history.

My health issues saved me from PE without making me fail. The first issue was my period. I'd have a terribly heavy flow for up to two weeks at a time. Less than two weeks later, it would start again. After a few months, I was fatigued, pale, and dizzy. They took me to the doctor and then subsequently put me on birth control to stem the flow. I was told to eat lots of dried apricots and prunes to supplement my iron loss. I got to the point where I never wanted to eat another sticky soggy prune.

I suffered from extreme abdominal pain. I'd curl into a fetal position and sob because it was so bad. My mother was called to bring me to emergency a few times. One night, in the emergency room, a nurse came with an answer for us. She asked me if I wanted my mother to leave so we could talk in private. I declined as I had no secrets.

The woman told us that I was likely suffering from a tubal pregnancy. I was still a virgin. I hadn't even been given a pregnancy test. I started to laugh. I was laughing deep from my belly at the absurdity of it.

I hadn't even seen a boy's privates, never mind gotten close enough to get pregnant. When it was determined I wasn't pregnant, there was no alternate idea. It was suggested I had gas.

My mother and I had a good laugh as farting was a terribly funny thing in our family. The diet of high ruffage, including beans, made it a common occurrence, even a competition from time to time.

I had numerous doctor appointments, emergency room visits, and calls to the medical hotline. Nothing alleviated the pain or supplied a reason for it. There were possibilities, but nothing proven, and no tests were offered. At one point, they said I might have gallstones, and passing them caused the pain. After a year or so, the pain eased and came less often, although it plagued me well into my adulthood.

Chapter Twenty-Three:
Rides to the Community

After spring break, I went home to visit Mom every second weekend. It wasn't comfortable being with my aunt and uncles anymore. I was a pariah at school. I needed the peace and quiet of the farm. It felt familiar compared to this world where I didn't belong. I missed my siblings terribly and loved going home.

Mom was engaged by then, and her beau was often over for evening dinners. We would laugh and visit over supper long into the evening. I basked in her comments about how grown-up I sounded. What a young lady I was becoming. I was happy that Mom was moving on and finding happiness. She had a nice man she liked, and he wanted her even with her passel of kids.

I slept with the kids, mindless of their bedwetting. I played and rough-housed with them and pulled them in the wagon to the orchard. We played tag and tickle games in the leaves. At least, that is what I like to think. The truth is, I have little memory of being home other than a few snippets here and there. I mostly remember waking warm and wet from the kids and staying indoors, reading my beloved books.

I didn't attend vespers or church as I wasn't welcome there anymore. I didn't work or interact with anyone at the farm as it was discouraged to have me participate in anything. I did visit my dear friend Susan and occasionally slept at her place. She hadn't been in the commune for very long, and it seemed she had a good grasp of life outside the commune's mentality. It was refreshing to have someone to talk to who had an open mind. I had so many conflicting feelings, for that matter, conflicting directions from adults in my life. I didn't know what to think or believe about myself or the world. I could speak frankly with her, and she wouldn't be angry about the questions I had. I questioned everything.

* * *

Sexual bullying started not long after my bouts of abdominal pain began. It all started after spring break with an incident at school. It was awkward and scary, and I didn't know how to handle it. A pubescent classmate found me alone in a classroom reading and came in to tease me. I don't know if he had a crush on me or if he was dared. I tried to deflect and parry our words and push away the conversation. I tried to say I'd be able to get away and he could never have me. He kept coming back with more and more examples of being able to force himself upon me. He would catch me walking to the bus. He would corner me in the vacant truck yard. Eventually, it got so bad I'd cry on the school bus on the way home on.

My older cousin was home from university and was able to draw the story from me in bits and pieces. I swore her to silence as I shared my fears. What happened afterwards was horrible. She had told my aunt and uncle, who took it to the local authorities. They took it to the other family. It was agreed to settle outside of court without talking to me about any of what happened.

I learned about everything through school gossip. By then, my life at school was at its worst. I had ratted on a boy for taunting me, and my family had used the law to coerce money from his parents. There was no longer any hope of building any friendships or fitting in now.

The health issues I suffered went hand in hand with stress. The biweekly rides on the bread truck to Mom's became abusive as the months went by. The driver picked me up every second Friday after school.

The commune market garden delivered produce to the nearby town's stores, and the route came my way on Friday afternoons. It was the perfect way to get me home to visit Mom and the kids. I'd bring a change of clothes with me to school on Friday morning and be ready to leave with the truck after school.

I had a favourite dress to change into as I followed the dress code when visiting Mom. I can still see that dress in my mind's eye. My friend Susan gave it to me. It was a long-sleeved ankle-length dress made of soft, stretchy cotton fabric with colourful flowers all over the black background. I'd skip out of last class early to change in the school bathroom from my jeans into the dress before hopping into the white cube truck to head home. I don't know why I dressed according to the strict dress code expected at the farm. I don't know why I bothered to continue to show respect to a place that had turned me away and spread terrible lies about me to keep face. I was respectful and docile every time I visited.

The rides started out uneventfully enough. The driver would ask me questions about my life and give me religious pointers. He had a whole houseful of women he looked after. Wife, daughters, students. He was familiar with how to draw a girl out. As the weeks went on, he became more comfortable with me and realized I had little fight in me. I didn't like to argue or be in confrontations. This worked to his advantage.

One day he started off with a birds and the bees talk to determine what I knew. It progressed to what I had done, which was very little at this point. He didn't know I read romance books or that I'd already been astride a lively young woman who was trying to show me how sex worked.

I didn't volunteer any information as his questions made me uncomfortable. When I expressed my discomfort over these conversations, he took it even further. He told me what a filthy slut I was, that it was my fault men wanted me. It was my fault because of how I looked, because of the dress that I wore. He would reach out to touch my thigh as he continued to expound on why it was my fault.

Apparently, everything about me was heathen, according to the little man who drove the truck. Once he started in on me during those rides, it didn't end. I tried to defend myself. I tried to say I wasn't what he said I was. He continued reminding me that children suffer their parents' sins tenfold, and it was a fact my father had a wayward eye. Here I was being told what a whore I'd be before I was even old enough to date, let alone have sex.

Sadly, it didn't stop there. He began to try and pinch my breasts or put his hand high up on my thigh. I sat so close to the door that I was on the edge of the seat. He would reach across the cab to pinch my thigh or my breast. I learned to keep my jacket on regardless of the heat. I twisted and turned as much as I could. He would still try.

He enjoyed my discomfort more than anything. He was an insignificant man who tried to make up for his physical lacking by bullying me. He lorded his auxiliary police badge like a kid showing off his power. He ranted and railed at me when I tried to stand up to him and told me I was built for fucking. He said it was my fault he acted this way because of how I looked, the lips that I had. He said I'd get my punishment from God. Sadly, for a time, going home was worth the rides. But they became more and more hellish as the weeks went on.

One day it was too much. He was on a full rant about how I'd die a whore's death. I'd suffocate to death from an obese man who died on top of me. I was horrified and devastated to be spoken to this way and have someone think of me this way.

Men were the head of the household, the Lord of the family. They were to be obeyed without question and never talked back to.

After this last verbal attack and being groped again, I went to my mother. I should've known better. Mom lit into me something fierce. She lectured me and demanded to know what sinful behaviour I'd done to cause this pious man to be tempted.

I left the house sobbing and went to my friend Susan's and stayed with her over the weekend until I could go home. I spent much of the weekend talking to Finn on the phone and hiding in my favourite escape: books.

Susan let me stay. Mom just couldn't see me as a victim of that horrid little man—a victim of the life they chose. She believed I'd done something wrong. I didn't see myself as a victim either. I thought there was something wrong with me, that I really was the harlot they called me. Susan tried to intervene with Mom on my behalf, but nothing would sway her way of thinking.

Then, like a miracle, he was gone. Not literally. He just wasn't the driver anymore. A new family came to live at the commune, and that man drove the truck.

I swear that perverts telecommunicate with each other. Or maybe there's a group, and they meet to swap names. Somehow, he'd heard stories about me. I only rode with him once, and he pushed me even further than the little man did. He tried to get me to let him do things and offered to give me money for meeting with him. I was shocked.

When we got home, I went to my Mom and told her what had happened. Obviously, I hadn't learned from my mistakes with her yet. She got so very angry with me and told me I was a bad woman and needed to stop being a tease to men. She said it was my fault that men treated me the way they did. I left her house sobbing and spent the night at Susan's again. She told me it wasn't my fault, and my mother didn't know how to react—how to deal with this. That she loved me and was upset and worried for me.

During the night, the strange new driver packed up his entire family and disappeared. Then the little man was back as the driver. I didn't dare speak to my mother again about the rides. I just shut my mouth and did my best to ignore the little man as much as I could. I think he'd been spoken to, for he didn't talk to me anymore and didn't touch me.

Other girls complained about him walking into their rooms without knocking. They said he would come in and watch them change. His youngest daughters knew more about sex at ten years old than I did. They learned from their home life, their older sister, and books they found hidden in their parents' room. He was just another file folder in the office that the staff ignored.

There were a few men who were parishioners of the church that were well-known for having these types of issues. They lived with their families at the commune or in surrounding towns. Some of them would repent, pray with the pastor, and swear not to sin again. Forgive and forget was the motto. Except when it came to me. I wasn't to be forgiven or allowed anywhere except, of course, to ride with that deviant little man.

My cousin started in on me about the same time. We were almost the same age and struggling to get through puberty without going sideways. I was all soft and chubby innocence, and he was raging hormones. We'd once shared laughs and adventures, and now that we'd grown older, he looked at me differently.

I remember the exact moment when the innocent play turned uncomfortable. My back has always bothered me since a bad leap on the mountainside. He would often massage my back, and one afternoon the massage went further. For my headache, he said.

His mom had taught him to massage her glutes—let's be honest here—her ass. My aunt believed that a butt massage would alleviate headaches. Weirdest thing ever to see her lying face down on the couch while my teen cousin massaged her butt. It always creeped me out, and I'd leave the room when my aunt had him rub her there.

That day he held me down and did the same thing to me. When I fought back, he just laughed and said no one would believe me. It felt awkward and wrong. I hated it. Fight as I might, it was difficult to dislodge him. I was telling him to stop and get off me. He claimed he could do as he pleased, and there wasn't a thing I could do. He could rape me and get away with it. I vehemently argued that I could easily call for help and get away. Then he pointed out that I lived in his house. He could find me and overpower me and do whatever he wished when no adults were home. He might have been joking, but my fear was real. After that, I never accepted another back massage and tried very hard to not be alone with him.

Unfortunately, that was impossible, and we had a few more heated arguments about his opinion of my sexuality and his ability to partake of my body if he felt like it. The trouble with my cousin finally pushed me over the edge.

It seemed like everywhere I turned, I wasn't safe. After the school year ended and my aunt and uncle left for their yearly family trip to Mexico, I packed up everything I owned. I left the house key in the mailbox as I was never coming back.

True to form, I maintained my candour and hope in my mother. I told her what had happened with my cousin, and she, in turn, told my aunt and uncle. That cemented my aunt's hatred of me. Mom gave me the summer to live with her, and after that, I had to find somewhere else to live. I was fifteen years old.

Chapter Twenty-Four:
Living With Great Uncle

After my mother told my aunt and uncle about me, I wasn't welcome there again. As if I wanted to see them. I also wasn't allowed to permanently stay at Mom's house. I had nowhere to go.

My dear friend and pen pal Paula was appalled by what had happened and suggested I visit her. You could buy a seven-day Greyhound ticket for two hundred dollars and travel anywhere the line went for seven days. It only took four days and three nights to travel from one end of the country to the other. Mom said it was okay for me to go, so Paula sent me the ticket.

Once the ticket arrived and I planned my move east, my mother's tune changed. Instead of keeping the ticket for safe keeping until I was to board the bus, she burned it and forbade me to go. When I told Paula what Mother had done, she was beyond frustrated.

"She could have at least returned it so I could get my money back," Paula protested. My friend was out two hundred dollars, and I had nowhere to go. Paula was angry and felt betrayed. Any potential trust and working together for my future were abolished by my mother's deceit.

I was so angry and frustrated. I didn't know what to do.

Talking to Mom did no good. She couldn't seem to be straight with me. I walked out of the house and went to Finn's.

His parents' house was about eighteen kilometres down the dirt road the commune was on. I had my Walkman blasting out Aerosmith's "Get a Grip" cassette tape in my ear, trying to blot any thoughts from my mind. I didn't know what to think or what to do. No matter where I went, nothing seemed to get any better. Within a few kilometres, I was caked in dust from the dry dirt road. My throat was parched, and water became my top wish. At a turn where the road went alongside the train tracks, I switched routes thinking the train tracks would be slightly quicker than the road. When I arrived, all I could manage was, "Water, please."

Finn and I hopped on his motorcycle and went down to the river. We kicked stones, cooled our feet in the river, and eventually lay down where we both fell asleep. When I woke, I had the funniest patchy sunburn. A triangle on my thigh, burnt forearm, and side of my neck. The rest of my skin still a blinding white.

There was little Finn could say or do for me aside from taking me back before dark. I held on tight as he drove the washboard gravel road wishing I could stay with him forever. For the rest of the summer, our afternoon respites at the river would be repeated when he could get away on weekends and evenings.

I managed to hitch a ride with a family going to the annual weekend of Christian revival meetings at the community I had lived in down south. The one where the heavens had opened and ruined my birthday dinner. I couldn't stay there, of course, but I could stay with my friends that lived on the nearby farm.

I felt right at home at Wilson's farm. Even though it'd been a couple of years. The girls and I still got on wonderfully but had outgrown weeding the garden for dimes and quarters. We didn't find lying in the sheet hammocks as entertaining either. We were growing apart in our interests as we navigated our teenage years.

I was drawn to their cousin, who was home for the summer. Jenny stayed in a nearby cabin on the property, and I decided to join her for the weekend. We stayed up in the evening talking about boys, the weird church rules we were raised by, and what our futures might hold. The second night we watched a meteor shower. Jenny and I had never seen anything like it. We stood there in the dry, dusty dirt, mesmerized by the bright streaks across the sky.

I was in such awe of the natural wonder that I leaned in and hugged Jenny. She didn't pull away. Instead, she wrapped her arms around me. I leaned forward and brushed my lips against hers. There was something about her thick curly hair and her golden skin that had me thinking about doing that all evening. Standing there together, watching the falling stars together, kissing her just seemed right.

Jenny didn't kiss me back. She pulled away and apologized to me. She was sorry, I was sorry, we didn't mean to mislead the other. It was an awkward conversation that thankfully turned to other topics sooner than later. I didn't question why I wanted to kiss her. It seemed natural to me and didn't warrant mental questions in my mind.

I left the next day, hitching a ride across the border with a commune student who was going home for a few days and offered to take me with her. She lived with her family a few hours into Washington state near Wenatchee. The dusty barren countryside wasn't anything like Seattle's lush oceanside landscape.

During the long drives to the community, to Washington, and back to Mom's, I pondered where I could go. I didn't belong anywhere. I was too much trouble for anyone, yet I didn't know what it was that made me troublesome.

Mom found a few farms that housed troubled youth down in the southern United States. She was willing to pay the fees to send me there. She hoped staying at a farm for troubled delinquent teens would set me straight. I wasn't fooled by the glossy handout. I was raised in a similar place with nasty things behind the façade. There was no way I was going.

When my father passed away, my great-uncle told me that if I ever needed anything to call him. That's exactly what I did. I needed somewhere to live. When I called Uncle Bill and voiced my request, he said he would think about it and wanted to talk it over with his wife and my mother. The next day he called me to tell me he and his wife Lisa agreed to have me come live with them. He was in his mid-sixties, and his wife her mid-thirties. I had extended family in the same area who I hadn't met. Arrangements were made for me to leave in two weeks' time. Mom got me a plane ticket to fly me to Vancouver, where they would pick me up and take me on the ferry to their home on the island.

Before I left, we had a big celebration. Mom married Rick. During all the drama of the summer and preparation for my move, I helped Mom plan her wedding for the end of August. The dresses had to be bought, and the suits fitted.

The four of us kids would be standing up next to Mom and Rick when they said their vows. The idea was he was marrying not only Mom but her children. Grandma and Grandpa came, as well as Auntie and Uncle and the cousins I'd lived with.

Then Mom was off for her honeymoon, the kids stayed with her best friend Nina, and I was off to live with Great Uncle. It was my first time flying. I was nervous and excited. I started practising my poker face so as not to give away how I felt.

Vancouver felt enormous after spending the last year in a town of less than five thousand. I was wide-eyed and awestruck at the high-rise buildings and the never-ending city. I could have gone from one town to another, two or three towns in the time it took us to navigate from the airport to the ferry terminal.

Along the way to the ferry, we stopped at a McDonald's for lunch. I'd never been in one before and had no idea what to order. I hadn't eaten meat before and was frightened to try a hamburger. Aunt Lisa recommended a fish or chicken burger. I tried the chicken and tried my best to eat it. Lisa had me try a bite of her fish burger. The fish taste made me grateful I had chosen chicken. The sandwich nearly came back up once we were on the ferry. The rumbling engines vibrated through my very being. It was hard to determine what was more exciting that day. The move to live with virtual strangers, the plane ride, the city, the ferry, or the mass of chicken in my stomach.

When we arrived at my new home, I was given a little tour and ground rules of what was expected from me.

I had my own room and would be enrolled at the local high school. I was to start grade eleven. I was expected to dust once a week as my chore, help with dinner dishes, and clean up after myself. My aunt was an accountant and started a ledger showing the money they received to care for me and how it would be spent. Some went to my room and board, and some was to pay for my extras, like clothing, makeup, and going for ice cream. It was the first time it was acknowledged by adults caring for me that they received money for my living with them.

To see it in black and white, on a budget showing funds to provide for me, was a reality check. There was money to provide for my needs instead of being a burden, instead of my mother having to buy it. At that moment, I realized my other aunt and uncle had received the same money for my care but refused to do any more than provide room and board. I asked Aunt Lisa how she had learned of the funding. Her response solidified my fear about Auntie and Uncle. They'd received the same amount prior to my moving out.

I was quite upset that my previous family received the same

income for me but had rarely gotten anything for me when we went shopping. I was treated as a burden. This ledger showed quite the opposite. I was furious, a feeling I was unaccustomed to.

Aunt Lisa, for her ill health and lack of experience with children, never acted as though she minded a teenager being in her home. She was kind to me. She taught me about music: Rod Stewart, Mr. Big, and Chicago, to name a few. We went shopping for clothes before school started.

I dressed way too old for my age. I wore button-up dress shirts tucked in over top of my T-shirts. No wonder I had trouble making friends. She took me to get my ears pierced and for ice cream. Lisa drove me to church every Saturday to support the religion I was born into. Whether I wanted to go or not didn't matter. I was to attend church.

Once, I was allowed to attend mass at the Catholic church with my other aunts, uncle, and grandparents. It was kind of fun with all the stand-up, kneel, stand up, sit down, kneel, stand up that was done. It was the same church my mother turned her back on when she joined the commune. I wasn't allowed to attend again. I was fifteen and too young to decide which church I wanted to attend. I was a chess piece shuffled about based upon alternating opinions of those who supposedly knew what was best for me.

* * *

I loved living near the ocean. I loved it all: the humid air, the rainforest, and even the giant black slugs along the road. There were huge overgrown blackberry bushes that filled the ditches. It was a beautiful place to live. I went fishing in the ocean with my uncle. I swam in the ocean at my great, great aunt's beach house. The water was so salty it left my lips sticky. I felt light as a beach ball, buoyant in the chilly water. It was a wonderful drama-free end to the summer. No one accused me of anything, and no one thought badly of me or my parents. At least nothing negative was said out loud to me. I was shown everyday life in a small oceanfront town.

I relaxed and breathed it all in. My health improved, and the physical pain disappeared. My depression dissipated. The open acceptance, everyday relaxed lifestyle, evening walks, and overall pace let me be a kid on summer vacation. It was a healing few weeks. The pain that blurred my life was no longer front and centre. There was no lump of pain pressing down on my chest, crushing my ability to breathe. I finally felt happy and safe. I felt like I had a future.

I was enrolled in public school and really enjoyed my classes. I was offered a whole wealth of knowledge about life and the world that I had no idea existed. Home economics was hard for me to take seriously as we learned to can little jars of preserves, little mini pies, and other foods on a small scale. After each project, we had to fill out a paper with what we had learned. I always put that I learned to do this on a smaller scale. It was pure cheeky teen humour.

I started to spend time with friends. At school, I hung out with a classmate that suffered from Fetal Alcohol Syndrome. Her mother drank too much while pregnant, and she was the result. Her face looked a little different than mine. Her huge eyes peered out from behind thick glasses. I liked her. She didn't judge me, and I didn't judge her. We would go for a walk at lunch and eat up on the embankment above the school.

There were also a couple of kids I got along with that lived in our subdivision. We went trick-or-treating together. I'd never dressed up before except for church. I felt awkward yet terribly excited to go out. I wore a large cape and hat. I carried an ice cream bucket for candy. I was almost sixteen and trick-or-treating for the first time. I spent a lot of time with the two classmates who lived down the street. They smoked and made fun of me for not smoking. I pretended I did and took a big drag of her cigarette. They had a good laugh when I couldn't inhale. It didn't matter that I didn't smoke or drink. We still had fun together.

My aunt wasn't happy with me being friends with kids who smoked. She didn't want me to spend time with them. But I wanted friends. What was I to do? I hung out in the garage with my great-uncle and watched him tinker. I shared my concern with him about my inability to make friends easily. He gave me some wonderful advice that I carried with me for the rest of my life. He said, "We can have many acquaintances in life, but are fortunate to have a few we can call a friend."

I got to be a part of a mock-up school election. It was so interesting to learn about the government and the different groups that shared running our country. This was all new and interesting to me. I had so many questions for the teacher and my peers about politics and what it meant.

I wrote long letters to my sweetheart, Finn. I also wrote long letters to his father. I really liked his father and felt a connection to my own through our friendship. He recommended I read the book, *Siddhartha*. It was a life changer for me. It gave me strength and a positive image of the future. I loved that book and carried it with me everywhere. In school, we read, *The Chrysalids*, another neat eye-opening book. We also read *Animal Farm* and *Lord of the Flies*. I was learning and reading about different ways to think, to view the world.

And then, just like that, it was over. One night I went for a sleepover with my friends down the road. The next morning my uncle pulled me aside for a chat. I had to go. It was too hard on his wife. The stress of having me was too much. I didn't understand. What had I done wrong? Why hadn't there been any warning?

I didn't dare press him too much because he was caught in the middle. I knew he had to stay loyal to his wife.

Now I had to figure out where I was going to live again. I called my friend Paula, and she sprang into action. She arranged for friends of hers in Vancouver to take me in. They found a local school I could attend while living with them. I was excited I'd still be able to attend school and have somewhere to live. Mom gave her permission for me to live with them. My aunt and uncle agreed to drive me to my new home in Vancouver. I packed my large trusty suitcase once again in anticipation of my new home.

The car ride started out normal enough. The winding island road to the ferry, the highway from the ferry toward the city. Then the Vancouver airport came into view. I was confused. We shouldn't be going to the airport. We should be going to an address in the downtown core. My questions weren't answered straight away. Then my uncle told me my mother wanted me returned to her. She hadn't wanted to tell me this and instead left it up to them. The car ride became very awkward and quiet the rest of the way. I was taken to the airport, where they checked my luggage and escorted me to security to make sure I boarded my flight. I still hadn't learned to stand up for myself and didn't think to try and leave the airport. I just sat in blind shock that I was going back. Back to a home I couldn't live in.

Chapter Twenty-Five: Fight For a Home

I was on a northbound plane heading to where I didn't want to go. I was frozen inside, numb with grief and confusion. Why had they sent me away? Why had everyone lied to me? What was going to happen now?

Once we'd landed at the small airfield, I walked inside the airport and looked around. I didn't see my mother or anyone I knew. I retrieved my luggage and dragged it over to a payphone. I called her. There was no answer. I knew she lived about an hour and a half from the airport. I didn't own appropriate clothing for being this far north in the winter. I wondered how I'd survive. I was penniless in a rural area, with the closest people I knew being Auntie and Uncle. Night was falling. I sat and waited as the clock slowly kept ticking on the wall. Each tick was a weight added to my shoulders as time crawled by.

Three hours after my plane landed, a vehicle pulled into the parking lot. It was my mother and Rick, my stepdad. I lugged my big suitcase to the back of the pickup and heaved it in. I got into the back of the little fold-down seat and asked what had taken so long. Her answer stunned me. She said she wasn't sure she was going to pick me up at all. She said they had stopped numerous times on the way for her to think it over. Mom decided to come and get me, but I had to leave within a week. I was dumbfounded.

Why would she force me to fly there if she didn't want me to stay? I had a home and a school lined up, thanks to Paula. Mom had ensured that wasn't available to me. Now I was far north, in mid-November, turning sixteen in a few days, and had nowhere to live.

I spent my sixteenth birthday at my mother's. No one acknowledged it, though. I may as well not have turned sixteen at all. The children didn't know it was my birthday and she didn't tell them. It was as if it didn't happen. That week passed in a blur. I'm not even sure I know if my mother lived in the basement or the upstairs of the house. I spent a good amount of time on the telephone. My friend Paula helped me all she could from across the country. Mom was dead set on blocking her every move to assist me. I didn't know what she wanted me to do or where she wanted me to go.

There I was, with a week to figure out the rest of my life. I was a little shell-shocked by all of it. I had no shits left to give. I didn't even know how I'd meet my basic needs of food and shelter. I was livid with my mother, and I told her so. She didn't want me, so what was I supposed to do? I had to figure that out myself. It wasn't her problem. I had to leave when the week was up. My existence in fight-or-flight mode had begun.

I stayed in the area as I had no money to go anywhere. I literally didn't have two pennies to rub together. At first, I went to Finn's and stayed there for a couple of nights.

His dad was super chill; however, I had to leave before his mom got back from her church retreat. She was crazy religious and would beat you with a broom if you tried to bring something as heathen as a jug of dairy milk into the house. While there, I phoned people I knew from church in the neighbouring towns. Looking for anyone who needed help around the house in exchange for a couch to crash on.

I slept in a loft above the den while at Finn's. His parents had built a beautiful log home on their dream acreage. Finn had mailed me a silver chain with a sweet sixteen pendant for my birthday that arrived days before I was sent north. Now that we were together, finally sleeping in the same home, I wanted a different kind of sweet sixteen birthday gift. I wanted him to take my virginity. He was the love of my life, the one I thought of the most and shared all my dreams with. Who better to take the next step of adulthood with than Finn?

After Finn's mom returned, he and I slept in his car in an abandoned field for a night. After that, he had to leave me to my devices. Finn had to get back to work with his dad at the local mill. He had dropped out of school to work full-time with his dad while trying to keep a roof over their heads. Finn's mom refused to work anywhere that might ask her to work on the Sabbath, or that promoted a heathen lifestyle, such as selling cigarettes. She never had a job. Better to love the Lord and lose your home than live in sin. She was a God addict. She couldn't give up the fix even if it meant her family wouldn't have food to eat or a place to live.

I slept on couches in exchange for babysitting or housework. I stayed with people who knew of me but were sideliners from the commune who didn't believe I should be ostracized and left to the streets. I lived out of my backpack with a few changes of clothes, a sleeping bag, a pen, and paper. I hopped from town to town in a four-hour radius, crashing with whoever would have me. People from the commune somehow reached out to the people I babysat for. They told them I was dangerous, evil, and to be kept far away from their family. The stories were horrifying and biased. I was an abuser, a molester, an addict, and a danger. This was Christianity at its finest.

Soon I had nowhere to stay. I went to Family Services to see if I could be placed in foster care so I could live with a family and attend high school. My family had to be contacted, which meant my mom, Auntie, and Uncle. Mother told the system I was welcome to live there, provided I gave up my dangerous ways. Auntie and Uncle were highly esteemed in the fostering community, and when they claimed I didn't need care, that was the end of that.

My mother refused to relinquish her legal rights to me. She refused to sign over her rights as a parent. I was denied foster care or income. I either didn't get the chance or think to ask why my mother didn't have to take me back. Not that I wanted to be with her anymore. Now I was just plain mad at the system, the world, and those in charge all around me. I stopped giving a fuck.

Christmas was coming, and I was running out of people I could turn to for a few days respite. One day I attended a Saturday service in the church where Dad's memorial was held. I was in the back room where the babies are kept to not let their cries interrupt the service. A strange woman came to me and offered me a home in exchange for childcare. I didn't know how to react. I didn't know why she'd offer this. What did she want? What was the catch?

Gavina said there was no catch. She'd heard of my plight and knew of my family. She wanted to offer me a home. I didn't know what to say. I didn't really have any choice. I accepted. I was given my own room, two adorable children to care for, and a schedule of what she needed from me. Plus, I was enrolled in the local high school.

It was surreal and felt too good to be true. After staying for a few weeks, I knew I had to tell Gavina what people would say to her. It was so hard to look her in the eye and say those terrible things about myself. Whether true or not didn't matter. That would be what was said. There were those who made sure no matter where I went, their stories would precede me.

It turned out Gavina had known all along. She was

Early days camping with Mom and Dad

Just an ordinary walk through the mountains.

A day's worth of canning in preparation for winter.

The look of freedom to paddle alone on a mountain lake.

A weekend of living in a Teepee and rapelling.

A tobogganing holiday in the mountains, always a fun time.

repeatedly contacted as commune members tried to bully her into sending me away. I was shocked. Shocked that she wanted me anyways. Shocked at the tenacity these people were putting into trying to end me. They didn't want me anywhere near anyone who might possibly help or care for me. Yet this woman from the very same church thumbed her nose at them and welcomed me into her home. It would never be forgotten and would carry me through many a dark time.

Mom changed her tune about me again. She called just before Christmas, not to wish me Merry Christmas, but to sing me Happy Birthday. I didn't know how to react to that. I politely said thank you. I also pointed out that it was almost Christmas. There was no offer to come home for the holidays. I still wasn't welcome to visit. She came to visit me and brought my siblings. It was awkward as she tried to act as though nothing bad had happened between us.

Gavina was livid on my behalf. She had no interest in hearing the stuff Mother had to say, especially the stories and excuses for past actions. In fact, when Mother thanked her for being my friend, she lit into her something fierce. She told her not to thank her, for she wasn't doing it for my mother. She was doing it because she genuinely cared about me. Mom left shortly thereafter.

My new high school did its best to get me into similar classes to what I was taking before. I didn't have the energy to try and make friends.

Gavina took me to get my learner's license and taught me to drive. She bought me a winter jacket. I even got to pick out which one I wanted. I felt like a burden and tried to select the best-priced one. It was nice to be treated like a young woman, not a pariah and burden. I fell in love with her children and loved looking after them.

Finn came to visit often as we now lived in the same town. His mom and dad were finally separated. His dad moved into an apartment in the logging town he had a job in. Finn worked at the mill with his dad, saving up money for the future. They had a sparsely furnished bachelor suite a ten-minute walk from where I lived. Occasionally, I'd go to Finn's and spend the night if his dad was working the graveyard shift. We slept on a mattress shoved up against the wall.

By then, Finn was up to no good, hanging with a rougher crowd. One night Finn and his buddy took unsellable stolen items and threw them off the eighty-metre suspension bridge. Finn shared what a fun rush it was tossing bulky items off the one-lane bridge. He gave me little trinkets from his B & Es: a jewellery box and bracelet.

I'd have been better off not spending any time with him, but I was obsessed with him and blinded by love. He was all I thought about for a few years. We spent as much spare time as we could together.

More often than not, when I'd close the door on my locker at the end of the school day, I'd see Finn walking down the hall toward me. This gorgeous Irish man/boy stood out like a diamond amongst stones. Rough edges, glowing hope, and strength to fight all that the world was throwing at him. And he was there for me. We would drive anywhere and everywhere, sharing our hopes, fears, and dreams for the future. Finn had compassion, understanding, and a sense of right and wrong that had nothing to do with God. He also had a terrible fear of ending up alone in a broken relationship like his father.

I attended church and hung out with some of the kids I knew from before. Some of them had previously attended the commune or had family members that had. Five or so of these small towns were all intertwined by church and family ties. We didn't get up to a lot as we lived in a hick logging town that had little to offer. We'd watch movies, chat on the phone, and sometimes sneak out of church for a nip off a bottle of vodka.

Sometimes we would make out. Finn and his friend Dick wanted to swap girlfriends. It was like Dick's girlfriend, Bailey, and I were a bag of candy to be shared. For some reason, we thought nothing of it. I declined any further fun with Dick as he was a terrible kisser. I was more than happy to play with Bailey, but sadly, she was only into teasing the boys.

One of my friends, Belinda, once lived in one of the homes that housed the girls at the commune. The same home whose family included the little man who drove the bread truck. Belinda's grandfather had served time for child abuse. Her uncle was a known person at the church to not be caught alone with if you were a young girl. Her father was said to have abused his two-year-old stepdaughter so much she was taken to the hospital bleeding from all her orifices. Whether that was true or not, I don't know. I do know he disappeared from their lives at the same time the stories started. It was a common way to live then. It was common knowledge that you didn't allow yourself to be alone with some of the men from the community, church, or commune.

Belinda went to the authorities about the abuse she had received from the little man. After taking her statement and her family's statements, they released her back to them. Shortly after, she retracted her story. She listed me as one of the girls who also suffered at the hands of the little man. The police came to the door asking if I'd come down to the station and make a statement. I didn't know what I was supposed to do. No one had listened to me before. I'd never gone to the police about it. Going to the authorities never crossed my mind. Gavina was supportive and explained what they wanted from me. She told me it was up to me if I wanted to tell the police about what he did to me, what I knew about him. I decided to go and make a statement. Not for his abuse against me but to try and save the next girl who got into his line of sight. He was the kind that liked to lord his power and control over others.

It didn't take long for the case to go to court. I barely remember the tiny courtroom. The judge was kind. I was scared and tried hard to fake a brave front. I tried not to stutter or break down into tears when asked questions. I was terrified, seated in front of this man who'd bullied me. His wife sat beside him, showing her unwavering support. I knew his family would feel a ripple effect from all of this. I knew how angry and embarrassed my mother was for me taking a stand against this man—against something everyone else was fine with.

After I testified, the judge and both councillors met and decided there wasn't enough evidence for a conviction. The charges were held. Because he was charged with an offence, he lost the right to be an auxiliary officer.

It was a small victory. He and his wife still ran a home for female students, which posed a continued threat to innocent girls. I knew the action from the commune toward any deviant behaviour of any man was to pray, ask for forgiveness, and then his slate would be washed clean. This enabled him to do it again and again.

NOTE: I recently learned this man has since been arrested and was sentenced to a year in jail for inappropriate behaviour with minors.

Chapter Twenty-Six: Life Unraveling

I cracked under all that emotional stress, even though I was in a safe home. Gavina was understanding and patient with me, strong and supportive. She didn't judge me or see me the way others did. She was the strongest, most independent woman I'd ever known, aside from Paula. I wanted to be like her when I grew up.

The stress was in part because I was bombarded with my mother's emotional calls. She'd either berate me or try to explain her reasoning for her past actions to me. I avoided her phone calls.

Then my body betrayed me. I'd lie there shaking and crying. I floated above myself and watched my body lying there. I wondered what was wrong with me.

When I was in the middle of these attacks, Finn would get Gavina. She'd put me in a hot bath and give me a body massage. Then she'd have me drink a glass of full-bodied Italian red wine and eat a thick piece of homemade bread. Her calm approach to my breakdowns helped me through the rest of my life. For in those moments, I could hear her talking to Finn. Some of what she was saying got through to me. She said I'd be fine—that I was under stress, and, in time, everything would be okay.

I hated myself for my weakness. I harboured the fear that I just wasn't trying hard enough. The trouble was the harder I tried to gain control, the harder I shook. Only when I stopped thinking and began to breathe did I calm down. My body's agitation slowed to a stop. Then I'd finally sleep. When I woke up, it was as if it had never happened. Maybe I didn't wake up at all. Maybe I hadn't slept but instead had somehow come back to consciousness. The stress, shakes, and fear of being insane were, in retrospect, anxiety attacks or PTSD.

I tried to spend time with kids my age. I went to a few house parties but suffered from such anxiety in groups I didn't know how to function. At one house party, everyone was getting wrecked. Kids were drinking, smoking pot, doing mushrooms, and God knows what else. I had a couple of drinks but didn't feel comfortable staying to do whatever kids did at a party. Heavy drinking and drugs weren't my jam.

Finn was in a deep conversation with friends and was in no mood to leave. A young man I knew said he would take me home as long as I drove because he was tripping. I'd never driven a stick before and did a terrible job on that little sports car over the numerous dips and bumps of that long dirt road. But we made it home alive.

I tried attending one more party, and that ended very badly. Again, my boyfriend was with a group of friends and couldn't be bothered to leave, so I got a ride with someone else. Trouble was he wasn't willing to drive farther than his house until the next morning. I woke to him pumping away on top of me. He wasn't much concerned with my opinion of that. The ensuing scuffle did little to dissuade him. I was too ashamed to tell anyone. I felt it was my fault for being stupid enough to think it was okay to sleep at a strange guy's house. If you go home with someone, you're asking for it, right? I didn't go to any more parties after that. I did my best not to think of it again and didn't consciously realize I was raped until I wrote this book.

I buried myself in books. I hid from reality by immersing

myself in stories. It felt good living in books. I read, *They're All Dead, Aren't They,* by Joy Swift. It wrenched my heart more than anything I could imagine. The story was an autobiography of a young mother who came home to all her children murdered. It brought her to God, which irritated me. It showed me how people need a reason, an answer to their whys. It was a great way to rip open my heart. It made me forget what had upset me. I came across another autobiography, *Runaway*, by Evelyn Lau. It was a dark, depressing diary of a street kid addicted to drugs and then introduced to prostitution. Dark and depressing fit my emotional state perfectly.

I felt I couldn't handle anything anymore. I attended school, babysat, and lived with Gavina and her family. I couldn't do any more than that, and even doing that was hard. I was in a good safe home, offered a chance to go to school, graduate, and then whatever future after that. But I had no dreams, no hope.

School seemed pointless. I wasn't smart and had no future there. College was never in my thoughts as it was discouraged at the commune. I didn't know how to dream of more. I was emotionally desolate. Living a regular life seemed like a farce. I felt I couldn't face anything deep, serious, or difficult. I couldn't do life as a teenager anymore.

Gavina and her husband hit a rough patch. Maybe it was the seven-year itch. I didn't know what to say to help them, for they both loved each other. It was too hard to see. In the spring, when Finn moved to the nearby town, I went to live with him to give them the space they needed.

My mother came out and took me shopping for dishes, pots, and some groceries. She boggled my mind. She was setting me up to live in sin as a little housewife at sixteen. I didn't know what to make of her behaviour.

I hadn't thought anything through. I had no job, no

income, and no interest in playing house. I had no knowledge of paycheques, budgets, and cost of living. Finn hadn't been sheltered like I had. His father worked himself ragged to care for his family. Finn was light years more worldly and mature than me. He was completing grade twelve at the alternate school and worked day shift at the mill while also selling illegal substances to make ends meet. He needed an equal, someone with the ability to function in the world. I wasn't there yet. I was too naïve and innocent.

As time went on, we lost respect for each other, and things went from bad to worse. He was concerned I'd become like our mothers: pious, religious, crazy women. We were taught that we became our parents, and both our mothers were everything he didn't want.

Finn's parents were high school sweethearts. They were good, strong Irish people. Then one day, his mother found religion. She found God. She became a completely different woman. She didn't cook any meals but vegan. She wouldn't even purchase the meat and dairy her husband and sons still ate. She didn't want it in her fridge. She'd go on religious rants over their heathen ways. She used a broomstick to chase them out of the house. She refused a divorce for years as she didn't believe in them. That example of intolerance stayed with me.

I learned a great lesson from their sad family circumstance. I chose not to force my opinions, diet, or beliefs on anyone else. My partner would be free to be themselves regardless of my personal beliefs. They should be themselves and try not to change into something they thought I wanted. That's easier said than done. It's not a good way to go into the dating world as a naïve young woman.

Finn had no way of knowing I wouldn't become like his mother. He just knew he wouldn't take the chance, wouldn't give us a chance. I didn't know how unhealthy we were. We continued our train wreck of a relationship. We were at a small gathering of couples where he was pursuing a girl. It was blatant and unhidden. I was the odd one out. To top it off, the movie playing was *Cliffhanger*. Something I couldn't handle seeing. Watching a man hanging off a cliff brought back terrible flashbacks. That movie and his callousness pushed me over the edge. I felt a hurt surround me with such a powerful force field that no one could enter.

I went to the washroom and searched the cupboards. I took all the pills I could find. He didn't care and told them to leave me lying on the floor. They carried me to the pickup when we left later that night.

I spent the next two days unable to move. Finn went on with his usual routine. Finally, I crawled out of the house and hitchhiked to the local hospital. They admitted me and pumped me full of fluids. I didn't know what I'd taken, and it was two days earlier, so it was simply a matter of letting my body recover.

My auntie and uncle came to visit me at the hospital. I wouldn't talk to them about why. My mother came to visit. She cried and lamented my situation. She asked if my father had abused me. All I could think of was the pain that must have caused her to say those words aloud.

I didn't tell her she'd done this to me. That she abandoned me time and time again and blamed me time and time again. I didn't tell her it was her actions that put me in the hospital. Instead, I said I didn't know why I took the pills, and I was fine.

I asked Mom to write a letter stating she gave me permission to be wherever I wanted and do what I wanted. I learned later this was called emancipation. I told her if she couldn't provide a home for me, then she needed to give me the freedom to search for one. She wrote the letter, and I left the hospital the next day.

Once released, I went back to Gavina's place. Paula

arranged for me to go east as soon as I felt well enough to travel. I was amazed by her belief in me. She'd sent me a bus ticket that my mother ripped up. She'd arranged home and school the previous fall, and then I was escorted north to be left homeless. Paula never gave up on me. Now I was going to live with her.

I rested and gained my strength back at Gavina's until it was time for me to go. This time, Paula left my ticket at the station ticket office. The ticket would be released upon proof of ID prior to boarding.

Chapter Twenty-Seven: Montreal

The bus ride across the country passed in a blur of days and nights. I don't remember the goodbyes or even who took me to the station.

I had a little pocket change, so I had money to eat at a few of the bus depot diners. I had never ordered food and paid for it all by myself. The menu was foreign. I was afraid of eating meat. Not for health reasons but because I was afraid it would taste yucky. I didn't want to gag and embarrass myself.

Considering I was at a greasy spoon diner, it's good I waited on trying meat. I stuck with grilled cheese. Even that was difficult to swallow. A processed cheese slice melted between squishy white wonder bread was a far cry from anything I'd had before. I ran out of change on the last day of the trip.

At a stop in Sudbury, a gentleman took pity on me. He wanted to buy me something to eat. I was starving and desperate, so I gave in and let him buy me a meal. The trouble was that so far, nothing I had tried over the past couple of days tasted like the food I was used to. I was embarrassed because I didn't quite understand the menu, and I didn't want it to cost too much, either.

I ordered a hot dog. I had never had one before, and it was more than awful. I wasn't familiar with mustard or ketchup. They just added to the weird, unfamiliar flavours. I carefully ate the bun, trying to secretly push the hot dog out the end into the napkin. To this day, I prefer my hot dogs flavoured with everything and well done. I like them overcooked into a charred mass of blistered lips and assholes.

As it turned out, the bus didn't go as far as Quebec, so Paula came to get me from the closest station in Ontario. Instead of going straight to Montreal, we went to spend the weekend at her dad's. It was a couple hours' drive into the country, where we spent the weekend with her father. At the time, I didn't fully realize the effort she repeatedly put into helping me. She was a university student and still made time to care for me. I have no idea what her father's opinion was on that.

He was always kind to me. We spent the Passover weekend with her family in her childhood home. I loved it there. It was filled with books, memories, and the neatest welded artwork I'd ever seen. Truth be told, I hadn't seen much art before. I watched the movie *Dune* while there and was absolutely in awe. The movie itself was interesting and yet a little frightening to me. I still didn't grasp what could be real and fictitious after having been lied to all my life. Possibilities are endless if you see those around you create their own realities.

There was so much to love about the house: the ambiance of a warm den with the sun pouring in, heaps of books everywhere, and a comfy stuffed couch. I didn't want to leave.

We went back to the city after the weekend. Paula had given up her apartment with a roommate to sublet a flat for us. I'd never heard of subletting. In this case, we were living in someone's fully furnished home while they were away. I had so many questions about how that worked. The couple she found to sublet from were bicycling across Canada. The idea of someone choosing to bike and camp across an entire country was intriguing. Of course, I had questions. I mean, why would they do that? Where would they sleep? What made them want to do that? How long would it take? My new life in Montreal gave me more questions than answers. Paula was always happy to answer and discuss any idea or question I put forth.

Over the next few weeks, I told Paula more than I told anyone. I was still a little afraid to show my scared young self. Too afraid to show my insecurities, my emotional fears, and my inability to function as a young adult in the world. I tried to fake my maturity and readiness to take on life as an independent sixteen-year-old. I pretended I had the confidence and worldliness I didn't yet possess. I jumped into life with both feet trying to find out exactly where I fit.

Living with a politically opinionated lesbian was a gift of love and acceptance after living with so many religious bungholes. There was no judgement. I shaved my head and left a lone ringlet on my temple. I took a black and red permanent marker to a white T-shirt venting my anger into all the bad words I could think of. I put my leather vest over my angry shirt and went proudly exploring, bald head and all.

I explored Montreal on foot as far as I dared go. I walked Mount Royal on a regular basis. It was my favourite place as it was a mountain of nature in the centre of a city larger than I could conceive. I rode the subway as far as it would go in every direction. I went into nearby high-rises at the end of each line. I went up as high as I could go, and I still couldn't see the end of the city. As far as I could see, there was concrete, except for the St. Lawrence River and Mount Royal Park. It was incredibly daunting to realize there was a world so large that this giant metropolis was just one of many on this planet. I realized how small and insignificant one person was. It made me sad in a claustrophobic way to know how inconsequential we were, like grains of sand on a beach.

Paula gave me an allowance that I used to see afternoon

matinees, buy subway tickets, buy my first pack of cigarettes, and whatever other things teenage girls spent their money on at that time. I knew that Paula was giving me a lot of money and spending a good bit on me on top of all her other responsibilities. I knew Mom wasn't helping her. I knew I should be working and earning money. I just didn't know how. I was too young, inexperienced, and uneducated.

To make a resumé, I'd need to lie about my education, and I couldn't use my previous work experience. Who would believe a twelve-year-old worked three months in a dunnage mill? Or, at thirteen, made vegan meals from scratch for thirty-plus people? Who at fourteen spent four months prepping and opening a bakery? I had work experience I couldn't use.

I had no marketable skills that I knew of. It wasn't like I could walk into a bakery, sawmill, or cafeteria and expect them to believe me. I didn't even know where any of those places would be or what they would be called. In hindsight, I could have easily looked in the Yellow Pages.

It was the summer of 1994. I read the newspaper. I didn't understand the talk of wanting to separate Quebec from the rest of the country. I remembered in 1990 when there were roadblocks that First Nations people put up to stop others from passing through their reserves. They always let us pass, though, as they knew we lived down a dead-end road with no other access. But how could Quebec separate? By building a wall? Putting up roadblocks with armed guards keeping people from passing by? I didn't understand it at all and added it to the many things I didn't understand and worried about in the back of my mind.

Then I discovered the classified section at the back of the newspaper. Things for sale, things people lost, jobs to have or wanted, and personals. I was deeply intrigued and set about trying them all out. I met a fellow who was hiring, but he wanted me to sell a magic vehicle cleaner. I had to sign up, buy it and then sell it and lots more. I wasn't into selling things to complete strangers. Heck, I could barely talk to them.

I showed up at a café for a job, but it turned out they were offering to give a free meal for someone to wash dishes. I wasn't looking to volunteer, especially at a popular diverse location with so many people. The café was warm and inviting with its brilliant colours, eclectic artwork, mismatched flatware, and musicians strumming away on their instruments. I didn't belong there. I wished I did.

I landed an interview at an office that dealt with printer paper and was hired. I was paid minimum wage for the first week of training and then commission only based on sales made. It was a telemarketing job. I was given a phone book and told to start calling and use a script. I learned it was best to call the west coast after lunch to catch them home after work. I just couldn't do it. I was embarrassed and ashamed to call a stranger and try to sell them a roll of printer paper. I mean, would they even get the paper? No one had that answer, and there wasn't any that I could see in the office. I was taught strict phone rules growing up. You called after eight a.m. and before seven p.m. Just like how you never just show up unannounced at someone's door. The job felt like such a scam that I quit after two weeks.

* * *

One weekend adventure, Paula took me to see McGill University. The sheer size was impressive. I had never seen anything like it. The architecture and layout reminded me of what I imagined when I read historical books. I was awestruck and wished I could attend lectures and be a student.

I knew better than to dream of that. I hadn't received

enough education, even if I could find the funds to go to school. It wasn't high school I wanted. I wanted to go to university. The failure at the Christian high school living with Auntie and Uncle left a lingering internal judgement that I was stupid. I had missed too much to start anywhere.

We explored some of the churches. They were so beautiful it hurt me to look at them. The carvings and stained glass were things I'd only read about. We walked home through the park— well, she walked—I skipped and bounced with my expressive energy and joy. As I carried on with my silly commentary, Paula made a comment that stopped me in my tracks.

"You know what," she said. "You could be an actress."

I thought it was a brilliant idea. I'd be an actress. I had the energy and exuberance for it. We took my headshot (my grade ten photo where I had long curly blonde hair) to a modelling agency.

The previous month I had thought change would be good and had buzzed all my hair off, leaving only a ringlet on my temple. The visit was an eye-opener. I'd have been perfect for a role they just had in *Are you Afraid of the Dark*. Unfortunately, they said, with my shaved head, I'd need to wait for a fitting role to come up.

Also, my mother's signature would be needed for the application. My letter wasn't enough. Plus, there would be a fee for them to represent me, and new headshots were required.

My dream was shattered. It was just one more thing Mom wouldn't let me do. Never mind the cost for a pipe dream. The appointment was informative, though, and it reminded me I was still too young to do much. I needed to stay below the radar.

Gavina drove out for a visit. She said she was in the area, she was actually quite a few hours away, but she wanted to see me.

Those two women, Gavina and Paula, showed me a love I'd never felt before. It was something normal, and yet it was foreign to me. No strings or judgement, just acceptance and always being there for me.

Gavina, Paula, and I spent the day exploring. Paula taught us that you could turn left at a red light when turning onto a one-way street. Something you don't learn when you live in the country. There were very few lights where I came from. It was mostly flashing yellows and stop signs.

We went for ice cream, which made my day. I loved going for ice cream. The hardest part was trying to decide what flavour to try next.

Chapter Twenty-Eight:
Exploring LGBTQ Interests

I read the sociology and psychology textbooks Paula brought home for me. They were a little dry. Actually, they were so dry I could barely skim a few chapters before skipping to the good part: the glossary at the back. I liked that better. It was to the point and had clear language. My world was expanding bit by bit, book by book.

I joined a women's self-defence class. It was scary but neat to learn to use my voice loudly and to move my body a certain way to break free. I joined a group for the sexually abused and went to a few of their meetings. I also joined a group for youth who were gay or undecided about their sexual identity. The ratio of abused people to gay appeared to have a big tie-in. At that time, almost everyone I met who wasn't heterosexual was abused in some way or another. Little did I know how common abuse was for any walk of life. I didn't consider myself abused, for no one had beaten me, forced themselves upon me, or left me in a battered pile of tears and blood. That was how I pictured sexual abuse. Little did I know that all those rides, those touches, those escapes from the men we weren't to be alone with were abuse. It never crossed my mind that the mind games, the push and pull from Mother, would be considered abusive.

I met a rambunctious redhead at the youth group. She was vivacious and full of life. She enjoyed the adventure as much as I did. We bought rosé wine at the corner store to drink in the park. We listened to the musicians while we snuggled on the soft grass. The physical contact was a balm to my sadness. We went to the movies and made out in the back of the theatre. Red had no qualms about making out at the movies, going so far as to slide her hand into my pants. I did. I felt shy about doing that in public. We went to pubs, sitting out in the warm spring evening air laughing over our escapades of the day. We shared pitchers of beer over platters of poutine—a delicious new extravagance. Red wanted more from me than I could give. She wanted a relationship and sex. I couldn't fully give either to her, so we parted ways.

I started to write again. I wrote word after word, page after page. I wrote all sorts of ways: free verse, stories, and essays. Essays were the easiest at that time. I had so many ideas, thoughts, dreams, and opinions I needed to confirm or disprove about life. I poured out my convoluted thoughts and ideas onto paper. I was free to write without it being burned, taken, or misinterpreted.

I kept reading and answering my favourite part of the newspaper—the personals. It was a world of dating and intrigue. You didn't have to be educated or smart, and anyone could take part. Well, you had to be a certain age, but changing my DOB was easy. There were so many people looking for people.

I started going on dates. On one date, he took me to a drag queen competition. It was amazing. I'd never seen such beautifully dressed women. I tried to find some tell-tale signs they weren't women. I decided that it was the perfection that gave it away. The perfect outfit, perfect big hairstyles, shiny layers of makeup hiding who the person really was. That was the only tell I could find.

I went on another date, this time to a mini-movie. We climbed a dark narrow stairway up to a shabby hallway. The hall had stained, tattered carpet. There were rows of curtains to slip in behind. There was a bench and a screen on a wall. There was a box of tissue at the end of the bench seat. It reminded me of a cross between an outhouse and a photo booth I saw at the mall. My date paid for the show. It made my mind and my emotions recoil while my body betrayed me. My mind was in shock, and my body's response shamed me. As we left, I asked what the tissue box was for. He nervously laughed. He whispered his explanation over fries at a burger joint. I never saw him again.

I never dated the same person twice. I wasn't looking for what they were. I was investigating what people were like. People that didn't talk about the Bible all the time and pretended to be good on the outside.

As I kept up my perusal of the personals, I came across different types of interests. I was open to discussing anything. I met women, women who were curious, women who wanted a gift for their man, and women who liked to have fun. As soon as anyone showed any serious interest in me, I ran. I was too lost to give anyone anything. I was only after the distraction, the adventure.

One young woman I met wanted to have a threesome with her boyfriend for his birthday. They were from different cultures, she was Greek, and he was Italian. Their families wouldn't allow them to be together. Soon they would have to break things off to marry the person their family approved of. They were a modern-day Romeo and Juliet saga that hit my soft spot.

She arranged for a hotel that was rented by the hour and told me what time we would meet. I'd never heard of hotels that rented by the hour or had beds that rattled and shook like an unbalanced washer. She was a beautiful brunette with long fake nails, perfect makeup and hair, and a modern, sexy outfit. I didn't care about any of that. I wanted to kiss her full lips. As my lips travelled across her neck and her cheek and nibbled on her lips, I found she tasted a little funny.

Over time I learned that was the flavour of the Barbie look. It was makeup.

We continued our exploration: me, her, and him. Her long dragon nails didn't feel so fun. There wasn't anything sexy about them scraping about inside me. Within moments we came to an abrupt halt. Even her boyfriend, who was happily thrusting away from behind her, came to a stop. As strange as it may sound, at that exact moment, we both started our periods. That afternoon we all earned our redwings. By the end of the day, the pristine white sheets looked like a massacre had happened, not an adult adventure.

Before coming to Quebec, I was called a whore, a girl destined to be a slut. This was long before I'd fooled around with anyone. In Quebec, there was no judgement. No one looked for reasons to call me a floozy. Instead, sex was considered just that: sex. It wasn't made into a guilt trip or a sin. There was acceptance of me. All of me, just the way I was. I grew in so many ways. I began to find the girl I thought I could be, deserved to be, and wanted to be.

In that journey, I found my sexuality. I was curious, worried, ashamed, and confused. Then I found my clit. I found fetishes. I found things you don't need to know. I found I was fine with my wants and needs. I was an avid and willing learner and participant to find all the pleasures and joy there ought to be. I read, investigated, and experimented. I wasn't ashamed anymore. I began to find the words for what is good. I loved sex and wanted to be good at it.

When I wasn't answering personal ads, I looked for work. It was difficult as I was a minor, uneducated, and didn't speak French. I cleaned someone's home. I worked hard and did my best, yet was remonstrated for a job poorly done and handed five measly dollars. I couldn't see what the issue was as everything was sparkling clean. I was properly offended at the miserly pay I got for slaving away on the stupid apartment with black and white laminate flooring. I refused to clean after that.

I answered an advertisement for unspecified work. A creepy man answered the door of the condo and tried to act fatherly. All he wanted was to take nude photos of me. I refused to pose for him. He told me that he could make me rich. He said there were men who would pay good money for the photos. There were also men who would pay $20,000 to beat me to the point that I almost required hospitalization. He told me women made great money doing it. He said after a couple of times, I'd be driving a fancy convertible and living in a great apartment. I wasn't convinced. I told him I wasn't a fan of convertibles.

Then he told me about a job that required me to eat a rather large meal and then let strangers watch me go to the washroom. I didn't understand. Did they want me to poop while squatting, similar to camping in the bush? Or was I to sit on a glass toilet so they could see through it? Or would I have to be high above them on some weird seat so they could be below? I just couldn't picture it. I didn't understand and didn't want to. I didn't reply to any more job offers from the classified section after that.

On the weekends that Paula went home to the country, I stayed in the city. Although I loved her family home, I'd had enough of the country. I didn't have the stomach for family anything anymore. Families reminded me of what I lost, what I didn't have anymore.

I enjoyed having the weekend to myself. I took the subway down to the gay section of town. There was a nightclub I liked to frequent. I didn't dare order a drink while there, for I was a minor and didn't want to get caught. I hung out on the sidelines, watching people. No one ever bothered me for ID, maybe because

I came frequently, I never drank, and I didn't cause problems.

I loved to watch one particular man dance. He wore jeans and a tight T-shirt with a leather studded armband. I had never seen anything like it until I watched the movie *Queen* in 2018. I was mesmerized by how his body could move to the sounds of the music. I didn't feel the music the way others did. I tried to move my body to the music and simply felt foolish.

* * *

In June, the entire street turned into a market. A festival they called it. Stores brought their wares onto the sidewalks. The street was blocked off by vehicles, and vendors set up stalls. It was incredible. I had never seen anything like it. I spent the day walking up and down, gawking at all the merchandise. My pale English skin was lobster red by the end of the day.

Mom and I talked on the phone on a regular basis. I still craved her love. I wished for a mother I'd never have. Her words were empty. I love you is meaningless without action. Mom reminded me repeatedly that my health benefits would only last for six months after leaving British Columbia. After that, I didn't have any health care. No mention to me that all I had to do was notify the appropriate agency, and my health benefits would start under Quebec instead of British Columbia. Another thing to add to my worry list of things I didn't understand and didn't know how to fix.

I decided I couldn't stay in Quebec any longer. I didn't have health care. The province could separate, roadblocks could be put up, and I wouldn't be allowed to leave. I had no future in a city where I couldn't work or speak the first language. I had to head west and figure out what to do. Paula was very supportive and didn't tell me to stay or grill me as to why I was leaving. She helped me get in contact with fruit pickers that were driving across the country. I could hitch a ride with them next month.

I had no actual destination in mind aside from my home province. No one expected or wanted me back. I travelled light with a wool blanket, all my writings, and a few changes of clothes stuffed into my Kelty backpack. I began my search for what I did not know.

Chapter Twenty-Nine:
Summer, Fall, and Winter

I had no direction. I simply rode across Canada with a van full of fruit pickers. I had no idea where I was going. I had no destination. Then we arrived in the Okanagan Valley of beautiful British Columbia.

I spent a few days working as a fruit picker and got enough money to buy a few cans of beans to eat. I was essentially penniless, homeless, and as emotionally twisted as a ball of yarn a cat got into. I needed to find a place to live.

I decided to join Mom on the coast for our family reunion. I made my way there by hitchhiking and sleeping on changing room benches. I met up with Mom and the kids on the ferry to Vancouver Island. Staying with Great Uncle was out of the question as his wife had made her position clear when it came to me. I was told I couldn't stay at the campground with Mom, so I slept on my grandma's couch.

That reunion solidified how much of a misfit I was. I felt the unspoken judgement and barriers put up against me. I was the black sheep of the family. I was the rebellious one. Everywhere I went, I felt like no one wanted me to stay. Not one person asked how I was with a genuine interest. I was adept at playing make-believe, that I was fine and had things under control. No one asked if I needed help planning my future.

In retrospect, maybe no one knew what to say to me. Maybe I couldn't hear their words of love and encouragement, or maybe there were none. Maybe I looked and sounded like I had it together.

After the reunion, I hitched a ride with Mom back to the mainland, where she dropped me off on the side of the highway.

She headed home with her family, my siblings. While I was in Montreal, Mom had moved to southern BC with Rick. He owned a small acreage and had only left it to get her. Now they were married, and he moved them to his home. I wasn't welcome there. I hitchhiked to a nearby town and stayed with an acquaintance. I was there for a few days, and they didn't ask me to stick around, so I stuck my thumb out and kept looking for a place to call home. Like Grandad always said, "Company is like fish. They start to smell after three days."

I hitchhiked here, there, and everywhere. I met people who wanted to help and gave me a meal and, at times, a safe place to sleep. I met men who were kind on the outside but angry and rude when I refused their advances. I was dropped in the middle of a large city as retribution. Thanks to that drop-off, I learned how to read a map. I slept in a phone booth as it seemed the safest place, as no one could get at me without pressing the door into me to enter. I tried to sound confident, and in control of my destination to all I spoke with. I told them I was trying to decide where to set down roots. I tried not to be afraid or lonely. Finally, I decided to head up north. Finn was still there, and I had a few friends there, too. Maybe they would help.

I slept in the bus station with the hope of getting money for a bus ticket home. Social Services would pay for a bus ticket for a minor if it was to get them home. The trouble was no one in my previous hometown would say I belonged to them. I wanted to be where Finn was. I loved him to the point of obsession. My auntie and uncle also lived there, but they refused to say I could come there. The only person willing to claim me was my mother. She was at the wrong end of the province, so that was no help. In the end, I hitchhiked.

I headed north with my thumb out. At the time, I didn't know I was hitchhiking on the Highway of Tears. Outside Prince George, a man picked me up and spent some time scolding me. He said he didn't want me to become another victim of the Highway of Tears. I'll never forget that man. He was a guide for the deep north, and half his midsection was missing. It was a deep concave scar from a shotgun blast gone bad. He was kind, concerned about me, and shocked that my mother let me traipse about Canada at my age. It didn't matter that I had a letter from her stating I was allowed to be wherever I was. He was concerned about my well-being. He tried to give me pointers on staying safe, including not hitchhiking. I will always be grateful to Rusty Savage for driving me safely through the main artery of the Highway of Tears. He even rerouted his trip to Alaska to take me to the front door of where I was headed.

So, there I was, back home, so to speak. I got a job working the late shift at a convenience store. It was the first real paying job to involve my social insurance number and a paycheque. Not counting the short stint of telemarketing I did in Montreal. I often walked or hitchhiked the seven kilometres to and from work. It was my first step toward independence in a world I was taught to stay away from.

And then there was Finn, my obsession. Finn—oil to my water—ice to my fire. I had left as a broken, suicidal mouse of a girl and come back a sexually confident, curious young woman who was building a new life. And damned if I wasn't going to fucking make it. I still didn't have a clue, but I was willing to try.

Within a few days, Finn and I fought as often as we made out. There were loud screaming and crying matches as we vented our fears and frustrations borne from our broken childhoods. The fights were followed by fierce and passionate lovemaking. We splashed in the lake, rode his bike from town to town, and explored local hiking trails.

On one occasion, we were exploring outdoor nature trails with a group of peers. At the end of the trail, we found a beautiful waterfall and a great pile of fallen rock. Amongst those, I found a small flat rock that fit perfectly in the palm of my hand. On its surface was something that went against all I was taught: a fossil imprint of a leaf. That meant the world was much older than what the church said. I didn't have Google to immediately answer all my questions. My questions moved to the back burner, but that fossil rock is still displayed with my trinkets collected over the years.

During this time, Finn worked and made a side income selling drugs with someone named Tiny. I wasn't very familiar with them, even though I pretended I was.

When I ate the mushroom cap he gave me, things went badly. The floor fell away, opening up to a great chasm. The floor was a bottomless rift. I was frozen with fear on the couch, unable to move. They laughed at me and kept portioning their product while I tried not to fall to my death from my perch. I declined to try any more magic mushrooms after that.

Then there were the teeny toothpick-thin joints: pinners that did little to affect me and tasted like paper. I was surprised people bought them. I learned later that Tiny had much better stuff to smoke.

The visit to Tiny's Sensi was something out of a novel. Sensi wasn't only the man's name but his aspiration as a teacher. We drove down a long, narrow, dirt road to a two-storey ramble shack. It housed a wizened old man and his middle-aged partner who looked like a child in part due to her weight and in part to whatever issues her gene pool gave her.

I sat very still and quiet, careful to be polite and not bring undue attention to myself. My ability to remain placid was shaken when a horse poked its head into the living room. I was warned Sensi wasn't a man to mess with, and they needed him to expand their business.

* * *

Finn and I took many drives to nearby small towns and villages to see people or make pit stops for things. Sometimes Tiny would be with us, and those rides involved transporting things I knew better than to ask about. A dirt bike was usually securely fastened in the back of the pickup in case the mood arose to whip through a gravel pit. One day, when we were out driving and delivering, Tiny insisted I partake of his rolled smoke.

Moments later, my eyes rolled back, my neck slackened, and my head lolled about. I came to on a log in the middle of nowhere. We were sitting by a beautiful creek that trickled through the valley. Finn was tying down the bike in the pickup while Tiny brought me around. I fainted or blacked out. What happened to me was unclear. What was clear was they were done and ready for me to get my shit together and get going.

Not long after, our fights came to a head. I cowered in a corner between the wall and the sink as he yelled at me and told me how crazy I was. Finn said he wanted nothing to do with me. He was sure I'd turn into his mother and that I was a nymphomaniac. I had no idea what that was, but according to Finn, it meant someone who was addicted to sex but couldn't have an orgasm or some such nonsense.

In that moment, cowering in the corner, I saw myself and saw what I was letting our relationship do to me. It had to stop. I was heartbroken and angry. We didn't see eye to eye on anything. Our values were completely different. We were both so screwed up from our childhoods that love wasn't enough. It was something we both agreed on. We cried, we fought, we made love one last time, and then we were done. I moved to the neighbours next door for a couple of nights.

While I was crashing on the couch, sleeping days as I still worked nights, I had a terrible dream. Sensi visited me, saying and doing things I didn't want him to, but I couldn't stop him. I woke to knocking at the door, and there he was, standing there. All he said was, "Did you like what I did to you? Remember, I can find you wherever you are."

I was terrified. I knew he was teaching his protégé, Tiny, to travel out of the body. It was a way to go places, do things, and see people without ever leaving your physical location. I didn't put much stock in that. However, anything was possible. Considering the adults who I'd grown up with, who created whatever life and reality they wanted, who knew what was and wasn't real. To me, it seemed like you could believe anything you wanted, and it would become your reality.

I felt more violated and dirtier after that terrible dream than I did when I woke to being fucked by that asshole after the party the previous year. I was downright scared and never wanted to see Sensi again. I didn't know if it was a terrible dream or if it really happened. If it was a dream, how come he knocked at the door right after he was done and told me what he had done? How was that possible? Was I going crazy like my ex had said? I had to flee.

I quit working at the corner store, and I reached out to a married girlfriend for help. She offered me their spare room for a small fee that I could pay back once I had a job. The fair came to town, and I got a two-day cash job making corn dogs. The roadies gave me free rides after my shift. It was a blast but not tempting enough to hit the road with them. That same weekend I got an interview and was hired for a full-time day job. I had a set schedule instead of sporadic late shifts.

The job was at a burger and ice cream joint in the centre of town. It was during that job that I first had the experience of my muscles being on fire. It was a burning sensation caused by repetitive motion for hours on end. After a few weeks, I got accustomed to the repetitious action.

Now that I had a job with a steady paycheque, I looked for somewhere to rent. Winter was approaching, and I needed to live close to town as I walked or hitchhiked everywhere. An Indian family had a basement suite available. It had the necessities, other than doors from room to room. The ceiling was low, and the heating vents were bare and exposed. It was affordable. To have a home that was my own felt amazing. I was tired of living out of my backpack, but living alone was terrifying.

The only consolation was that there was always someone home above me. The entire family, parents, grandparents, and children all shared the same house. One of the single female family members slept on a narrow bed in the laundry room off the entryway. They all worked hard, some holding multiple jobs, working together toward their common goal. It was a lesson of hard work and sacrifice.

During the first couple of weeks in my own place, I slept on a board laid across two upside-down milk crates. My army survival sleeping bag may have been warm but left much to be desired regarding comfort. My uncle came to see me and brought me a smoky, stained mattress he had salvaged from a burnt residence for me to sleep on. It was more comfortable than the slab I called a bed.

I excelled at my job, and my bosses loved me. That good old work ethic gets people every time. I was given a small title, a quarter an hour raise, and a key to lock up each night. Once a paycheque, I'd splurge and have dinner at the all-you-can-eat salad bar at Mr. Mike's.

One day, after a long shift at work, the police picked me up as I walked home. They said they had a few questions they needed to ask me down at the station. The fear and shock were as cold as the hard plastic chair I sat in. The fear made me feel like I needed to vomit. The officer wanted to know things about Finn and Tiny.

At first, I thought it was about drugs. I knew not to say anything. Besides, I really didn't know that much. Then I was told it was about a missing man from a neighbouring town. His wife was on the radio and news station asking for anyone with information to come forward.

The man's remains were found, and that's what the police wanted to talk to me about. Someone had seen Finn and Tiny digging in a field at night and had called the police. They found a fresh grave with the missing man's remains in it.

The man, as it turned out, was a local cog in the wheel for a well-known drug dealer and business owner. He'd lost favour and then disappeared. He didn't have a good death. According to the police, his teeth were knocked out. He was dragged down gravel roads behind a motorized vehicle and then buried in a gravel pit. That gravel pit was on the same road we'd driven on the day of my blackout. It was determined his body was dug up and buried on my ex-boyfriend's parents' land. That second burial is what was witnessed and tipped to the police.

I just listened and tried not to cry. The detectives kept asking where we were on specific dates. I kept saying I couldn't remember. I told them I wasn't seeing Finn anymore, and I couldn't help them. I had nothing more to say and left without making a statement. I slowly walked home with their card crumpled in my jean pocket, my mind in turmoil. Pieces were starting to fall into place, which before held little consequence.

When I got home to the safety of my basement suite, I reviewed my calendar. I felt like throwing up. As the dates and the places were laid out, a cold chill rose up my spine. I knew what the timeline was saying. Mom may have forced me to stop writing a journal, but I wrote snippets on my calendar to track what I was up to. The calendar showed the probability was beyond doubt. I was to upset to notice the tears streaming down my cheeks.

I was in a pickle and needed someone to talk to. My uncle was as supportive as he could be, coming into the shop from time to time for ice cream and to say hello. He always tried to give me good advice. I went to visit him, and we sat outside on the steps as Auntie wouldn't allow me indoors. Shortly after I left, I heard him calling Auntie to unlock the house and let him back inside. She had locked him out for talking to me, his niece. I felt so guilty I never reached out again.

It took me a few days of thinking after talking to Uncle before I went back to the police station. This time I shared information on what I knew of Finn and Tiny's whereabouts on the days in question. They were mighty interested in my calendar and took copies of the weeks in question. I knew it was unforgivable to be a snitch. I knew Finn would never forgive me. That broke my heart. I knew it was the right thing to do for me, for the crime committed. What he may have done shook me to my core. The lines between us were boldly drawn now.

Life went on day by day. Aside from a constant chill of fear and avoidance of some people, nothing happened.

I kept working and got a weekend roommate. Celine kept me laughing and enjoying life. We'd kept in touch after I left home. She and her siblings were fun and always up for an adventure.

I admired her confidence. She knew what she was worth and earned twice what I did. I tried to grasp what she did differently to earn more. I didn't have any qualifications or confidence to go after a different kind of job that would pay more. For that matter, I had no clue what kind of job I could do that would offer a better future. I felt invisible and thought I was good for nothing more than cheap labour.

I kept up the writing I'd begun in Montreal. I called it free verse, for in no way was it poetry. I entered contests and publication offers found on the backs of magazines. I won a publication in a booklet of mixed poetry. They said I won, but they wanted me to send them a cheque, so I could get a copy of the book.

They returned my cheque as I hadn't signed it. I'd never been taught banking. When I opened my own account to cash my paycheques, no one told me how to write cheques. Lesson learned.

I began to want. It was an uncomfortable feeling. Want wasn't allowed in the commune. Grateful, giving, subservient, turn the other cheek, give away half of what you have to those with less—that's what I knew. Now I wanted things. I wanted army boots with laces. I wanted music, books, clothes, friends, and acceptance. Wanting was new to me. I had no experience in want or how to get.

I met a couple of kids my age at the arcade. Over pinball games, a friendship formed. I met another Red, aptly called that for her beautiful red locks. She had a sense of humour that kept me in stitches. Red and I would wander the lone main street looking through shop windows at things we knew we could never afford. Red introduced me to her friend Hazel, and the three of us became fast friends hanging out a couple of times a week at the arcade, the movies, or my place.

Celine's eldest brother and his wife invited me over for

dinner and a tattoo. Free food, something to do besides being alone in my basement suite? Hell, yes, I was interested. I wasn't really into getting a tattoo, but the couple needed someone to be the first guinea pig in their new business. I picked the smallest, most relevant one I could find and placed it where it would be easy to hide in case I was possessed by the Lord and found God. As he gave me the tiny little tattoo on my shoulder, I was astounded at how the little buzzing machine could cause such an irritating discomfort.

I recalled a giant of a man from my childhood with tattoos all over his body standing before us in church, telling us of his conversion to God. How his tattoos would forever remind him of his sins.

It turned out the couple wanted me to be their guinea pig for a tattoo and me in their bed. She was attractive enough, and I did enjoy kissing girls. I just didn't have the hots for them. When there's no spark, fondling is rather like a belly full of cold stew you wish you didn't eat. I couldn't bear to continue with the foreplay and stopped. I asked to be taken home.

I literally sat up from leaning into her naked body with her breast in my mouth and said, "Okay, I'm done now." They must have wondered, WTF! They were great about my change of interest. I was taken home and never saw either of them again.

* * *

I called my mother every weekend like clockwork. I craved her love and acceptance. On one such call, Mom told me Mr. Willis was passing through town in a few weeks and asked if I could join him for dinner. The Willises were family friends as their children had lived with us and attended the commune academy. Mom arranged a time and place for us to meet, as I didn't have a phone and had no way to contact Mr. Willis once he arrived in town.

I was rather excited to be going for dinner. Seeing someone who knew my past life and my parents felt comforting. It was an escape from work and sitting in my lonely, barren basement suite. I put on my best new-to-me clothes and walked the half dozen blocks to the fancy restaurant.

Mr. Willis and I had a quick hug hello outside the restaurant and then went inside to be seated. The lights were the proper dimness of an evening restaurant. The music played quietly in the background. He ordered a bottle of wine and appies while we perused the menu. It was a rare occurrence for me to be in a fancy restaurant. I was careful to not order anything expensive. I also didn't want to order anything too inexpensive, so I settled in the middle with a safe chicken entrée. Safe because I could probably eat chicken, and it was priced in the middle.

The evening was quiet and nice. We chatted about a time gone when I had a family and knew life was no different from the sheltered commune. He caught me up on how his children were doing. They were young adults now and attended a Christian college down south.

We had dessert and finished the wine. Once the table was cleared and the bill paid, we made ready to leave. He offered to give me a ride home as it was dark. I gratefully accepted and hopped into the front passenger seat. Before I had time to latch my seatbelt, he reached over and gave me a hug. It wasn't just a hug. It came with hands groping and a wet tongue flicking toward my aghast open mouth. Thankfully he didn't fight my quick ducking, flailing arms, and wiggles.

Words were another matter. I was berated for not giving a proper thank you for the meal I'd eaten. Fortunately, and sadly, I was becoming quite agile against piggish men who thought I was an easy morsel for them to take. I got out of the car and walked home, steaming mad at the end of what was a great evening for me.

The next time I spoke with my mother, I shared my shock, anger, and betrayal toward this man who I thought was a safe person. My mother's response hit me in the gut like a punch. She said, "Oh, I forgot to mention that about him."

How could she? She'd arranged this dinner. She arranged the time, the place, with this man. She arranged it with her daughter, who was but a child-teen, still in need of guidance, in need of protection. She'd simply forgotten to tell me she was setting me up with a known pervert. It was one more reason not to trust my mother.

* * *

Throughout this time, I still suffered from abdominal pain, although it was much less often than I had when living with Auntie and Uncle. The doctors arranged for me to have exploratory surgery, where they would go in through my belly button and fill me with air to take a look around. It was a day surgery, and I'd be released once I successfully woke from anesthesia. I told them I was too terrified of needles to have an IV, so they put me under and then put in the IV.

I woke vomiting from the gas used to put me under. Because of that, it took me longer to recover. I lied my little heart out to the nurses and doctor and told them I had someone to stay with me overnight in case there were any complications. I took a taxi home and hobbled with difficulty down the steep old stairs to my suite.

The red cleansing dye still discoloured my skin from surgery. The pain of the air travelling inside my torso, trying to work its way out, was much more painful than I had anticipated. The next morning, I had thought to go for a walk, but after a block, I had to turn around. The surgery revealed little. They had removed a few small cysts on my ovaries, which I was told were probably the cause of my pain.

Celine and I celebrated my recovery with an order of beer and weed from a taxi driver who did trunk sales. We hung a blanket from the ceiling as a backdrop, then dressed up and took photos as if we were models. I loved photos and always tried to have a disposable camera handy. I couldn't afford a real camera.

* * *

Thanksgiving arrived cold and dreary. I asked to work, but we were closed for the holidays. I walked to the public rec centre with an indoor pool to go for a swim, but it was closed. I walked home through the deserted town, trying not to feel sad and alone. It seemed my only entertainment would be to smoke a joint and start the puzzle I'd splurged on. That was my Thanksgiving.

I began to meet more people, although no lasting friendships were built. I met a couple of guys who worked at a restaurant. I'd go chill at their place sometimes. We would get high and listen to Pink Floyd. Lying on the floor with my eyes closed, I'd let the music carry me away. Nothing else mattered at that moment. I was happy, warm, safe, and enveloped in the most incredible music I had ever heard. I started dating the one roommate Ben, more out of loneliness than attraction.

The end of November was upon me in no time. It was my seventeenth birthday, and I spent it working. Mom sent flowers to my work. I was giddy with excitement. My boss asked me why I was so happy, and I explained that if I kept waiting for big things to feel joy, then I'd rarely be happy. To not be happy was a waste. I decided to choose happiness as much as I could. I didn't add that

I had a pile of sadness inside trying to overwhelm and overtake me. I hadn't told anyone it was my birthday, and Celine was out of town. I spent that evening at home, alone. I tried not to dwell on how alone I was at times when families got together for feasts of food and laughter.

I started to hate holidays. They were anything but a warm fuzzy time for me. I went to Mom's for Christmas. I had mixed feelings of excitement and fear on that bus ride. Thankfully Mom was waiting on time at the bus depot.

I couldn't afford to buy gifts for my siblings, so I made them. I made cross-stitched pictures for everyone. The amount of love I carried for my siblings caused a painful ache in my chest. I wanted to hug and hold them but could only do so for a few days at most once or twice a year.

It was no secret I wasn't wanted there. That I wasn't to stay long. It was a prime example of unconditional Christian love at arm's length.

A few short weeks after Christmas, I got a call at work from my mother. Mom had never called me at work before. This was urgent. She had received a threatening fax from Finn's mother that implied I should leave town now or else. It made no sense to me. Surely nothing was going to happen. It was a prank. The threat didn't say I was in danger. However, Mom said she and my siblings would be in danger if I didn't leave town. I didn't want to risk it.

Arlene, a friend I knew from living at the commune, was now in Ontario and offered me a spare bed. Another young woman I knew, Beth, lived nearby.

Mom gave me the thousand dollars she had saved from the monthly stipend the government sent her to care for me. I didn't even know she got money every month to help care for me. Within two days, my suitcase was packed, my few belongings stored with

Gavina, and a bus ticket bought. There was little ado made as I said my goodbyes to the few friends I'd made.

Ben, a fellow I was seeing sometimes, wanted to come, but I refused to even discuss it. I was running from something that was supposition. A claim Mom and Finn's mom made that I was endangering them by staying. It was a fear based on accusations. All because I was a rat about Finn and Tiny not being with me like they said while that poor man was beaten and murdered.

I was the worst alibi they could have chosen if that's what they'd done that afternoon I blacked out.

Chapter Thirty: London

I was rather comfortable crossing Canada. I understood the bus system, convenience stations, and purchasing of items. I even knew a few meals I liked. This time I had money, more than I'd ever had before. I had little experience with budgeting and no real concept of trying to bring enough money in. I didn't realize how little I had in the face of living expenses.

Arlene and Beth were waiting at the terminal for me when I arrived in the hick town they lived in. I arrived during a terrible blizzard, and we were snowed in the first weekend. I hadn't seen either of the girls in years. It was great to be reunited. We'd all lived in the commune together when Dad died. Beth was a child of religious believers and previous residents of the commune. Beth was my rock, my guardian when I was falling apart after Dad died. Arlene was a student and friend. We were camping buddies on a few survival trips way back when. Now we all were reunited thousands of miles from where we first met.

Once the snow stopped and the roads were cleared, I signed up for grade eleven for the third time. I had to face the horrors of navigating another large high school once again. True to my habits, I spent most of my time in the library.

Instead of reading Christian romance or historical novels, I switched to cults. I read about David Koresh, and how he'd once been in the same religion I was born into. Beth and Arlene also attended the same high school even though they graduated from the commune high school. When they went to enrol in postgraduate classes outside the religious education system, they discovered our school wasn't accredited. That meant that prerequisite classes had to be taken again to apply at a college or university. I can only imagine the feelings of betrayal, frustration, and anger that information must have caused those who had spent years working and living in the boarding school that now had no diploma.

I struggled emotionally. School was forgettable at best. I had no interest in my fellow classmates. There was no common ground to build upon. The girls were supportive and helpful when they could be but had their own battles to face. We made the most of our time together, going out dancing and doing the usual things girls do together.

Beth lived with her uncle while she finished going to school. She had her life all planned out, including children and career. I was a little jealous, I didn't have a plan. Arlene, like me, didn't have a family to help her. Yet, she had a plan, a goal for a career that required night classes while attending high school. I didn't understand how she supported herself while she attended school.

I asked Arlene what she did to pay her bills since she didn't hold a job either. Arlene wouldn't or couldn't really answer me other than I didn't qualify for the arrangement she had. Whatever that was supposed to mean. I met the son of a farmer who, by the third outing, mentioned he thought I'd be the perfect wife for him. I might not have had a plan, but I knew I wasn't going to be a wife anytime soon.

One day, after school, I couldn't find the girls in the parking lot. I thought I'd been abandoned and misled by my girlfriends. I walked through rain and sleet. There were no cars driving by to even see my extended thumb. Once I arrived home, I jumped into a hot shower where I stood shivering and sobbing until I was thoroughly drained and warmed. In a moment of reckless emotions, I took scissors to my freshly grown short curls and cut my hair short, leaving clumps sticking out every which way. I was angry, hurt, and now had a horrible-looking haircut. When the girls came home, they helped me trim my hack job. They did their best to give me a cute pixie cut of curls.

Don't touch your hair when you're upset!

All this because I didn't know how to communicate and misunderstood my friends. Or I was crazy. I didn't dare speak of this fear aloud. I had already faced my fears that I was mentally unstable while I worked out west. I had asked my boss if I was crazy, and he assured me I didn't fit the symptoms of being crazy. I was told these were growing pains. It did little to alleviate my hidden fears. I embraced smoking weed and drinking to quiet the voices inside. I was willing to try almost anything and embraced forgetting my life with abandon.

* * *

A few months after arriving in Ontario, I was picked up by the local police and brought in for further questioning regarding Finn and Tiny's alleged crimes. The interrogation room was larger than the last one. A camcorder was in front of me for the interrogation. I didn't know what I could possibly tell them that hadn't already been asked and answered. I was shocked with the reason for their searching me out.

A few young women's remains were found in close vicinity to where he had hidden his drug paraphernalia. I hadn't told them where Finn hid his stuff because I didn't know. Somewhere across the highway in the bush from the apartment was all I knew. The police couldn't prove who killed the young women.

They wanted to blame Finn and Tiny. They wondered if satanic rituals were performed using the women. I didn't understand and couldn't fathom them doing anything like that. Sensi, maybe, he creeped me out. But those young men? No, I couldn't see them doing anything like that.

I was disturbed at how easily I was found. Not thinking through that by enrolling in a school under my name created an easy trail to follow. The police wouldn't tell me how many women's remains were found, and I had nothing I could give them.

The interview left me feeling confident that it was a good thing I'd told them what I did the previous fall, permanently ending any sort of relationship with Finn. I didn't tell anyone I was picked up by the police.

I questioned my choice of first love. As if it was a choice. I had loved Finn from the first moment on the riverbed kicking stones while our parents visited.

* * *

As spring arrived, so did reality. I was running low on funds and had no clue how to start an income stream living on rural farmland.

Beth, Arlene, and I continued to go out dancing, watch movies together, and overall had loads of naughty fun. We went to bars, shopped across the border, and flirted with boys.

All the while, I struggled to understand how they managed their lives, finances, and plans for the future. No matter their answers, the light bulb for my future just wouldn't turn on. I didn't have anything I wanted to be or do. I had no dream career, no dreams of marriage or children, nothing. I had ideas, but I had no idea of the steps I should take to get there. I didn't want a white picket fence, two-point-five kids, and a dog.

I'd left Ben, my boyfriend of sorts when I moved out east. A few months after my move, he and his friend decided to move east as well. They moved to the nearby city of London.

By the time Ben arrived, I was broke and unable to pay my share with Arlene. Ben would let me stay rent-free until I got on my feet. So, I moved to London to live with Ben and his friend Bill. I left grade eleven for the third time in two years.

Living with these two young men, I learned about food banks and free holiday meals. It was embarrassing and odd to go line up for food. It was even worse to go line up for a free meal with other unfortunate people. I didn't like it and chose not to do so after Easter.

I needed a job. I searched the want ads and hoped for something, anything I could do for money. I tried being a private dancer. Growing up with virtually no music and no dancing, my rhythm was non-existent, as was my confidence. Cleaning jobs often required a driver's license and a car, both of which I didn't have. Finally, I found a job at a fast-food joint, and I worked the closing shift.

The bonus with that job was I got to make my own meal free of charge at the end of the shift. Thankfully it wasn't a burger joint as I was still very much vegetarian, and veggie burgers weren't a thing yet.

To me, the city was a vast flat world of concrete where humanity blended into a sea of unimportance. It had a large city park but nothing like Mount Royal in Montreal. I missed the quieter, slower pace of the country.

During the honeymoon phase of living with Ben, I thought we should be like a family. Bill moved out, and Ben and I shared the apartment. We were a couple. I was raised to be a good housewife and mother, so the next step would be that we had a child, right?

Bad idea. As soon as I found out I was pregnant, I realized

it wasn't a good idea. Reality set in. I was dating an unemployed loser in his mid-twenties who had no job and played pool for free drinks and the occasional jackpot. And he was overweight.

We slept on a mattress on the floor, and our shabby couch came from the alley. There was no way we were fit to bring a child into this world. He, on the other hand, saw no such issues and employed every trick in the book, including tonsil hockey with my girlfriend to get me to keep the baby. How cheating was a good idea is beyond me, but I guess it soothed his battered heart.

Ben realized we were done, and he went back west to his family. I stayed to complete the doctor's appointments. I took to sleeping on the floor in the main living area as I felt terribly alone and afraid in the apartment all by myself.

I called Mom and told her the news. I told her we'd split up, and I'd be having a procedure called a dilation and curettage. The D&C would remove tissue from the inside of my uterus, ending the pregnancy. After that I was going to move back west.

In our conversation, I let slip that I couldn't stand how he had to lift up his belly to place it on my ass while we were doing the nasty.

She then shared something that I have felt sad about ever since. Mom said she hadn't enjoyed sex since she got married. Said it wasn't so bad with Dad. Said she was lucky her current husband, my stepdad only wanted to maybe once a week. She said you just plan your shopping list or think of the things you need to get done while they do their business.

I was appalled. I mean, what about the reason you're having sex, you know, the big O. I felt so bad for my mother that she didn't enjoy sex. It sounded like a death sentence to me. I never wanted to feel that way about sex, ever. I may have had moments where I wondered why or if we were almost done, but I still enjoyed it for the most part. It made me sad as everyone should be able to enjoy physical interaction.

Little did I know the high percentage of women who never had an orgasm or who can't have one from intercourse.

My mother wanted me to give the baby up for adoption. I'd seen how that had worked out for my adopted brother, Daniel. She even offered to raise the baby and tried to pressure me into giving her the unborn child. I'd hear of no such thing. I wrote a lengthy letter explaining that even though I was *killing it*, as she put it, my way would be fast and painless.

Mother's lifestyle killed you moment by moment, day by day. The child would have no choice or education to live any life other than the one deemed by her God. That didn't work out so well for me. I tried to be kind in my letter, to not hurt her feelings any more than I had to. I was honest. She didn't want me and hadn't for years. She wanted my child so that I could still get into Heaven. She'd never get it.

That conversation between Mother and I poked a hole in my bubble of belief that it was my fault. That I was to blame somehow for all the bad things in my life. I was angry. My mother fought hard for a baby that wasn't even to eight weeks of gestation, and yet she never fought for me. A volcano of anger burned inside me.

Paula drove down from Montreal and stayed with me while I had the procedure. The time passed in a haze of emotional and physical pain. She was with me every step of the way and stayed with me until I healed enough to be mobile. She never once uttered condemnation for my getting pregnant and having an abortion. I felt confident in my decision that bringing a child into this world at that time wasn't the right thing to do.

Once I recovered enough, I was on a Greyhound back to western Canada. This time I was headed to the southern end of BC to the town I was born in.

I saw no future staying in London. I was still searching for a place that felt like home, somewhere I belonged. I hadn't been anywhere that felt like home for so long.

Chapter Thirty-One: Into the Streets

The return to my birthplace was rocky. I knew no one and had no established resources. The Okanagan Valley was the first place I felt like I belonged. It felt like home to me in a bittersweet sort of way. I had blurry happy childhood memories of the towns and highways that I now wanted to call home. It was a feeling unlike anywhere else. I decided to make a life for myself there.

I started off in a women's shelter and got my bearings. First, I needed funds to get a place to live. That wasn't an easy battle. I was seventeen and technically a minor. It'd been four years since I left home. I wasn't eligible to be a foster child. I was too young to get a welfare cheque.

As a minor, I could apply for independent living. It wasn't easily acquired. I submitted the application with high hopes. When I called the office about my application status, the case worker kindly explained that I wasn't eligible for youth assistance. It was because when she contacted my mother, she was told I was welcome to come and live at home. I was shocked and angry. I argued the application's denial as much as I could.

Too little too late, Mom.

I was frustrated to tears. In a moment of clarity, I asked the case worker to ask my mother if I was allowed to attend high school while living with her. Within the week, I was approved and had a cheque to pay for a room in a shared house. I now had a monthly allowance to pay for a roof over my head and enough left to buy ramen and potatoes to eat for the month. It was a small victory.

Mom wanted me to come home and live there permanently. I didn't understand her newfound interest in me. Why did she want me four years after she'd turned me away? Maybe it was the suicide attempt, the murder rap I was witness to, the D&C I had. Maybe it was because she saw me beginning to stand up for myself and manage on my own instead of being at her mercy.

I didn't know why she wanted me, but I did know that she was too late. I had seen enough on both sides to know bullshit was everywhere and nobody could be trusted. I had asked Mom if I could go to school, promising to wear a proper full-length dress when home and change on the school bus. I was denied. Homeschool, not leaving the yard would be mandatory. If she'd said yes, I might have fallen for living at home. Instead, I politely declined.

I was now independent with a clean slate away from anyone I knew. I didn't have to look over my shoulder here. I wouldn't see Finn driving down the street. The heartbreak over Finn hadn't lessened. I still missed him terribly.

That fall, I started grade eleven again. The administration didn't know what to make of me. I was a minor on my own with no adult to send report cards to or to notify if I missed school. I produced my emancipation letter Mom had written to help them understand.

I didn't want to talk to the other kids. There wasn't any common ground, and I didn't want to pretend there was. My classmates' biggest concerns were things like not being allowed to go somewhere, not liking their lunch, or wanting their parents to buy them different clothes. I couldn't relate.

I was often hungry and didn't enjoy my haphazardly cooked meals. I splurged for pizza on cheque day once a month. Then it was back to Mr. Noodles, potatoes, or bread. If I needed clothing, I'd go into a thrift store and put it on in the changing room. Then I'd cross my fingers and hope I wouldn't be noticed leaving the store. I stole cans of beans and potatoes from a discount store when I didn't have enough food to last me the month.

I started to hang out at the smoke pit even though I couldn't afford to smoke. Those kids didn't talk about trivial things and had similar issues to mine. They didn't judge or ask questions I couldn't answer. It was here I met dealers and pushers, wannabees, and lowlifes. I didn't fully realize the direction I was going. I slowly entered a world no parent wants their child to be in. Once I found these new friends, I attended school less and less and eventually quit altogether again.

* * *

I grew up in a place where your word meant something. Where you gave the shirt off your back to those in need. When Gordon, one of my new friends, came to me in a bind, I helped him. He and his friend, Matt, were about to move into a small two-bedroom apartment, and Matt had bailed on moving in with him. The deposit had already been paid. I felt terrible for his situation and told him I'd move in. We were both on government assistance, and it was a necessity to have a roommate to afford somewhere to live unless you lived in a single room. I agreed to this move sight unseen. I didn't realize the kind of run-down places people lived in. My neighbour helped me move.

He was shocked at the state of the unit. He offered me his spare room if that would keep me from moving into the rundown dump. I couldn't take him up on his offer for two reasons. He was a single man, and he could have ulterior motives. Plus, I'd given my word that I'd move in. I shut my eyes and mind to the conditions of the rental and unpacked. The shortest description I can give is that they were later condemned and turned into a parking lot.

Once I moved in, Matt stopped by and told us he'd changed his mind and wanted to live there after all. Gordon forgave him for breaking his word, and we became three. Matt stayed in my room with me. We shared a mattress on the floor. My two roommates were young men from rough childhoods. Matt thought he was a little gangsta. He wore saggy pants that hung down below his ass. He played rap music at a stupid level. Gordon was a little more mature. He was from a rough neighbourhood back east and had hoped to make a go of things here.

During those few months together, we lived like losers with no money, no jobs, and no future. Matt collected cigarette butts to break apart and roll smokes. His favourite place to collect them was the hospital, as they often tossed half-smoked ones. Matt asked me out for dinner once and took me to the hospital cafeteria. I didn't see this lifestyle as a rosy relationship of any kind. I didn't know what Gordon did with his time. I didn't ask; he didn't tell. We were all struggling to survive.

Our place was the worst shithole I had ever lived in. The rental door wouldn't latch shut, so we used my couch to keep it closed. The window became our exit and entrance. The tub backed up with something black when you flushed the toilet or did dishes. Having a shower was tricky because you didn't want your feet to be on the bottom of the tub while the water ran. It was best to plug the drain and let the tub fill while you showered, then let it drain after you got out. The stench while it drained permeated the unit even with the door and window open. The metal accordion heater did little to warm the place. I was grateful for my warm army sleeping bag.

I couldn't find a way to live off the hundred bucks I had left over after paying rent. I'd buy a bag of potatoes, a bag of flour, and a case of Mr. Noodles and hope I could make it last a month. I still stole cans of potatoes occasionally when I was really hungry. You could eat them cold right out of the can. It was a shabby life, no matter how you looked at it. The cold winter air blew right through the walls. It was an unpleasant and scary way to begin my adulthood.

The guys used to go into a peeler bar for whatever they needed, so I walked around the block while I waited. I was too young to enter the establishment and felt awkward watching old men drink beer while watching a girl gyrate around a pole while the sun shone brightly outside.

One time, this red car pulled up, and the guy told me to hop in. I declined, saying I didn't need a ride as I was waiting for someone. He kept insisting and proceeded to circle the block to park and try his luck again. The guys came out just in time, and we were off. They had a good laugh at my confusion as to why some random guy insisted I wanted a ride. I had no idea until they explained that a girl could walk down the street to get a ride and some cash. It wasn't that I didn't know about prostitution. I just didn't know how people went about it. I had read *The Happy Hooker* by Xavier Hollander and had taken mental notes on ways to seek and give pleasure. She was a madam that ran a pleasure house. There was no mention of walking down the street in the book.

That man in the red car continued to try and followed me for months. I learned that he managed a large grocery store. He felt no compulsion to leave me alone. I avoided him the best I could for as long as I could. It took me almost a year before I threatened to expose him if he didn't leave me alone.

I spent a lot of time with Melena, a girl I met at the smoke pit. She was rebelling against her political father because he moved her away from all her friends and childhood home for his career. Her response was to hang with me and try out drinking and drugs. She was the first person I felt close to in a long time. I didn't feel inadequate or naïve when I was with her.

I was totally infatuated with Melena. I'd do anything she wanted to try to please her. I was to chicken to try and kiss her as she wasn't into women. Damn shame because I wanted to kiss her until I was drunk on her affection.

Instead, I was teased terribly by her as she had figured out her power over me. She didn't care about the squalor of the apartment. She was happy to get high or drunk and hang out. She'd stand over me on the couch, shaking her hips until her pants fell off because she was more comfortable without them. Looking back, I wish I'd been brave enough to grab her and show her what happens to a tease.

* * *

Paula had moved west to complete her doctorate in Vancouver not long after I had moved to the Okanagan. I visited her once. I envied her path in life and the culture and style Paula and her friends had. They talked of things in the world I barely understood. They listened to jazz music, had chunky, colourful furnishings, and made foreign dishes from scratch. I wanted to live like that but had no clue how to go about it. I knew without a doubt my current life wasn't good enough. I was too embarrassed to let others know how I lived. I withdrew from Paula, Gavina, and my mother.

Melena wanted to party and try different drugs. I joined her. When faced with decisions like that, I just asked myself, "Why not?" I mean, we couldn't judge Brussels sprouts as nasty without trying them, wouldn't drinking a bottle of Jose Cuervo be the same? It was stupid logic that I'd use for years.

One time we ended up joining a group of people that were going for a drive and trip up the mountain. I liked mountains; I was born playing in nature, and it sounded fun. Melena and I managed to get a Snapple jar of moonshine and some tabs of acid. We all met at a brightly lit gas station in town. Everyone popped acid and washed it down with a swig of moonshine that may as well have been swamp water. We climbed into the back of the camper and enjoyed the ride up to the mountain.

I'd never been to a ski resort before. I'd been to a ski hill that had a few brown cabins and a matching brown chalet for hot chocolate, but that was it. I wasn't prepared for what I saw when we tumbled out. I was shocked and couldn't tell the difference between the acid trip and reality. I thought I'd been dropped into a real-life wonderland. We were surrounded by brightly painted cabins and chalets that sported nostalgic Victorian architecture and style. Some had lattice trim, some were A-frame, and some had large, exposed wood beams. It was like stepping into a little village, a cabin colony filled with bright, vibrant colours. And there was snow, lots of snow. I thought we had entered a different world altogether. I couldn't comprehend what I saw. I lay down in the snow and giggled as I tried to make snow angels. By the next morning, the terrible pain of gut rot and an inability to sleep or get comfortable mentally and physically were overwhelming. I never did acid again.

After we got back, I met Jim and Jen. They had their hands in a few things, including drugs, tattoos, and using the system. They had two adorable little girls I tried to stay away from. I didn't want to become attached to them. I wasn't interested in building a bond with anyone. They also sold and smoked weed. They liked to party and take things to the physical level, the same as I did. I found Jim and Jen to be much better company socially and in bed than my younger friends. I grew apart from Gordon and Matt as I preferred Jim and Jen's company. We spent many a night up to no good. I discovered porn magazines and videos and was an avid learner.

November was an eventful month. I spent my eighteenth birthday with Jim, Jen, and their gang of friends that came and went. I got a tattoo and a man as gifts from them. He was a few years older with long hair. A pretend Fabio who liked to play the *I'm-sexy-and-you-want-me game.*

He wanted to give me something special, so we sat on the stairs with the door closed behind us for a semblance of privacy. He had handed me a key on a necklace. I asked him what the key was for. He said, "It's the key to my heart."

I burst out laughing and lost all respect for him in that moment. Here was a complete stranger, given to me for the night as a birthday gift, who wanted to play romance when animal sex for the night was all he was for.

Who the hell did he think he was? Did he really think I was that stupid? That I needed lines of bullshit? I ignored his stupidity for the evening. I enjoyed my present and then never spoke to him again.

Meanwhile, Melena's parents got smart about her behaviour. She disappeared from my life when her parents found out what she was up to. I was devastated to lose her. I adored her. In a lonely world, she was my person.

We had a little Halloween party with numerous kids popping by. A girl there said Gordon raped her. Gordon hadn't raped the girl. We'd all been there when they went into the bedroom for alone time. We all heard them doing it. The entire apartment was less than five hundred square feet.

Apparently, she was too embarrassed to take her tampon out before having sex, and it got lost inside her. Unsure what to tell her parents, she went to the hospital to have it removed. It was then she claimed rape. She was too young, and her parents would kill her if they'd known what she was up to. It was easier for her to lie and ruin a young man's life than risk being grounded and disappointing her parents. Shortly after, Gordon left town as he was charged with rape and couldn't stay for the trial date for fear of getting time.

I took to heart what she did to him. For her to find it easier to ruin someone's life rather than be honest with her parents made me wonder what kind of relationship they had.

Shortly after Gordon left, Matt took off for the coast to live with his mom.

It was December, and I was alone and had to move on. I needed to find a new place to live. Preferably one that wouldn't be bulldozed down. That required having at least one roommate to afford to live somewhere. I couldn't even afford the shithole's rent.

Jim and Jen had a proposition for me. I could become their second wife. We would all live together as a family. Men, wives, and kids sharing everything.

I couldn't do that. I was raised very differently, and while it didn't look like it from my actions, I did keep some of those values. Especially when it came to children. I had very strong opinions on protecting and raising children. I couldn't join them. I wanted so much more from my life.

I was also afraid of the drugs and what they could do to me. Being with Jim and Jen involved a daily lifestyle of various drug use.

One morning, after a night of partying, I went to dress and leave before their kids woke. I couldn't find my clothes because I realized I had no idea what I had worn the night before. It was like I'd blacked out for a few hours and then woke from a dream I couldn't remember. It scared me because I didn't want to become an addict like the guy who lived with his parents and shit himself in the church by doing bad drugs. Needless to say, that friendship ended shortly thereafter.

* * *

Andy was a pusher I'd met the previous fall at the school smoke pit. He was a welfare bum who sold drugs. He was now my only supplier since I cut ties with Jim and Jen. Instead of just getting weed from him, I began to spend time there. He had a cat and an iguana for pets, and his apartment was heated. I was afraid to be in my cold empty place. I still hadn't found a new rental.

Andy suggested we get a place together. That's how I began my first common-law relationship. I didn't have any other options besides him.

We found a two-bedroom basement suite and moved in. I was unwilling to live in sin and had to have my own room. Even though I'd shared a room with Matt before, it was an unexpected interim. Moving in and sharing a bedroom on purpose, I was unwilling to do. I had to keep a semblance of a front that I was a good girl for Mom. I wanted her approval. It was a shitty little basement where even the bright white paint couldn't lessen the darkness. The ugly green stove was used to hot knife hash, not to cook. It was affordable and a huge leap better than where I'd been. What I didn't realize until after we moved in was that Andy had told the government we were a couple, and now our cheques were combined and reduced. I wasn't sure what I was more upset about. Being common law or having even less money.

Kenny, a man Andy worked for, needed a place to stay last minute, and true to my upbringing, I invited him to rent my room until he got on his feet. I moved my stuff into the idiot Andy's room and let Kenny have mine. That action meant a lot to Kenny. It started a friendship that would save me during another cold winter and last a few years.

Chapter Thirty-Two: Losing Finn

I learned about a drop-in youth centre. A street clinic for youth and street people. I started dropping in every few days, even if just to have someone to say hello to. The nurse explained STDs to me. I only knew of bad ones like AIDS and HIV. The nurse, Amy, offered to give me the Hep B vaccine, which I accepted.

While living in that basement suite, I met a pretty, green-eyed blonde who lived in a group home up the street. She was buying what Andy was selling. She was hot, fun, and let me do all sorts of things to her. One minute she was snorting her Ritalin medication off the dresser, the next, I had my face buried between her legs, making her scream my name.

I didn't understand why she wanted to snort her medication. When I asked, she said it was more fun that way. What did I know about medication? I didn't take anything medicinal. The medication I grew up on was burned tree ash and ground-up roots. We called them charcoal, goldenseal, and echinacea and used them for everything. If she wanted to snort Ritalin, that was fine, but I wanted none of it.

Andy tried to get in on our friendship, but I told him in no uncertain terms he wasn't needed or wanted. I'd lost all interest in him as he wasn't an alpha male. He was lazy with no interest in bettering his situation. Something that was high on my agenda.

When she asked me to be her one and only, I declined. What would the purpose of a relationship be? I was fighting to survive one day at a time. She was living in care, putting in her time until she was an adult. Our lives were both a mess and not to be combined.

Kenny, Andy, and I moved into a bigger place and found a house with two bedrooms and a huge loft that could be used as a bachelor suite. I found a free bed frame and mattress and set up my room.

I found a summer job at the local cadet camp and worked as a salad girl for the officers. It was nice not to rely on a government cheque. Having a job gave me a reason to get up and do something. It also provided almost enough funds to survive. I needed that job, that purpose.

Try as I might, I struggled to sit on a couch all day and watch the tube with Andy. I was used to being busy until I crashed, so inactivity was difficult and boring. I didn't understand most of the references made on sitcoms and Saturday Night Live. I did enjoy the WWE wrestling, where men like Stone Cold Steve Austin, Mick Foley, Triple H, The Gravedigger, and Goldust acted crazy on stage.

The crazy way they talked made me laugh. At first, I was upset by the violence, but once it was explained that everything was staged, that even the stage itself was on a spring, I was able to relax and enjoy the show. Stone Cold was sexy as hell. Mick Foley as Mankind in his wacky leather mask tearing out his hair while loudly claiming that he had feelings really tickled my funny bone.

Kenny was fun to hang out with. He turned forty that year. He sang in a garage band, went 4x4ing on his way to and from picking up his packages, and liked to go out on the lake with his friend on their boat. It was nice to be able to just enjoy the day out doing what felt normal.

An old classmate had moved in with us to finish out the school year when her parents moved to the coast. It boggled my mind that her parents let their teen daughter move in with us. I would never let my own daughter do that if I'd had one. It was nice for me to have a girl my age to hang out with, though.

On my days off, we would all go out and bake in the summer sun at the lake. She and I were broke ass teenagers who could only afford an Old English bottle of beer for five dollars. We would pop a straw in the bottle, suck it back, and enjoy the buzz while it lasted. All that time in the summer sun turned my hair into an orangey, blonde mass of curly crazy waves. I'd stopped wacky hairstyles that involved shaving parts of my head, stopped dying it blue, purple, and black, and let it grow out. My pain was dulling, and I wasn't as angry, so I didn't need crazy angry hair.

We had a few good times over the summer. One night about eight of us got together for a boating excursion. Half our group was wrecked on acid doing dumb ass stuff. Buddy, who owned the boat, was tripping hard and yanked all the wires from the battery. While Kenny tried to talk him down and figure out how to get the motor up and running, the rest of us went exploring at the resort we'd docked at.

People randomly grabbed shit they found, thinking they needed a life jacket or chair. One girl just about drowned trying to go for a swim. She had to be fished out of the lake. I was a little buzzed from my beer and the Mary Jane I smoked. I watched them trip out.

It was funny and scary at the same time. If Buddy was losing his mind just from tripping out driving the boat in the middle of the night, what would he do if someone said something wrong? What if something set him off on a violent tangent? I kept my trap shut and was glad I didn't do acid. I hoped to God Kenny could get the boat running. Thankfully he did, and we all got back to shore as the buzz wore off. That was the last midnight boating trip we did.

That summer, I learned Finn was dead. I heard months after he had passed. I had no contact with anyone I knew from my time with him except my mother. This was before Facebook and the ease of social media and the internet.

After Finn died, Gavina tried to find me and bring me back for the funeral. My mother pretended not to know where I was. It was a fluke that I called Gavina and found out Finn was dead. I was heartbroken. It didn't matter how things were between us. It didn't matter what he had involved me in. I loved him from the moment I laid my eyes on him by the river when I was twelve years old. He was gone. There was no chance to make things right, to grow and reconnect. He was dead. One more thing to block and drown from my memory.

Finn's accident was a matter of debate as to whether it was a planned accident before trial or merely an unfortunate event.

He was riding his motorcycle in the wee hours of the morning when a cab came out of nowhere. Finn's bike skidded into a concrete barrier in his efforts to avoid colliding with the taxi. My heart broke for his parents. To me, losing a child would be far worse than losing a parent. At some point, you bury your parents. A parent should never have to bury their child.

Chapter Thirty-Three:
Nineteen & Homeless Again

At the end of the summer, Kenny slept with a minor. She was fourteen. And my so-called boyfriend, Andy, was getting it from a few other girls. I didn't care. I wanted nothing to do with him. We all parted ways with some bitterness as we judged each other's choices.

I got laid off from my summer job, had no income, and had no home. I was back to square one: alone and broke. It was such a painful blur that I don't remember where I went next or what I did. I lost almost everything. What didn't fit in my Kelty pack went into the back alleyway for passersby to pick up.

At one point, I ended up staying in a bachelor suite with a woman and her girlfriend. The woman was in her early thirties—her girlfriend was almost fourteen and legally in her care. The government cheque provided them with an income to survive as she didn't work, and the teen didn't attend school. I guess they lied well enough that they believed her to be an acceptable guardian.

My bed was on the other side of a sheet hung from the ceiling. It did little to save me from hearing their sloppy sex. It disturbed me greatly to know this fourteen-year-old girl from an abusive family was being fucked by an obese butch woman who should have been looking out for her and not taking advantage.

The slurping, slapping sounds made my skin crawl as though claws were being raked across a chalkboard.

Right before my nineteenth birthday, I found a damp, dark basement to move into. I was glad to be away from them and their circle of abuse. A few days later, they broke into my place and stole my tiny black and white tube TV out of spite. They said I owed them extra money for sleeping on their floor. I didn't care. Take the damn TV. I was free of them.

There was no celebration for my birthday. Turning nineteen was the same as any old day of the year. I was alone, hungry, and broke. I tied black garbage bags together to make a makeshift shower curtain. Showering was a scary dark experience that left the bathroom floor filled with puddles.

I'd slosh through the slush and snow to The Mission to get free bread. I didn't have winter boots or a jacket, so I piled layers upon layers to stave off the cold when I went out. I couldn't bring myself to stay for the sermon to get the free hot meal. I had loaves of stale bread, a bag of frozen peas, and a tub of margarine to eat. I started walking the streets when I couldn't stand it any longer. I needed money for food and had no other way to get any. I didn't even have a phone number to put on a resumé. Not that I had the confidence to face an interview had I been offered one. I hid behind a brave, positive front as I tried to get by.

On one of those cold, wet walks to town, Kenny stopped to give me a lift. We went for coffee to catch up, and he offered to buy me lunch. On the way home, he stopped at a store and bought me warm, dry winter boots and tossed out my torn, soggy shoes. He invited me to his work Christmas party that coming weekend. I had never heard of company Christmas parties. It was great fun. There were tables laden with food, similar to the church potlucks I had growing up. There was a bar, and everyone was given two tickets each for free drinks. There was a raffle which meant everyone had a ticket for a draw toward the many prizes and gifts. He won a nice warm winter jacket, just my size, that he gave me. Now I had boots and a jacket for the winter to keep me warm and dry. It was a false boost to my confidence in things getting better.

* * *

Mom, Rick, and the kids came to town near Christmas Day. It was an easy way for them to see both me and Rick's son, Anthony. A winter picnic at the park with the misfits, so to speak. Rick's ex-wife Gladys brought her four children, including Nancy. Mom brought my three siblings, and Rick awkwardly sidelined the debacle.

I was ecstatic to reconnect with Nancy, as I had lost her number in the shuffle of recent moves. We first met years earlier when Mom and Rick had brought me with them to meet his son, Anthony, shortly after they were married. Nancy was Rick's stepdaughter from his first marriage. The way she and I figured it was we were like sisters, having both had the opportunity to have Rick as a stepdad. She was older than her siblings, just like I was. She had a different kind of mom, just like I did. And we were almost the same age. It was enough to bond us as sisters.

Nancy and I started to chat on the phone now that we had each other's number. I didn't have a phone, but the girls who rented the upstairs did. They would let me borrow it from time to time. Nancy was going to be eighteen in the summer and was ready to live on her own. She and I talked about her moving in with me. It seemed the logical step to Nancy, and I was happy to not be alone. We had wanted to be sisters ever since we met, and this was perfect. From the start, my mother refused to let me have anything to do with Nancy. Now Mom had no say in my life. I was happy for the companionship and potential help with renting a better home.

Nancy moved in before the end of January. Her bed and dresser fit at the other end of my long narrow bedroom. Her mom, Gladys, bought us a shower curtain as a housewarming gift. Honestly, it's the little things that can make you happy when you have nothing.

I still walked the streets occasionally to get enough money to buy us food. Nancy wasn't on welfare like I was, and neither of us had a job. I took it upon myself to find money to feed us until things got better. I warded off the bitter winter cold by wearing multiple layers of leotards and pants, not caring to try and entice men with my body. I hated walking the streets. I hated the men that wanted blowjobs in their cars. I hated the taste of condoms almost as much as I hated what I was doing. I saw no other way to put food in our bellies. Nancy needed protection and help getting on her feet. I'd had enough bad things happen to me, so what did it matter now? The emotional darkness and hatred of my existence fueled my desperation to get out of the life I floundered in.

I searched for work and continually lost self-confidence in my ability to get a job or to even be worthy and capable of a job. I used the phone number for the girls upstairs for call-backs, hoping they would tell me if someone did want to set up an interview.

I had no appropriate clothing to wear or money to buy any if I did get a job. It was winter in a small town, and no one was hiring. I continued to see Kenny. He made it his mission to feed me a few times a week. My stomach was so shrunken I was barely able to eat even a quarter of the restaurant portion. Thankfully doggy bags were available. I felt safe with this man, who was almost old enough to be my father. He didn't have issues I needed to listen to. He didn't want anything other than my companionship and, of course, what my body could provide. I had a few guaranteed meals a week and somewhere to hang out that had a comfy couch and television as I tried to pass the cold winter days.

Kenny's house was a stand-alone rental that he shared with his business partner. When he was off at his legitimate work, the roomie was busy keeping everyone stocked up on products. Cheap cigarettes, joints, or baggies of various sizes of weed were available, and of course, something a little stronger for those who wanted to fly a little higher. I didn't stick my nose in things that weren't my business. I was happy with sitting in the other room watching TV on a big screen.

Kenny and his roommate had such a booming business with clients lined up outside their place that the cops waited in the lineup with everyone else when they busted them. No one even noticed until they came in and slapped the cuffs on Kenny and his roommate. I didn't even know they were there until they came over to talk to me. I was hauled off to the police station with everyone else, just not in cuffs. Later that night, I was released to go home and warned that these men weren't good company to keep. I found them a far site kinder and safer than many gentlemen I had met. I wasn't leaving my meal ticket, my friend.

* * *

Nancy was pretty, confident with peers, and comfortable navigating the world I was still almost completely unaware of. I felt protective of her and yet a little envious of her ease. We were polar opposites in our ability to gain employment, friends, and social life.

By spring, Nancy had a job pumping gas. With Nancy working, we could afford to rent a two-bedroom apartment. No more damp, dark basement suite for us. After we moved, the style in how we kept house became glaring opposite. The one thing I could control, and was good at, was keeping everything neat, tidy, and clean. Nancy was the complete opposite. Old crusty dishes and mouldy Slurpee cups caked themselves to the blanket over her easy chair. The sink overflowed with dirty dishes that would have to soak for half a day before the dried bits would come off. Never mind the cat litter all over her room. It made my skin crawl. I began to feel resentful of her ability to do everything better, yet she couldn't keep the damn house clean.

Nancy liked to go clubbing, meet sexy young men to party with, and have fun. Nancy also seemed to like partying with men who liked snow. I was worried about stronger drugs and didn't want to be living with someone who spent the weekends snorting blow. I even tried to be like her, but it felt so awkward that I didn't try often. I hid from groups, people my age, and anything I might not have control over. I preferred to stay in at night and be out enjoying the daytime, preferably in nature. It was a living arrangement meant to end. Each of us going our own way.

Around the same time that Nancy and I were growing apart, Kenny and I were as well. I was knocked up again, and no way was I having a baby with him. He already had a child that he never saw or wanted anything to do with. What the heck would a bum like me and a grown-ass man who was already a useless father do with a kid? Nothing, that's what. I felt terrible that I was going to have a second D&C. I knew better than to tell Mom. I begged the doctor to tie my tubes to no avail. I had to either have had a few kids already or be over thirty for them to be willing to end my chances at motherhood. I was livid and vowed to never make this mistake again. Thankfully the street clinic got a new type of birth control called Depo-Provera that came in a needle dose every three months. I didn't care that birth control made me emotionally sick and crazy. I wasn't taking the chance of accidentally making another human. Kenny and I saw each other a lot less after that.

After Nancy left, I moved to a house that rented single rooms to people. You shared the main kitchen and living room but weren't to leave anything out, ever. I had a small fridge in my bedroom for my food. I had no job in sight and had given up trying. I enrolled at the local drop-in school to try and get my diploma. I struggled with depression and my inability to make a go of a decent life. At the street clinic, I'd lament my situation. What I was doing obviously wasn't working, but what was I to do differently? No one had the answer.

* * *

I had a girlfriend my age from a nice blue-collar family that I spent time with on and off over the years. We hung out, played cards, listened to music, and smoked pot. How we even met is beyond me, as she was a high school student, and I was done repeatedly trying to attend school and live on my own. She was given a nice reliable Subaru for her graduating year.

One time we drove to a nearby town that was big enough to have mainstream restaurants. We went to the Cheesecake Factory. It was a splurge trip for us to have a nice treat. She knew how I loved cheesecake and missed what my mom used to make.

There were so many choices it was overwhelming. I finally chose the mixed berry. I waited with barely contained excitement. My mouth was watering in anticipation of the delicious treat soon to arrive. I hadn't had cheesecake in years.

What arrived was slightly concerning to me. A wedge of white and berry-coloured marble with a thin graham crust sat upon my plate. I gingerly took a small bite and was shocked at the unfamiliar flavours in my mouth. This wasn't cheesecake. I didn't know what this was, but I knew for a fact it wasn't cheesecake. I waved the waiter over and shared my confused disappointment as I had wanted the berry cheesecake. He assured me my plate held such an item, but I couldn't believe it. I was led over to the large cheesecake display to search for what I was looking for. Nowhere did I see Mom's cheesecake.

The disappointment was bitter in my mouth. I didn't understand. What was the item I was served made of? Why it was cream cheese with berry syrup laced through atop a graham crust. Cream cheese in a dessert? Wasn't cream cheese for bagels? I'd had them for the first time when living in Quebec. Apparently, it was also creamed with sugar for cheesecake. That poor waiter must have had a hard time not laughing at my shocked dismay. I never tried cheesecake again for years. My childhood treat was destroyed forever.

Maybe if I'd known it wasn't made with tofu but instead cream cheese. Maybe if I hadn't been stoned, I just might have been willing to have an open mind when tasting it. Almost everything I ate in the world was different. It wasn't anything like I'd had before. I knew that, expected that. But at that time, because I had an expectation of what I was getting, I was disappointed.

It took me a few lessons in expectations before I realized it's better to go in with an open mind—be ready and excited for what may come. When you're not expecting a creamy white filling with thickened berries on top, the swirled berries and cream can be delicious.

Chapter Thirty-Four: Life With Samantha

One day, as I walked out of the drop-in school, I saw *her*. She was standing there, talking to a boy. My heart came to a stop, then restarted at an alarming rate. It was Melena, the girl who was like a best friend to me for those few short months. She had disappeared the year before when her parents got smart to her skipping school to be with me. I went up to Melena, overjoyed. She looked me straight in the eye and crushed my heart with a single lethal blow.

"I don't know you," she said and then walked away.

I was devastated, almost beyond the ability to move. I was inconsolable, completely lost, and ready to die. I proceeded to go to three different walk-in clinics to get the maximum dose of Tylenol 3s I could get for pain. My tears and sobs added to my story of physical pain. I don't know why seeing her and the subsequent denial of friendship hit me so hard. Maybe because I had no one. I was alone unless I could provide someone with something they wanted. I knew in the centre of my being I could never rely on anyone to ever truly be there for me if my own mother couldn't be.

I had adored Melena. She was my best friend for a short time. This denial, this slap in the face, was too much to bear. I took a handful of pills and began the long walk back to my lonely little room. I gave up. I was tired of the constant struggle that I saw no purpose to. It wasn't a conscious suicide attempt, but it was a conscious effort to end any type of feelings and emotions. I was done fighting. I had had enough of being all alone with no reason to be.

My sobs had slowed to hiccups, and my tear-stained cheeks were dry. My shaking was down to an angry gesture or two as I vented aloud, stumbling up the steep hill. A van drove past, slowed, and reversed. It was a random guy I'd met at the beach. He offered me a ride.

Once I got in, he introduced me to Samantha, who was sitting in the front passenger seat. It didn't take long for Samantha to deduce there was something wrong. I felt ill from the pills and thought maybe it was best I didn't get a ride. When I explained why, she took me under her wing then and there. She took me to her house for a few days. After a good finger down the throat and a shower, I went to bed in her spare room.

Once I was nursed back to health, Samantha told me she'd teach me how to get high the right way. It was then that I was introduced to *the pam family*, as I called it. Lorazepam, also known as Ativan, Diazepam, also known as Valium, and my favourite, Clonazepam. The right pills for happiness that didn't make you sick. Samantha berated Melena's cold-heartedness to me and called her a worthless spoiled rich kid. Samantha assured me that though I was broken-hearted, there were better people out there who deserved my affection.

Samantha was from back east and had lived in a large city before. She was tough, scary, and the kind of woman I wanted to be. If you showed her respect, it was fine. If you didn't, she might clean your clock. I learned about theft at a whole new level with her. She'd pull into a gas station, fill up and drive away. She'd fill a grocery cart with anything you might possibly want to eat, walk it out to the car and load it into the trunk, not even bagged. One time she got the store employees to pick up a television, haul it to her vehicle, and load it up for her. I'd never met someone with balls like her. Or with such a klepto personality.

I didn't mind, though. I had new clothes that fit. I had shoes, bedding, and all the food I could dream of. I was flying high on little pills, happy as a clam. Samantha would get her scripts filled by a few doctors every month to have the supply we needed.

It didn't matter which ones I took. They all sent me to a place where the world was rosy. It wasn't cold, lonely, and filled with danger when I had them—when I was with her. Sometimes she'd put a bottle of panty remover (Southern Comfort) up her sleeve when in the liquor store for a treat. Along with the pills, we would smoke weed to top off the rosy glow. I introduced her to Kenny, as he was my main weed supplier.

I gave up my bedroom rental and moved in with her. We pulled our mattresses into the living room and slept there. She showed me television shows like *Rosanne, Days of Our Lives,* and my favourite, *The Dame Edna Show.*

Lying on the floor, riding a wave of beautiful high, laughing, did my soul wonders. When I didn't understand the humour, Samantha would explain it to me. She insisted I was missing out, not knowing about the yellow brick road. So, we watched the wonderful *Wizard of Oz.* I didn't really get it, but I appreciated the effort to get me caught up on all that I'd missed. We often wore matching outfits, my favourite being track pants with matching jackets. I had a few, but my favourite was the one that was bright turquoise with purple accents. One morning Samantha drove us to the beach to watch the sunrise and drink Champagne. The bubbles tickled my nose and poured out of the bottle when I tipped it back for a swig. We were celebrating life.

My depression lessened as I found a way to more than just

exist on a day-to-day basis.

As summer came, so did the colour of my cheeks and the weight to my skeleton. I was almost a hundred pounds again. I spent time with either Samantha or Kenny, sometimes both. We would go on road trips together when Kenny had deliveries or pickups in neighbouring towns. We smoked weed, listened to tunes, and ate McDonald's. Things felt good except when I'd faint. Sitting in the middle of the front bench seat, one minute, I'd be bopping along to AC/DC, and the next, we would be on the side of the road with Samantha slapping my cheeks. We never did anything other than get me something to drink and fresh air when I fainted.

* * *

It was while living with her that the courts found me and flew me back to stand witness on the murder trial. Tiny was the only one left alive. That fact alone put a ball of cold fear in my gut. The man Tiny had supposedly committed the murder for was said to be a long-term heroin addict. He was a successful addict as he owned a small business as a front for the shipments of drugs that he brought in. He accidentally overdosed and died, which eliminated his voice in court. Paranoia had me thinking it wasn't an accident. Finn's accident was questioned as well. I was terrified and didn't want to be there. I was ashamed of my past relationship with Finn. I was scared to say the wrong thing. I did my best to botch everything I said, making myself a joke of a witness, therefore, not a threat. After court, I went back to Samantha's, where she promptly helped me disappear into a mental fog of happiness.

I hardly ever had to do anything yucky for money. When I did, it was for more money, and Samantha usually joined in, which made it fun. We found a few men who regularly wanted our company instead of their wives, which gave us the money we needed. Going into another woman's home and bed reminded me to never believe the fake fairy tale of love and marriage.

Life wasn't such a hand-to-mouth struggle anymore. I wasn't fainting hardly ever now. I had become a healthy weight. My daily stress was diminished to almost nothing.

The high of happiness that came with the pills also came with a downside. Samantha would end friendships over misunderstandings that could turn violent in a heartbeat. The bouts of angst and flying off the handle were unpredictable and occasionally frightening. All the contacts we had were street people, criminals, or others wanting to fly high. When things hit the fan, it got ugly and got dramatic fast.

After one such violent outburst, the upstairs tenant's grow-op came to light, as well as cops and everyone's eviction. I was lucky to have been with Kenny when that happened. During Samantha's run from the scene (prior to the police showing up), she called Kenny's cell phone. She needed a ride once she'd ditched the *borrowed* vehicle. Samantha never owned a vehicle. She always borrowed them. I was so high at the time I searched the bedroom closet for her until he pulled me out, forcing me into the car to get her.

Samantha moved in with one of her clients, and Kenny and I found a cute little two-bedroom house to rent together. The house had a sagging porch that gave it a country house feel. I loved the front mud room and created a little lounge area where I could smoke. I had a love-hate relationship with smoking. It was expensive and gross, but it also kept my hands busy and forced me to breathe and think. Kenny didn't smoke and disliked it. We scavenged carpet from the dumpsters behind flooring shops, and after a few trips, we re-carpeted most of the house. With the plywood flooring hidden and our furniture set up, it felt almost like a home.

Kenny and I visited a friend of his who was recently paroled after a stint for murder. I was careful to keep my eyes on the floor and asked to wait outside as soon as I politely could.

There was a black dog with brown markings chained to a concrete block in the middle of a dusty patch where a lawn should have been. I was told her name was Penny. This poor dog had no food or water and no access to shade. My heart ached for her. After a few conversations, Penny came to live with us. She was taller than I was when she stretched out on the bed with me. I adored my beautiful Rottweiler, and she was devoted to me. I had a home, a dog, and someone who looked out for me.

I went back to just smoking weed. Samantha kept a low profile off the grid somewhere. It took a while for the drugs to clear my system. As they did, the happiness stayed. I was feeling better even when I wasn't in a glowing Clonazepam haze.

Kenny worked a Monday-to-Friday job and still had a side business going. I kept my mind clear of most of that knowledge, although it was easy to see the lumps of cash being stashed for road trips and the sawed-off shotgun under the front seat. Then there were the packages loaded during our road trips. The nice thing about his road trips is they sometimes went into the countryside where Mom lived. He would drive the extra hour to take me there for a quick visit. I'd bring the kids gifts that should have been acceptable. Anything from me was considered tainted, though. For example, the remote-control car was broken down, the body was removed and replaced with plain wood.

That summer, I was able to work at the army camp again. It wasn't much, but it kept food in my belly and paid for my portion of the rent and the gas I had to pay for rides to work. I usually walked the three kilometres as the weather was beautiful.

I was laid off when the camp closed at the end of the season. There wouldn't be enough Employment Insurance to last over the coming winter.

Kenny had a cell phone and let me use his number for my resumé. I didn't realize cell phones were a big deal, part of the new era of technology. Everything was still so new and strange, and I wasn't able to differentiate between new to the world and new to me. I thought cell phones and pagers had always been a thing.

I answered an ad for a seasonal winter job as a maid at the ski hill. When Kenny and I arrived, I was shocked to be at the same place I had tripped out on a couple of years previous. It was a real place, not an acid trip. I gained a lump of confidence that day. When the interviewer asked me if I had any questions, I asked her if I had the job. She didn't hesitate and told me I could start the next Monday. I left ecstatic to have a winter job. It was twenty-two kilometres up the mountain, and I'd have to hitchhike on the days Kenny worked. The days he could drive me, I'd pay five dollars for gas. I didn't care. I had a paying job that would keep me with a roof over my head and food in my belly.

Turning twenty was the most normal birthday I'd had in years. I didn't get a cake or party, but every day for a week, Kenny hid gifts around the house for me. He was trying his best to make me feel special.

I picked up a job working nights as a cook at a factory out of town. It was fifteen kilometres in the opposite direction from town than my day job. I don't know how I managed to talk the couple into giving me the job. I had no clue about cooking everyday meals. I mean, I knew what eggs were, but I hadn't cooked them before. The men were patient and kept their judgement to themselves, thankfully. They taught me how to make eggs over easy or however they wanted them and what the requests meant. I was so tired of working four nights and five days a week that I was seeing dark spots swirl in the fluorescent lighting in the halls. I quit the night job after I had enough cash to buy Christmas presents for my siblings. It was a mutual dissolvement of the job as word had gotten back on my inability to cook.

Mom brought the kids out for a Christmas visit over the holidays. I was ecstatic to see them. I had gifts under the Christmas tree for them and Mom made spaghetti for dinner.

The gifts this time would be okay; I was sure of it. I had gotten them LEGO sets and plastic animals.

* * *

With winter and the exhausting schedule, a deep feeling of tiredness and depression settled into my bones. I began to sleep as much as I could. I was pulled deep into a dream state that I knew I needed to be in. I often slept to leave my consciousness, to go back to the dream world. I could feel in my bones that it was very important that I finish the dream.

During those dreams, I sat at a table with my dead father and my dead ex-boyfriend, Finn. I couldn't recall their faces when I woke, but I knew it was them. We sat and talked about things they needed me to know. Every time I woke, I couldn't remember anything besides sitting with them at that little square card table. The talks were as though I was taking lessons. Near the end, they let me meet my children. I couldn't remember if I had a boy or girl, just that it was important that I got to meet my child. And then, just like that, they were over. The dreams ended and never returned. I never saw them again, even though I wanted to more than anything.

I knew I needed to keep moving. This wasn't the life for me. Living with a dealer, a man old enough to be my father. I needed to keep going toward something. There was a life for me that I couldn't picture. It wasn't what I was currently living; that much I knew.

The break-up was hard on us both. Kenny had saved me. He helped me get on my feet. We split up our belongings, each taking turns or compromising over items we had bought together.

Kenny disappeared after that. I hid from him as I knew he had the connections and ability to punish me if he wanted. I learned later from Samantha that he went downhill rather badly. He got messed up with harder drugs, debt, and bad people. Samantha said he told people it was because I left him heartbroken and that he regretted making me pay my own way. Kenny didn't realize I knew there was a future out there for me that neither of us could begin to fathom. And it had nothing to do with paying my own way.

Chapter Thirty-Five:
Finally Earning Money

I moved into a two-bedroom unit in a four-plex in a blue-collar neighbourhood. I quickly got to know most of the neighbours. I had a roommate to help with the rent. I became friends with people living on the same street.

I met other desperate hard-working men and women who struggled against stacked odds to make a go of life. Now my friends were folks who worked hard to catch a break. I felt grounded and able to navigate life a little.

I was now an adult. I paid bills, earned money, had a bank account, and I had utilities and a phone in my own name. I mostly knew how to do this now. The valley I lived in felt like home in a way nowhere else had. Maybe because I was born there, maybe because it was a small town surrounded by hills, mountains, and lakes. Maybe because I was finally managing a little.

I spent more and more time with the friends I made. I felt comfortable with them. They didn't have the pretenses the white picket fence people did. I was tired of pretending to be okay, tired of pretending to be a well-adjusted young adult.

I was twenty years old, didn't drive, didn't have a full-time job, and didn't believe in anything much other than being a good person. I also believed in the power of *why not?* Why not try or do something new? Even though my new friends accepted me for who I was, it felt superficial. I had built a great wall around myself, and I didn't let anyone in. I wasn't communicating with anyone I'd known before moving to this town. I was grateful for their love and friendships, but all I wanted to do was hide in my world.

I began a work routine of winters at the ski hill and summers at the army camp. The trouble was in the time in between, there was no income. The wait for Employment Insurance (EI) was too long and not enough to live off. I had to choose between paying rent or utilities. Food didn't even come into the equation. I was looking at disconnection and eviction. I needed to make a little fast hard cash or be back on the street.

I was sick of asking for government assistance (welfare). It was less than my EI cheque and wouldn't save me. So, I stuck out my thumb and hitchhiked to a nearby city an hour away. There I'd be able to blend in and make some fast cash as a street walker. I could pick up a few clients (tricks or punters, as UK slang goes) without seeing anyone I knew. I hoped that after a few trips, I'd have my rent and utilities paid with enough money left over to buy some food.

I got a ride right away, and the gentleman, upon hearing I'd be heading that way a few times, mentioned he would be sure to keep his eye out for me from then on. I never hitchhiked on that road again. I bought bus tickets instead.

That summer, I met two men who would shape my future. Maybe they didn't shape it so much as show me by example.

I found the trolling street right away. A woman came up to me and told me I was in her spot. She was too skinny, too scabby, too shabby, and a little off her rocker. I told her to never mind, that I was just hanging out for a bit. She got huffy and went to get reinforcements. A few minutes later, she came back with a young man about my age. Tim sent her off to sit on a bench while we had a chat. Apparently, he owned this section of town, and I had to pay a fee for hanging out. This fee would help keep me safe. He shoved the tip of something up against his pocket to emphasize his strength. He had a gun and would use it even though he wouldn't show it.

I didn't buy his line of shit. First off, the only person threatening my safety was him. His gun would draw attention if used. His skinny little friend was off hiding in the bushes. I told him as much using some tact as I said it. I then told him I'd be hanging out there for a little while, and then I'd go on back to where I'd come from. My way with words must have left an impression because we became friends of sorts. His skank moved on to another block, and she left me alone. I didn't pay anyone a dime for protection while I waited for clients to drive by and decide to take me for a spin.

I learned a lot about Tim in those few summer weeks. He was out on parole and living in a halfway house. My guess was he had nothing better to do than pretend he was a tough guy who made money off the weak. I had no problem with that, as I was getting the hang of pretending I was tough. At least, I thought I was. Maybe my youthful appearance and childlike innocence, blended with my ability to converse beyond street talk, inspired some to want to protect me.

I still stayed in touch with Samantha. Every now and then, she'd have some work for me. One day she called and said she needed to bring a client over to my place. She said this guy wanted something extra. What are friends for, right? Samantha arrived with a white-haired man in a business suit. He was holding a shopping bag. We called him John. I learned that he was the manager of one of the local businesses. It was a small enough town that we knew he had a wife and a couple of kids in college. John pulled out his wife's old-school cotton nightgown. He put it on and crawled around on the floor while Samantha made him clean things. He wanted her to yell and hit him, to shove her high heel up his arse, and do other painful, ridiculous things to him. And he wanted me to walk about in my panties and watch his degradation.

As he crawled about the living room in the nightie, clothespins hanging off his nipples, I lost it. I hid in the kitchen with a hand towel over my mouth to control my hysterical giggles. I refused to come back out until they were done, and John left. I just couldn't watch a man behave like that.

After a few jobs with Samantha and a few more trips to the city, I paid my outstanding rent, got up to date on my utilities, and stocked my fridge. Work would start soon at the army camp, and I'd have a regular paycheque coming in. A couple of clients said they wanted to see me again and would call me for company. It was a much-needed income cushion until the paycheques started.

I met Duncan on one of my trips to the city. He met me on the street and took me out for lunch. He was a young man, only a few years older than me. He seemed nice enough. I met him when he was bored, sitting on disability because of an ankle spider bite gone bad, driving around looking for a friend, literally. He liked to give me little gifts like jewellery, shopping trips, and, best of all, he offered to teach me to drive. I didn't mind spending time with him as we were similar ages, and both had dreams for our futures. We ended up hanging out on a regular basis and built a friendship. What he really wanted was a relationship.

We went skydiving a few times. Silly little me, terrified of heights, agreed to jump out of a perfectly good airplane for kicks and giggles. The instructor was clear; once we had climbed out onto the wing to drop, there was no turning back. The pilot would fly in such a way that you had to let go if you didn't voluntarily drop like you were taught. I don't remember if I was first, last, or in the middle of the group to jump. I just remember hanging off the wing of that little Cessna, looking back into the plane at my instructor, wondering what the hell I'd been thinking. No way was this a good idea. Why in Sam Hill I should let go and fall was beyond me. Then I remembered it was too late to go back, and I had to drop.

I let go of that wing and promptly curled into a fetal position and shrieked. We were taught to hold our body spread eagle. Arms and legs out straight so we wouldn't end up in a spin or some such dangerous situation. I did none of that. I shrieked like a banshee until my parachute opened. I could go on to explain the beauty of the valley spread out below as I pulled on the handles to guide myself to land on the strip below me. I can't tell you that because all of that was blurred out by the heart-stopping terror I felt and the head rush from not quite fainting from my long shrieks. I had two more jumps to complete the lessons we signed up for. I did them but was no more successful than the first time, as every time, I curled into a ball of terror until my chute opened. I went one more time on a tandem jump, so I could try jumping from ten thousand feet. It was just as terrifying and not worth the ride once the chute opened. I wrote that off my bucket list of things to try and put it on my never-do-again list.

Duncan teaching me to drive was an incredible gift of freedom. He let me drive his pickup around, and I got a feel for driving in the country and city. I got my driver's license days before the law changed the waiting time from thirty days to two years to become an independent driver. We got into our first argument when it came time to decide what kind of vehicle I should have. He wanted to buy me an almost new car. I felt that wasn't right when first learning. I wanted a shit box. I won, and Duncan got me a great deal on a rusted-out, zippy little hatchback. I loved that little car. The freedom of having a vehicle was life-changing. No more hitchhiking and walking to where I needed to get.

Duncan was full of ideas for us. He took me to a shop called Bell that offered cell phones. They would give you a cell phone if you signed a contract to pay every month for two years. We got two phones, one for each of us. I put my name and social insurance number in all the right places and signed on the dotted line. I was now the proud owner of a cell phone. It was half the size of the one Kenny had had.

Not long after that, Duncan asked me to marry him. He had a diamond ring and everything. It was probably a romantic proposal, but it wasn't memorable. I wasn't in love with Duncan, and he didn't know me well enough to love me.

Duncan could offer a life I thought I was searching for, or at least a step toward it. So, I said yes. He suggested we move to Calgary to live with his sister until we could get on our feet. I didn't have any career or financial prospects living in the tiny town that felt like home. A move seemed like a good idea at the time. A moving company came and packed everything for me. And just like that, we moved to Calgary and into his sister's home.

Duncan's sister was nice and welcomed me with open arms. Her daughters were adorable youngsters. Duncan and I quickly settled into city life. He started truck driving, and I landed a job at an adult's only store. I was terrified of driving in a large city. I'd carefully map out each turn and list street names that came prior to the one I was to turn on. The four to eight-lane traffic hurtled along at eighty kilometres per hour, and it overwhelmed me. I had no time to give that fear life. Instead, I ignored it and forced myself to drive.

I worked at all three locations the Love Shop had. They preferred me in one particular shop. I had brought up sales by sixty percent in their worst location. I was eager to learn and knowledgeable about the products. I was happy to explain them to customers or just leave them alone to shop in solitude, whatever they preferred.

At one point, Duncan announced he wanted a joint account where we pooled our money. I hedged and put off having an appointment at the bank as long as I could before I caved in. I didn't like the idea and wondered at Duncan's ability to face life.

He complained a lot, was bad at budgeting, and appeared to struggle with being honest. We had lived with his sister for over two months now, and he showed no signs of wanting our lives to continue to grow and morph as it should. Duncan's lack of interest in helping pay for food and living expenses, never mind getting our own place, made me anxious.

One day, while Duncan was at work, his sister invited me to go with her to take his kids their Christmas gifts.

I was shocked and tried not to show it. I didn't know Duncan had kids! What kids did she mean? She swore me to secrecy before taking me. As it turned out, Duncan was married with a couple of kids. On the drive to his wife, or estranged wife's house, the story came out. His family took turns letting him live with them. Even though I had met him while he lived on his own, she told me it didn't usually last long.

The kids and wife were kept hidden from him for their safety. She knew where they were, and they kept in touch. His sister wouldn't get into detail on how he was a danger or what had transpired. By not knowing the reasons, my imagination ran rampant with worse-case scenarios. I was shocked, and my silence probably spoke volumes.

I didn't say anything and kept my own counsel over the Christmas holidays while I thought about what I should do.

I made an appointment with the bank. I opened my own account and took my name off the joint account Duncan and I had. I applied for a credit card. I'd always been taught debt of any kind was bad, but I needed a financial cushion to live on while I ran. I gave my notice at my job. My boss didn't want me to go and offered me a loan to stay and get my own place. He really didn't want to lose me because I was an asset to his store on the main trucking route. *Breaker, breaker one nine. Pop into the Love Shop on your way through. A cute redhead is there.* But I couldn't stay, I wouldn't stay. It was a huge city where I knew no one and didn't belong.

Duncan arranged for the moving truck with all my household belongings to hold delivery until we had a place. Now I needed them to reroute my stuff. Since he arranged the move, they didn't want to ship it back to BC without his say-so. After some strong conversations, they were finally willing to reroute to a new destination. I just needed to provide an address.

I called Nancy and offered to buy her a one-way bus ticket to Calgary so that we could drive back together. Driving the Rogers Pass in early January alone sounded scary and lonely. She offered me her couch for a few days until I got my own place.

I'd miss the safety of being with someone like Duncan. He taught me things like banking, driving, and having a cell phone contract. He also set himself up at my expense. I was young, dumb, and had fresh credit to play with. Even his cell phone was in my name. I needed to cancel Duncan's phone as soon as I got away. In retrospect, I was very lucky I learned about his wife when I did. Duncan had no time to get more than a cell phone and a joint bank account with no line of credit out of me before I cut everything off and ran.

I waited for Duncan to go to work before I packed up the car with my belongings. I didn't dare let him know. His sister was supportive and helped me sneak off. The only thing I didn't have was his cell phone which I wasn't really worried about. I could cancel that number as soon as I was gone. I wasn't heartbroken. The engagement was a means of survival for me, not love.

I was off to a new chapter. Back to my old stomping grounds, where I had connections and friends. I had no job and no home, but I ran an ad in the paper for a cleaning business. I called it a cleaning business—cleaning men's pipes.

Chapter Thirty-Six: Let's Talk About Sex

Sex was a mixed subject (and maybe still is) for me. It wasn't talked about when I was growing up, and it was taboo unless married. Stay pure until marriage, don't talk about it, separate the youth, so they don't try to have sex.

Perverted men obsessed with sex were forgiven, and though parents tried to not let their daughters be alone with these men, some were still victimized. The men were welcomed as members of the community regardless of what they'd done.

There was no sex-ed, safe sex, or learning that sex is okay and nothing to feel guilty about. There was no intermingling without accusations from the adults that inappropriate things were happening. It created an obsession for some. So many mixed messages about it. Sex is bad. Wait for marriage. Men take it. It's the woman's fault if he does, and so on.

Mom tried to have a safe sex talk with me. I was twelve when she told me I'd be worse with men than she was. I remember standing in the bathroom watching her curl her hair. I'm not sure what prompted the conversation. Most likely, it was my habit of asking questions. Mom told me about condoms and her beaus. She told me that condoms had probably come a long way from being made from sheep's intestines. Mom went on to say she was a bit loose with her affection going further than she should have on the first date. As in all the way. The way I understood these lessons was that I'd be worse than my mother. Essentially, she was saying I'd be a loose woman as she was, but worse. I felt that condemnation from her and the church for years, how I was destined to be carnal.

According to our religion, sins of the parents are lived tenfold by their offspring. I'd be even worse with even more men. In *Patriarchs and Prophets*, by Ellen G White, a chapter addresses parenting, as do numerous other volumes. "Spare the rod, spoil the child" was a common line. "The sins of the parents will be visited upon their children because the parents have given them the stamp of their own lustful propensities." (Testimonies for the Church 2:391, 1870.)

At that time, I was still reeling from Dad's indiscretion with the teenager I had thought to be my friend. Then I was told I'd be easier than my mother, who said hello with open arms on her first dates.

Back then, we lived in a house full of young men. I hit puberty and fell in love with half of them. All daily activities were closely monitored so none of the academy students could explore the beginnings of passion. There were no healthy examples of dating. Just segregation or marriage. There wasn't anything in between.

I was curious how sex worked as I couldn't picture it. I didn't even understand my own body other than privates were dirty and not to be explored. I didn't understand the tingling feeling between my legs, like an itch that needed to be scratched. I didn't have the courage to kiss the girl who had me astride her trying to explain sex. I was so distracted by wanting to do things that I couldn't comprehend what she was saying to me.

I didn't dream of marriage or kids or a white picket fence. I dreamt of a life with Finn, but what that life looked like wasn't clear. I didn't want any of the lifestyles I knew. I was worried about waiting until marriage for sex. I had a great fear that sex wouldn't always work right between the couple, and then what? You're stuck for the rest of your life with someone, and sex doesn't work. It was very concerning to a pubescent girl.

When I was sixteen, fighting for a home, I started having sex with Finn. I was almost as obsessed with sex as him. I couldn't get enough of it, of him. I wanted to ride him all night long and into the day. We had sex so much that we rubbed ourselves raw and needed to take a rest. I still wanted him, in my mouth, in my hands, all over me. He was overwhelmed by my affection. He wasn't nearly as sexual as I was. We did it everywhere, any time. In the lake, in the car, driving down the road, at high noon or midnight. We even did it while he was driving. Finn called me a nympho, a sex addict, as though it was bad that I liked it so much.

I was game to try anything. I didn't believe in love and marriage. I was up for anything as long as it felt good and no one got hurt. I didn't see sex as something special. I had seen time and again that men viewed sex differently. I wanted nothing to do with the church's ideas of God, love, marriage, or sex. I wasn't familiar with healthy ways to have a relationship. I craved affection, and sex was the best way to get it. For me, it was a win-win situation.

Having been raised that either you were a good girl a man wanted to keep or a cheap girl to be shunned left me conflicted for years. I couldn't silence the inner voice telling me I couldn't embrace sex and have a relationship at the same time. That inner voice choreographed by all the childhood judgements told me I wasn't the kind of girl a man would ever want for keeps.

By eighteen, I was an avid fan of sex and set out to study it and learn about how to make it feel good for me and for who I was having it with. I wanted to be more than good at it. I wanted to be amazing.

I had read the *Happy Hooker* by Xaviera Hollander as a teenager. I was in awe of her confidence and ability. She had no issues with treating sex as a delicious way to please and earn an income. Xaviera enjoyed pleasure with both genders equally.

Once, when I was sixteen, while browsing in an adult bookshop, I came across a passage that shocked me and sent me straight to my bedroom to scratch that itch again. It was then I discovered my clitoris. After that, I discovered sex could be good, great even. I read articles in magazines like Cosmopolitan on how to please your man. I came across an amateur porn film with a few couples on a weekend getaway. They were told to have loads of sex and film it. That porn was enjoyable, as everyone liked it. As opposed to the videos where the woman sounds almost like she is in pain while the camera tries to get the best shots regardless of the reality of position and comfort. As the years went by, I learned about what worked to give me pleasure. I embraced my sexuality with gusto. Most of the time, I didn't feel I was a harlot like the predators tried to say, like my mother believed.

I learned to love myself and to enjoy sex to the fullest, the best I could. At twenty, I was saddened by the knowledge that my mom thought sex was a time to lie there and review her shopping list. Me, I loved how good it felt, the power of making a man or woman lose themselves in the heat of the moment. I had no qualms about my sexual interest in both genders.

Getting that job at the adult store was perfect for me. I got to learn all about the toys and products available. I wasn't shy in talking to the customers about the products. In fact, just the opposite. I often had other items I thought they might want to hear about. I was more than willing to discuss the advantages of the products and offered suggestions for other ones that might be of interest.

I strongly believed sex is what made the difference between

roommates and a relationship. Maybe I had heard too many times how after marriage, sex stopped. It was my favourite activity, and there was no way I wanted that kind of relationship for my future.

When my days with Duncan ended, I had hard choices to make. I was headed back home with no place to live, a job, or savings. I had a credit card with a small limit to tide me over. I decided to run an ad for happy-ending dating and see if that could bring a lucrative income while I figured out what to do. My shiny new credit card would only last so long. I needed to be able to take care of myself.

I had given up on being able to earn a livable income. It was obvious that I was uneducated, plus there were no jobs I was qualified for that would pay rent, utilities, and food. Crazy, I know, to need all three of those things.

My new chapter in life wouldn't have minimum wage work offset by welfare. At twenty-one, I was going to be a hooker and let everyone be damned.

Chapter Thirty-Seven:
Becoming Independent

After a few days back in BC, I found a nice central basement suite that lined up like a storage unit or a prison cell, depending on how you want to look at it. The entrance walked into the kitchen, the bathroom was at the far end, and the bedroom was off to the right. There was no sitting room or entertainment area. It was basic, came with covered parking, and fit my belongings. Best of all, it was dirt cheap and included utilities.

I reconnected with some old friends and acquaintances, half-heartedly looked for a job, and settled into life. I went back to the street clinic, reconnecting with the street nurse and social worker. They were the closest thing that felt like a family to me.

I talked about becoming a cook. Cooks always had jobs as we would always need to eat. How to get to that point was beyond me. I thought about being a truck driver. I liked driving and was used to being alone. It would be a perfect job. I didn't pick up a phone book to look for driving schools. The thought never occurred to me. I gave up on my idea of being an accountant once I realized I flipped numbers without knowing it.

My mother came to visit me once while Samantha was over. She came alone without the kids, which was something she'd never done before. She was a little in awe that we both could walk away from men, simply taking what we could carry. She was shocked we were willing to start from scratch instead of putting up with the bullshit. Mom wanted to know how we did it. Her husband, my stepdad, was a sorry piece of flesh with little-man syndrome. He liked to act proper on the outside, but he was an emotional bully and a Christian asshole on the inside. She wanted out but didn't know how. Maybe she was scared. Scared she wouldn't make it to Heaven to my dad or afraid of how she'd support herself and the children. Or maybe she didn't have the backbone yet. Samantha and I both had enough crap in our lives. We weren't going to let that be in our home environment: our safe place. I felt sad for my mother. I couldn't quite understand her lack of fight for herself or my siblings.

Not long after that visit, I sat at my table having an apricot brandy for breakfast while I fingered the candy bowl on the table. I had read about apricot brandy, candy bowls, and other such things that seemed so refined and cultured. I used some of the things I read about to build my life. I didn't want to be plain and boring, a nobody going nowhere in life.

My finger came across something in the candy bowl that wasn't candy. It was a little orange pill from the pill family I liked so much. I hadn't done any pharmaceuticals for a year. I kept to the odd drink or puff of whacky tobacky. I sat there, sipping my morning brandy, looking at my newfound prize on the table. I didn't have any plans for the day. I might as well catch a little ride. That one little pill led to months of blurred images as I rode the wave of drug-induced happiness.

I had two cell phones, a number for each town that I ran ads in the paper offering a happy ending date. I'd drive anywhere for a date, never worrying about rejection. A nice dinner, drinks and laughter, some great physical exercise, and leaving with a few Benjamins kept my bills paid. In fact, I was left with extra. I could now buy new clothes just because I liked them. I met handsome young and middle-aged men too busy for a relationship, too married to be getting any at home, or whatever their reasons were. It was a win/win situation.

Samantha got her hands on some morphine pills, and gosh darn it, it was the best ride. It was better than smoking crack. Crack came with a healthy dose of guilt because if you smoked it, your future was on the line. There is rarely a return from addiction, and crack was high up on the list of bad contenders in my books.

Pills, however, that was a different story. They were legal—doctors prescribed them. They weren't dangerous like crack or heroin. And for someone like my friend Samantha on welfare, prescriptions are covered. Not birth control, of course, but the good drugs, the safe drugs, were covered. Or at least I thought they were safe.

So, there we were, Samantha and I, taking pharmaceuticals and riding the wave again. Then we added morphine to the mix. Sweet lord, that was a big wave to ride. I remember Samantha standing in the kitchen by the stove. She was built like a brick shithouse. She was tough, strong, and had breasts the size of summer watermelons and legs meant for running. The visual of her with my spaghetti fork in hand scratching her back had me in stitches. She'd reach around with one breast or the other getting in the way, trying to get an itch that kept moving. I almost fell off my chair laughing as I watched her. I vowed never to fall into the morphine scratch and managed to keep my word. Thankfully we didn't have an abundant supply or access to more morphine.

I had a few repeat clients from my ads. I'd often bring Samantha as my plus one when I went out for safety and companionship. I met nice and proper gentlemen and husbands who had no qualms about bringing me into their wives' beds. I didn't want a husband. Between the clients and my friend Danny,

I was clearly reminded why I never wanted to be the girlfriend. I preferred to be the other woman who knew what was really going on.

I liked Danny just fine. He was sexy, funny, and had an entrepreneurial mindset. If things were different, I'd have loved to be his girl. I saw how many girls he did it with, how he hid it from his lady. I never wanted to be the woman who thought she had the perfect life while other women were screwed in her bed, on her sofa, on the kitchen counter, or in the bathroom.

Danny worked on building a future outside of the illegal world. The problem was, he banged everything along the way. I sold my engagement ring to him after we had a good round of bumping uglies together. He bought it for his old lady. I never forgot how he did me and then bought my ring as a gift for her. I never wanted to be a *her*. I preferred the open honesty of offering a date with a happy ending than being the woman thinking her man was all that.

On a visit with Danny, he brought up how computers and the internet were taking off. He told me how I could start an online business. Instead of being hands-on with men, I could entertain online instead. Make a lot of cash and not have to be *doing what I was doing*, as he put it. It was sweet of him to think of my best interest like that, but I wasn't convinced. For starters, this wasn't my future, it was just for now. I was also smart enough to know once your stuff is out in the electronic world, there was no taking it back. I wish now I'd learned about the internet and computers because I learned decades too late. I missed that boom of technology that many made a fortune on.

I tried to learn about the rules of being a girl. My friend, Nancy, knew all sorts of things about physical appearance and rules of behaviour to get what you wanted. There was so much work that went into looking different than you normally would. I just didn't get it. I was fine with a swipe of mascara and maybe a touch of blush or lipstick. I wasn't a huge fan of shopping and didn't know or care about name brands. I didn't understand all the rules about dating that Nancy was trying to teach me. She tried to teach me about flirting, playing hard to get, and the rules of how long to wait for each thing.

This was all to get a guy to want you for a girlfriend and then a wife. I wasn't sure I'd ever want that. It seemed like a lot of work when I could just be myself. I tried clubbing with her, and it was akin to torture. Awkward dancing at a meat market where you couldn't hear yourself think didn't interest me.

Nancy came to me for help when her roommate stole her car and gave her a shiner and bruised jaw. She tossed all Nancy's belongings in the front yard and took her car for a joy ride without permission. I got my street family to help store her belongings, and I took polaroid photos to document her beaten face.

Then Samantha and I paid her roommate a little visit. We went to try and get Nancy's bird as she was beside herself without it. Samantha told me to stay in the car and keep it running. Nancy's roommate was given a little lesson in how not to treat my family, and then we were off. No bird was retrieved, but a stern warning was left. No physical damage was done, but a knife may have helped remind her of what not to do to people. It was the way of the streets. You stuck together. Apparently, Nancy's friend was more knowledgeable about dating rules than loyalty and street family rules.

A week later, I was hauled in and charged with assault with a weapon. I denied everything and refused to give a statement. I cried when I was fingerprinted and cried even more when they photographed me. I was released on my own recognizance with a date to appear in court more than six months later.

Nancy wasn't too concerned about the charges I faced. In

fact, she was upset we'd taken steps to protect her. She wasn't to ask for my financial assistance to set her up as a stripper, though. The local bar had weekly wet T-shirt contests offering the winning woman free drinks. Nancy had won that week again. While there, a gentleman suggested, she become a poll dancer, live an exotic life, and move to Vancouver. For an entrance fee, of course. Over the next month, I ended up lending her two thousand dollars to get waxed, dyed, dressed, and Barbied up to fit the roll.

I went with her to Vancouver for the first few weekends of work while she got settled in. I covered the cost of gas and hotel rooms as we enjoyed the adventure together. While in Vancouver, she partied with her coworkers while I went exploring. I loved being near the ocean and walked for hours during the day, soaking up the salty air. On my last weekend there, I happened to let a couple pick me up for a date when I sat and watched Nancy perform. They told me about the Leonardo da Vinci exhibit they had gone to see in Victoria. I'd heard of him and wanted to go see for myself. When I got back to the hotel, I called the front desk for help. They were able to book me a seat on a bus tour that would take me to Victoria. Once there, I'd find my way to the museum to see his exhibit.

Upon admission, I was set up with a Walkman and headphones to hear all about the exhibit. As I walked about, I was awestruck by how smart he was. I was amazed by the ideas he had in the era he was from. I mean gears, parachutes, a flying machine thought about in his time. It was a captivating day for me. I was too excited to be disappointed that the Mona Lisa wasn't on display. I bought a notebook and a tank top with her portrait on them. That day was the highlight of my year. I went home with thoughts of a different life than mine. There was so much more to the world.

A few weeks after leaving Nancy in Vancouver, I learned she'd made up with her ex-roomie. They were besties again, which meant she took her side on the criminal charges. Nancy, who was supposed to be my sister, took the accuser's side and wrote an affidavit to assist her charges against me. The same person who she had run to for help.

I was devastated, angry, and confused. That's what family does. Protects, helps, avenges. Nancy's friend crossed the line with her personal belongings and beat her up. Of course, we would step in and let her know not to ever do that again. That's what family does.

Nancy knew I ran with a rough crowd and lived by those rules. I didn't understand why she'd betray me like that. I lost trust in my one and only sister-friend, who had known me the longest, who was also seeking a life unlike what we were raised in. In trying to help and protect her, I was charged with a very serious offence and made enemies with a large circle of peers. Her peers. Between her betrayal and the criminal charge, a deep depression seeded itself in me.

Chapter Thirty-Eight:
Overwhelmingly Lonely

I decided to move out of my tiny basement suite. I found a nice little old log cabin in the farming district of our municipality.

Spring was on its way, bringing the pretty foliage to life. The cabin was not round logs but square cut timbers. It had hardwood floors, all sloped and sagging with age. The walls in the kitchen were made up of shelves upon shelves painted white. I loved everything about the rental. It was just my style. There were no neighbours around to bother me and beautiful horses in nearby fields.

I fell into a deep depression there. Maybe it was coming off the pills; maybe it was the loneliness. The knowledge that I was truly alone gripped me with despair. The friends and acquaintances I had were only good-time friends.

I was wise enough to know that no one was truly there for me. I couldn't sleep at night. I was suffering but didn't know how to fix it. I didn't want to be an addict like Nancy's mother. She had four children from different men, and they were all in the system because she was on a heroin binge again. In my limited world, I saw that I had two choices: the Bible or heroin. I didn't want either. All I knew was I didn't belong anywhere or to anyone.

I got into a routine of sorts. I'd have breakfast and a

paralyzer at my favourite pub. I loved that creaky old pub. The clientele were friendly, hard-working folks. The waitress knew my name and order. The chef was happy to make me a loaded veggie omelette even though it wasn't on the menu. His eagerness to please may have been partially due to the tongue-down-the-throat occasion from when I was new to town.

I learned how to smoke a cigarette and eat my meal at the same time. I learned by watching the other patrons. I listened to how upset they were at the new laws making smoking in pubs and bars illegal. We smoked anyway. I loved to chill out in the darkened corner of that old building as I waited for my phone to ring.

Often, I'd drive around the back roads and enjoy the beautiful valley I got to call home. I'd read, write, or have a nap. That would take me into the evening when I'd go for a drive downtown. I watched people and said hi to acquaintances. Occasionally I'd catch a girl hanging out on a street corner looking for a ride. I'd suggest she get a ride with me. I'd offer her safer work off the streets, working for me. Then I'd take her to my home, take my new dildo for a test drive on her and then take her home.

I was constantly struggling to find the life I wanted, a place I belonged. I didn't want a life like the people I knew. I didn't want the life I had. I didn't know how to get the life I wanted or what it even looked like.

I had an epiphany in the wee hours of the morning that sent uncontrollable sobs through my body. I realized we are actually and truly alone. That I'd always be alone. When it came down to it, there was only numero uno.

I called my aunt and uncle, mindless of the time, and asked her if that was what she meant. Years back, she had said that in the end, you only had yourself. It was a hard and depressing thought.

I cried so much they could barely understand me. I ended up saying never mind and ended the call.

They must have called my mother as she came and made me lunch the next day. She brought her whole wheat spaghetti and home-canned tomatoes. The kids ran around the backfield, playing in the tall grass. They set off firecrackers they'd managed to get their hands on. That got the police called to our door because the vacant place next door had a recent shooting. The idea that gunfire sounded the same as the firecrackers set mother and I off in a set of giggles. Our humour was always there, the ability to laugh in the face of anything. She taught me that.

After that, I decided to pull up my big girl panties and get on with life. I'd make myself happy one step at a time. It wasn't easily done, but making that decision was a big step. I tried to get out during the day and tire myself out enough to sleep. I started smoking weed to find happiness, to feel relaxed. Okay, I didn't start, but I began to use it for that as opposed to recreational.

I bought a beautiful quarter-carat diamond ring for myself. I was in a relationship with myself, marking myself unavailable with that ring.

I tried hanging out with Kenny again. We went to a bush party and slept on a mattress in the back of his pickup. I just couldn't reconnect with him. He belonged in the past. I was struggling, but I slowly got past my deep-abiding depression and feeling unwanted and not belonging.

Chapter Thirty-Nine: Lost in Oblivion

Going to the youth clinic for street kids gave me a purpose when I had none. I really liked the nurse and the youth worker there. They kept saying I should write a book about growing up like I did. I wasn't ready yet. My story wasn't over yet. I didn't have the ending I needed before I wrote it. I was in the middle of living it.

I asked them again and again how to meet nice people. People who weren't street people going nowhere. I wanted to meet people who weren't fake, like the people I knew from growing up with a church family. They didn't have an answer. It took me years to realize how. You need to be a part of something to meet like-minded people. It could be that you like the same sports team, or you're an outdoor enthusiast, or comic collector and fan, or even a churchgoer. It didn't matter what, you just needed to join a group, and over time, friendships with other members grew. But no one told me that.

At their request, I went to a board meeting to speak on behalf of the clinic and its needs. The funding was always difficult to acquire, and my voice was beneficial that year. It was terrifying to sit at a table of board members and directors; however, I felt the need to speak worth the anxiety.

One day, as I walked through the park, I saw a couple of young men I hadn't seen before. I went over to say hello. One caught my eye. He wasn't much taller than me. He looked to be my age but didn't possess the airs most peers had. I felt people, sort of like seeing an aura or reading their cards.

Jesse felt great, a balm to my soul. I asked him if he wanted to come home with me. He said yes, but there was a catch. His friend had to come too as they were travelling together. So, his friend got the couch. I fell in love that day. It was the start of a summer whirlwind romance. I was crazy about him and wasn't ashamed of it.

We talked in the bath together until the water was cold. We rolled around in bed, exploring each other day and night. We ate, slept, took road trips, and did couples' photo shoots at rustic buildings. You name it; we did it. I asked him to marry me and bought him a gold wedding band. I already had my diamond engagement ring I bought myself.

It didn't matter to me or raise concern that he was living out of a small shopping bag. Jesse had no money, no residence, and was down to hang out for the summer. He lived in a remote northern city but liked to come down and bum around in the summer. Considering my teen years, this didn't seem weird at all. His dad owned a store, and he worked there over the winter months. Eventually, Jesse's friend found his own lady friend, and we saw less of him.

One night Samantha, Jesse, and I were all sitting around the table visiting and sipping on gin and juice. Okay, that's an exaggeration, but we were all sitting around the table with a bottle of vodka front and centre. They were having a deep debate over gangs who ran the west versus east coast: the Crips, Snakes, Bloods, and the HA.

I was bored and uninterested, so I took myself off to the powder room to refresh my nonexistent makeup. One minute I was sitting on the toilet going pee, and the next, I heard a gunshot that had me off the toilet and yelling, "What the bloody hell!"

The two of them looked rather repentant. They had placed the handgun on the table between them. There was a bullet embedded in the window frame. Three feet to the right, and I'd have had an extra hole in me. I told them that someone was shot next door not long ago and that mere firecrackers had brought the police to my home. I grabbed the handgun and left. I figured the best place to take it was to my dealer, Danny. He would be able to get rid of it or at least store it short term. I called ahead to say I was coming over and said nothing of the actual reason.

On my way there, I ran into a roadblock. There was no avoiding driving up to the police. My bloodshot eyes made me look like I was mid-party, which I was. I claimed I was on my way home from working at the factory. I was asked to pull over and walk a straight line. My heart was knocking around in my chest as I stepped out of the car. It was hard enough to walk a straight line in a tight mini skirt and platform heels without the heart palpitations blurring my sight. Add to that the fear that they would search my car and find the gun added a tremble to my step.

I don't know if it was the skirt or the agility of my step, but they let me go. I almost cried in relief as I drove away. Danny refused to take the hot item off my hands. He had no connections to help me get rid of it, either. I ended up stuck with the gun hidden under my spare tire for a few weeks while I tried to find a way to unload it and get some money out of it. Not knowing what possible crimes that piece may have been involved with made it unwanted to most. I got pulled over for a broken taillight before I got rid of it. That scare made me willing to take the only offer I had, no matter how lowball it was. I didn't want to get pinned, for God knows what that gun may have been used for.

That incident didn't damper my relationship with Jesse, although I did set some very clear boundaries about crime and weapons after that. I found out he was younger than me. That was a first for me, liking someone who wasn't years older. Maybe it was his old soul that attracted me. We were like two peas in a pod, laughing and talking endlessly. We went everywhere together. He would wait in the car for me if I got a call to see clients. Before the days of smartphones and immediate entertainment, he would nap while he waited. My source of income wasn't an issue or even discussed. He didn't do anything for work and was, in fact, living off my income. It didn't bother me that I paid for everything. I liked being able to pay for things. I wasn't interested in finding a different job as minimum wage wasn't a livable income. I wasn't keen on going back to having to decide whether to pay for food or my heating bill. I liked having both and having money left in my pocket.

It turned out Jesse was a heroin addict. I had no idea and never saw him use it, but Samantha told me. She knew I was too naïve to see the signs. Samantha made him talk to me about it. He decided to quit using. He went to the clinic for Methadone as a way to fight his addiction. He suffered from withdrawal pain deep in his bones between doses. I felt bad for him, but I also thought if you were to put yourself into that position, you needed to pull yourself back out. What I didn't know is that many can't or won't.

We were having a late breakfast at the pub, and I got a call. I didn't like the sound of the voice on the other end. I said I was busy and ended the call. Jesse asked what the call was about, and I said it was a potential client. My refusal to take a job upset him something fierce. We got into a raging argument and ended our breakfast early. As I drove home, he began to punch my windshield. Within five minutes, the entire windshield was shattered, held together by the laminated plastic.

I screeched to a stop on the side of the road. It was a quiet road between large fields of alfalfa. I tossed my keys onto the floorboard behind my seat and leapt out of the car. We met in the middle of the road, and I attacked him as though I was a Billy goat. My head down, I ran into him with a full body slam. We wrestled and fought like that for a few minutes. I kept head-butting him away from me and into the ditch. I was livid and saw nothing of what was around me. I realized I was standing in the middle of the road with my summer dress unbuttoned past my waist. My breasts and underpants were on full display. There were cars lined up on either side of the road, watching us play out our dramatic difference of opinion. I jumped back into my car and locked all the doors. Thankfully I located my keys quickly and started the car. Jesse made a dive for my hood and hung onto whatever he could get his hands on. I geared up in record time and was revving fifth within yards. I hit the brakes, leaving a trail of rubber. He flew off the hood like an unwanted bug.

My windshield was a mess. I needed to park my car somewhere. I knew the cops would be coming and would want a statement at some point. Little flecks of glass fell to the dash as I drove. I squinted through the webs of shattered glass and tried to stay in my lane. I'd need to buy a car. I'd also need to find a new place to live—again.

Danny, wonderful as always to me, agreed to deal with my car. I left it parked out back and took a taxi home. The adrenaline and weed blurred my mind as I set about getting a new place to live, another beater car to drive, and all the arrangements that came with those tasks. The police told me that medics had taken Jesse to the hospital to be checked over before he was taken to the police station to go before the judge in the morning. I refused to press charges, but the cops said it was out of my hands. Crown would be pressing charges as they had numerous witness statements from the bystanders that had seen us fighting. I guess tossing him off the hood of my car was acceptable in that scenario.

I found a cute two-bedroom apartment with immediate occupancy. I went to Danny to ask to borrow his truck to move my belongings.

Anytime I went to Danny's, I usually hung around and visited for a while. If his house cleared out enough, we would have a delicious tryst. It was the way of our friendship. As I sat there, I mentioned the home invasion with a weapon charge I was facing. I had court coming up in a few months, and it was weighing on my mind. Danny was concerned. He explained the seriousness of the charges and possible repercussions. Until that conversation, I hadn't thought much of it. The so-called victim had no violence against her person or property. I was in the car when the altercation happened. None of that mattered however, innocent until proven guilty is not always the case. It didn't help that the original victim, Nancy, was now standing in court protecting this bully.

Danny said I needed to get a lawyer, a good criminal lawyer from out of town. Not only was I out the two grand I had lent Nancy to get on her feet, but I was also now going to be out thousands to defend myself. I went to some of the harder criminals I knew and was recommended to a gentleman from a nearby city that represented others in their circle. I called the number and had an appointment booked in a few weeks' time.

I settled into my new place, bought a new junker car, and got a girl as a roommate. I met Mindy by chance as she walked by Samantha's place at the same time I was leaving. She was from a broken home and didn't have anywhere to go. I offered her my spare room and a job. For a fee, of course.

Mindy was happy to entertain men for a fee. She didn't

have an issue with paying a small percentage to me, the house, for keeping the clientele coming.

I refused to make up with Jesse until he cleaned up his act. It was something that had to happen before he could be with me. I wasn't about to support him and wait for it to maybe happen. Jesse stayed on his destructive path. He stole and sold whatever he could to get high. He showed up at my apartment and peddled his bike (stolen, I'm sure) down the steps, ultimately crashing. The wheel bent badly enough to make it unrideable. I hardened my heart and threatened to call the police if he didn't leave the apartment grounds at once. I wanted nothing to do with an addict that wasn't willing to change.

Mindy and I did everything together. I was glad to have a friend. We drove around and played loud music on my souped-up stereo.

My car was a five-hundred-dollar piece of shit that was rusted and dented. The stereo, speakers, sub, and amps cost more than the car did. You could hear the sound system thumping AC/DC or Dr. Dre a block away.

I took Mindy with me and then left her at the mall when I went to visit the lawyer. After paying the fifteen-hundred-dollar retainer and agreeing to pay the additional three grand by my court date, I had legal representation.

The lawyer wanted to see me for a longer consultation in a month's time to go over my case. The court date wasn't set for a few more months giving him time to prepare and me time to get the cash together. I felt slightly relieved about my pending court date.

Mindy and I were a pair of young girls that men enjoyed being *friends* with.

One man became a regular client that enjoyed our company, although Mindy wouldn't let it be three-way. He reminded me of Michael Landon with a beard. I felt comfortable around him. He even had daughters our age, he said. Not creepy at all since he was having sex with us. He showed us a large greenhouse he had going. Marijuana for medical purposes, he said. He also had bottles upon bottles of morphine to ease the health issues he had.

Another regular client liked to give us his wife's clothing and perfume since they were in the middle of an ugly divorce. A different man from out of to town brought his toddler to hang at the apartment while he ran errands. I sat him down and gave him an ear full for that bad choice. You don't leave a child with a woman running on the wrong side of the law that you don't know. His response was to ask me to be his girlfriend.

I was losing more and more respect for people and their idea of relationships. I upped my daily intake of weed to combat the sadness of the world.

* * *

My brother ran away from home and came to me. Daniel couldn't live that way anymore. He had almost talked our little sister into leaving as well, but she wasn't ready yet. Daniel was only thirteen at the time. He was done with the fighting he saw between Mom and Rick. He was done with being condemned every step of the way by that pious jerk. Daniel was done with the life, or lack thereof, he had.

Rick was a strongly religious man, devotedly grave and solemn. He was an emotional bully in the name of God. He was the God of his household and expected the children to be solemn little pupils. He didn't believe in children having lessons aimed at their age and instead would expect them to sit through adult sermons. They were not allowed to fidget, play, or laugh. They were so strict the local church asked them to stop coming if they couldn't meet in the middle with their religious views. Mom's hair stopped growing, her eczema worsened, and she began to suffer from health issues. Her skin took on a yellow hue, her weight dropped to under a hundred pounds making her five-foot-five frame look gaunt, aging her well past her true age.

When I'd go on my biannual visit, I'd smoke a big fatty and get high as a kite so I could face the sadness I felt after seeing her and seeing how the children lived. This unhappy, unhealthy Christian lifestyle was lived for their God. It broke my heart to see the kids growing up like that, to see Mom so sad on the inside and so alone there with him. Every time I went to visit, it would cause a huge fight between them. When Daniel came to me, it was no surprise. I was expecting him. I expected all of them at some point.

I took Daniel to social services to try and get them involved with Mom. Daniel told me my stepdad was making my sister uncomfortable with the way he tucked her into bed at night. If it felt wrong, it was wrong. The social worker met with us at a coffee shop. As she conducted the interview, she asked me questions as well. What my concerns were and why. Was I looking to take my three siblings into my care? I explained I had no formal education, no viable future career, or the ability to financially care for the children. Without remorse, I openly shared that I worked as a self-employed woman of the night to support myself.

I felt I wasn't good enough to raise the children in my current situation. She took Daniel and my information all down in her notebook and promised to investigate it. I held little hope knowing how well the lies would roll off Mom and Rick's tongues.

I also knew my baby sister, now eleven, wouldn't say anything hurtful. Matthias, at nine, didn't have much of a voice yet about his upbringing. Regardless of education or religion, the welfare system didn't want to take kids if they didn't have to. They had a roof over their heads. Emotional abuse is not acknowledged as abuse, they were not physically abused, and there was no drug or alcohol abuse. Leave them be seemed to be the motto.

I wasn't equipped to care for a gangly growing teenage boy who was in the midst of puberty. I did my best to show him all the things he shouldn't do, watch, or want for his future. I bought him endless bottles of ketchup. He wanted it on everything, including toast. Daniel was in touch with his biological father and wanted to live with him. He'd come into the picture after Daniel's biological mother passed away. He knew who had adopted his son and followed our family from the beginning. Apparently, when the adoption papers were mailed, they had our last name all over them instead of being anonymous.

It was decided my brother should go live with his birth father, Josh. I offered to make the short road trip. Mindy, Daniel, and I bundled into the car and headed out. It would be a full day of driving for the round trip. It saddened me to see his emotional suffering, thanks to human flaws and the idealism of wanting to get to Heaven above all else. After a brief introduction at Daniels's dad's, Mindy and I headed home. Daniel was excited to start a relationship with his birth father. I spent the drive home smoking weed, blasting rock and roll, and trying to forget the pain. I belonged to no one, didn't believe in anything, and couldn't care for anyone. I wasn't good enough to care for anyone.

Chapter Forty: Downward Spiral

I spiralled down a bad path, and I took Mindy along for the ride. We took all the bottles of morphine from our client when he wasn't home. He never locked the door, and I knew he wouldn't do or say anything. He couldn't, considering what he had growing in his basement.

The tricky thing about pills is even when you're flying high as a kite, you think you aren't. It was easy to pop another pill any time we felt we weren't high anymore. We were so high I forgot to run the weekly ad for entertainment. We forgot to eat. Hunger wasn't something either of us felt anymore.

I found hundred-dollar bills hidden in the wastepaper basket and other random places. We made a point of getting out for a daily drive to enjoy the beautiful scenery. We did it hidden behind dark glasses.

An example of how out of it we were, was a light bulb moment I didn't have until my thirties. One time while driving, I pulled up in the left turning lane, and as I waited for the light to turn green, the car in front of me put their vehicle into reverse and rolled back into me. Not a big hit, just a rolling coast, a light bumper-to-bumper hit. I was livid. I put my car into park and jumped out, yelling at her for hitting me. The lady locked her car doors and windows, trying to keep a safe distance between us.

Years later, I'd realize I had most likely rolled into her, not pressing my brake totally to the floor. I probably scared the bejeezus out of the poor woman. Goes to show how stoned I was without even realizing it.

The trouble with morphine is that you aren't hungry. Blissfully, joyfully happy, but not hungry. I wasn't even smoking as much weed, which accentuated my loss of hunger. By the middle of summer, I had lost so much weight I had an unhealthy gaunt look. I made Mom look healthy, and that was an achievement. That prompted the street clinic nurse to give me an ultimatum: gain weight or be hospitalized in the next week. I stopped at the local bakery on the way home and picked up a Black Forest cake to eat. Not a slice, the whole cake.

I was out of morphine and hadn't seen Samantha in a while. I smoked weed and thought I'd try to clean up and find a better way. Again.

Mindy wasn't fairing much better than me. She was messed up something fierce by her family long before I met her. I don't know if it was her family life or if she was born with demons she had to battle. Either way, she now scared the crap out of me. She'd cut and burn herself and banged her head on the wall repeatedly.

In desperation, I put my foot through the bathroom door to break in and stop her from burning herself from knee to thigh with the curling iron. I was scared for her and didn't know what to do.

Everything came to a head between Mindy and me on the drive home from seeing my lawyer. Thankfully the morphine had run out in time for me to be sober enough for the meeting regarding the home invasion charge. The lawyer was confident that not only could he easily defend me but most likely get the charges dropped based on a cross-examination of Nancy and the photos of Nancy's battered face and neck.

On the drive home, the stereo was cranked loud enough to rattle our fillings. The relief from such good news gave me a sense of euphoria I hadn't felt in a long time.

We were almost home when Mindy reached over and grabbed the steering wheel. She gave a hard yank to the right, and the car swerved into the deep ditch and tumbled down the road, flipping a few times before landing upright in the ditch.

I was in shock, with blood dripping down my face. Mindy was crying, and her foot was stuck at an odd angle near the door. There were empty bottles at her feet. I had an ashtray full of wacky tobacky butts. This was bad. Bad, bad, bad.

When the ambulance arrived, I went and sat in the extra seat of the ambulance while they removed her from the wreck. I made sure I cried and shook, that I showed the physical signs of shock.

My forehead was bleeding from a small gash above my eye. They placed a butterfly bandage on my eyebrow to stem the bleeding. It was the same eye I had a scar on from cutting my eye as a toddler playing with car keys. Now I was adding another scar to remind me how lucky I was. At the hospital, Mindy was taken for X-rays and admitted.

I needed to check myself out before any tests or questions could be asked. The hospital wouldn't discharge me unless I could prove I wouldn't be alone for the first twenty-four hours in case of complications from my concussion.

I called and talked Danny into telling the nurse I'd be with him so I could be discharged. I took a taxi home and passed out. The day had started out stressful, had a great middle, and ended terribly. I was exhausted.

The next morning, I paid Mindy a quick visit at the hospital to make sure she was okay. While there, I got a signed note from her stating she had pulled the steering wheel. I gathered up her journals documenting her self-injury and the note from her to give to my lawyer, just in case shit hit the fan again.

Now I had even more problems. Mindy had lied about her age. She was a minor for a few more months. To top that off, her dad was a cop a few towns over. The hospital believed she was a heroin addict, juicing up through her feet. The health officials were mistaking her scratched feet as injection sites, not the morphine itches they really were. One more example of jumping to the worst conclusion.

I went to the pub for breakfast to celebrate my shitty news. I ordered a double paralyzer and an omelette. I lit new cigarettes from the old ones before they burned out.

My car was totalled. My stereo system was stripped by the asshole tow truck driver. I'd been lied to and duped again by someone I thought was my friend. I was filled with pain and anger. I was livid at my helplessness at that exact moment.

I woke later that day, naked, in my living room. I followed the trail of clothing to the haphazardly hanging blinds.

I had cloudy memories of being woken by a police officer on the front lawn of the apartment complex. I must have stumbled off and then broken in through the window as I didn't have keys. Hazy memories hung at the back of my consciousness. I was in an old rundown house somewhere along my walk home. I had wandered through it, leaving my purse and taking a random sandbag ashtray instead. I couldn't recall what house I'd been to and never found my purse or belongings.

I lost my camera, ID, keys, and general paraphernalia. Yet I still had the thick wad of cash in my back pocket. Small blessings, I figured. My life was in chaos, and the light at the end of the tunnel wasn't shining. It wasn't even a pin light yet.

* * *

I was a mess the night before court. I understood the plaintiff had a passel of friends to back her, including Nancy. I'd see them sometimes driving through town. They would laugh and use Italian hand gestures when driving past me. Samantha and I sat in court next to my lawyer, waiting for our case to be called. The fact that my friend, the girl I loved like a sister, sat on the opposing side hurt more than I cared to admit. The betrayal cut deep. Court broke for lunch, but I couldn't bring myself to eat. I was a ball of nerves. The outcome would affect me forever.

At the end of the day, the judge was about to have any cases left booked for another day. Then he laid eyes on my lawyer: they were old classmates. The clerk was remonstrated for making him wait all day. Court stayed in session, and our case was brought forward. Evidence by the crown was brought forward. There were signed affidavits claiming the victim had answered the door to a woman who warned her to stay away from Nancy or else. The plaintiff claimed to have been violently attacked by a knife to her temple.

My lawyer then rebutted with defense exhibit A, the photos of Nancy's face and neck showing prominent bruising. There were affidavits from myself and Samantha regarding the abuse and subsequent visit to said victim. The judge then called the plaintiff, Nancy's friend, to the stand, the one who said we assaulted her.

The more questions he asked, and she answered, the better I felt. Did you take Nancy's car without permission? Did you throw her belongings out into the courtyard? Did you assault and cause the bruises shown in the photos? Yes, yes, and yes, she said. Did you get hurt when the knife was pulled on you? Yes. How did you treat it? Did you call an ambulance? Did you go to a clinic or doctor's office? Did you require stitches or a Band-Aid? No, no, no, and no.

The defense had no reason to say anything. The crown looked as embarrassed as the witness. The more the judge asked, the more the so-called victim made herself look like a fool. In the end, the judge reprimanded her for her behaviour.

"Young lady," he said. "I can't even call you that. Your behaviour is an embarrassment. This situation should never have happened in the first place." He banged his gavel, and that was that. The case was dropped. The three of us signed a peace bond and agreed to have no contact and keep a distance.

I didn't go out and celebrate. I was exhausted and needed to change my life. I went home to do some soul-searching and decision-making.

I needed a new, better life. I needed to leave these people behind and change everything. I drove from one end of the Okanagan Valley to the other as I searched for somewhere that felt like home. One place reeked like manure. Another was too quiet, another the city too large. I couldn't find the right fit. I settled on staying in the same town in a quiet little basement suite that was within walking distance of downtown. I got a job at a gas station but couldn't bring myself to show up on my first day. Working for minimum wage wasn't going to happen. I was used to a handful of Benjamins after a couple of hours of visiting with a regular client.

I decided to enrol in a few correspondence classes at the local college. It was time for me to clean up and not do any more pharmaceuticals. I decided that weed and the odd drink were okay, but no other drugs. Pills were my kryptonite.

Chapter Forty-One: Finding a New Way

Coming clean was hard. Being alone was hard. Samantha always said you need to like being alone with yourself. I preferred companionship.

I made myself go outside for a walk every day. I'd walk to the bookstore or the pawn shop and add to my collection of VHS or books. I started keeping food in the fridge and eating. I took herbal supplements like St John's Wort to combat depression. I only took work from my regular clients. Most of all, I kept clean.

My body was still suffering from the car accident. Some days I couldn't stand up straight from the tight band of pain in my back. The pain in my jaw was horrifying. I'd often plunge my face into a pillow as I screamed in agony. A chiropractor helped me walk upright. No one could help my jaw. No answers were found except to offer me a prescription for a pill that was in high demand on the street. I didn't trust myself and sold them at a bulk price before I had them in my possession for a day.

As my mind and body healed, I found random little things. I found two leather handbags filled with pills, Percocet, otherwise known as Oxycodone. I wasn't sure I had the strength to keep them long enough to sell them. I didn't trust myself not to take one and flushed them all. I slowly began to heal, gain weight, and think clearly.

I went on road trips to my old childhood homes. My first childhood home high on the mountain overlooking the valley was only a few hours away, a day trip. I drove to the old barn I was left in as a child when Dad went to check on the forest fire. I drove past the old church that was turned into a one-room school. I drove around suicide corner all the way up to my old roundabout driveway. The cherry tree still stood in front of the porch. My family was no longer here. I didn't belong there.

The drive to my second childhood home was no better. There were fewer good memories there. We moved under duress, and the pain from that trauma still put a rock in my belly. I stopped by the farm I stayed at as a girl while my parents got us ready for that move.

Back then, we had all been young pubescent girls roaming the fields and dreaming of our futures. This time we had little to nothing in common. I couldn't be truthful about myself to them or their mother. My life wasn't good enough to speak of out loud. I had to fabricate a different truth.

After I left their house, I stopped beside the river. I sat in the hot sand, deadly whirlpools swirling past me, and sobbed. I sobbed for the life I once had. For the life I could have had if Dad hadn't gone over that cliff. I sobbed for the mother I desperately wanted. How was I supposed to become something better when I had all this pain, when I had nothing to give? I had no heritage. Our family had no traditions. I sure as hell would never willingly live the commune life.

I called an acquaintance from over the years and asked her if she wanted to go on a road trip with me. We headed north to my last home, where I lived with my family. Twelve hundred kilometres, a couple of tanks of gas, a dozen hours of driving, and I was there. I was back at the gas station I had biked to when I first left home at thirteen.

It was well past dark, and I had no destination in mind when I hit the highway. Now idling at the side of the road at the exit to Alaska, to the commune, I knew where I wanted to go. I drove down the one-way dirt road past the entrance to the commune and toward Finn's family home.

The graveyard was ironically not far from where the murdered body was found. I parked with my headlights shining on Finn's tombstone. I sat on the hood of my car and drank my cold beer in silence. I loved Finn so deeply, so purely. He had possibly committed a crime second only to child abuse in my eyes. I tossed my empty beer bottle into the cooler and unbuttoned my 501 Levi's as I walked to his grave. My girlfriend gave a squeal of concern as I squatted down and pissed on his grave. I had my closure. My goodbye to my first love, my first everything.

I stopped in at friends' and even Auntie and Uncle's on my way back home. I didn't stay long. The north held nothing but pain and sadness for me. There wasn't anything there other than reminders as to why I had walked away in the first place.

My past held nothing for me.

* * *

I strung Christmas lights along the door frames and window of my home to add a cheery light as I continued to hide in the dark. My twenty-second birthday and Christmas came and went as though they didn't exist. I tried not to feel too depressed or alone.

I took Christmas lights to Nancy. All wasn't forgiven, but I knew she probably felt as wretched as I did, alone on the holidays. I was still deeply offended she had stood against me in court. But no one deserves to be alone and bereft over the holidays. I had little to give but a visit and some holiday lights to offer some cheer.

While I was there, she informed me that her boyfriend thought she was too good to be working as a stripper. She had quit and now worked for minimum wage. She didn't know when she'd be able to pay back the money borrowed to start that line of work.

How warped is that, I thought. I worked in a worse industry earning the money she was happy to take, and now she was too good to shake her ass to pay me back. I didn't know what to say to that. I kept my silence even though I now added resentment to my feelings of betrayal. When I left her apartment that day, I washed my hands of our sisterhood.

* * *

Over the holidays, I watched endless classic cartoons. I slept, ate, and slowly gained weight. Correspondence classes required more than I'd bargained for. I didn't know what questions to ask or how to go about doing the work. Once I opened the textbook, I felt overwhelmed and out of my depth. I was deep in a fog of pills when I signed up and hadn't learned how to contact the teacher. I needed guidance on how to do the lessons and hand them in. I wasn't ready for that step yet.

It was one day at a time of maintaining sobriety and not wanting to kill myself. It was an ongoing battle that plagued me when things got dark.

Mom came to visit with the children not long after Christmas. Even Daniel came as he had moved back with Mom. He wasn't ready to live with a father he didn't know, even though he was his biological father.

Daniel had a connection to Mom, the woman who raised him since birth, since adoption. Daniel forced himself to swallow his hatred for Rick to be with her.

They stayed at my favourite hotel a few blocks from my

place. The hotel had a creek running through it, a large garden, a pool, and a restaurant in the centre. The three-storey building was built square around this centrepiece, with balconies facing inwards to enjoy the foliage. The warm, humid air felt great compared to the dry cold winter outside.

She brought a man with her from my childhood. I didn't remember him even though he had lived in our house for about a year. I was six when he moved back into the world. He was heartbroken to hear the distorted version of my life that Mom shared.

They showed me photos from my childhood to ask if anyone in the photograph had molested me. There was no facing the realities of the trauma Mom inflicted on me, of the men who had tried to hurt me, and her adamant stance that it was my fault. Mom was trying to find someone to blame, and child abuse from others was the easier route.

When Mom talked about my lifestyle, she made it sound so much worse than it was. Mom seemed to think I was a drug addict doing hard drugs and living an evil lifestyle. Which to her, I guess I was. To me, I was managing darn well, considering those I had met and knew.

She needed a reason to explain my street life, my not being Christian. The fact I was repeatedly turned away was conveniently forgotten. The man she came with gave me the heebie-jeebies. I didn't want to be alone with him and wanted my mother and sister far away from him as well.

I was helpless in this, of course. I didn't remember him, but he recalled me with great fondness. He gave me beautiful photos of myself as a young girl playing in the forest. He also stuffed a giant wad of cash into my pocket. Awkward doesn't even describe that feeling of him sliding his hand down into the front pocket of my Levi's. Mom made sure to point out he sold his prize rifle collection to help me. As though I owed him somehow for doing that. They wanted me to find a new lifestyle.

While Mom and I visited by the pool as the kids continued to splash and play, I told her I forgave her. At first, Mom didn't understand what I was talking about. She probably didn't realize the depth of pain and betrayal she had caused by turning me away again and again before I was even sixteen years old. I was letting go of the trauma she had unwittingly inflicted on me. I told Mom I understood she felt she had to choose between being a mother to me or a mother to the three younger ones. They obviously had to come first. I'm not sure what prompted me to say that. In hindsight, it was one of the best things I could have done for our relationship.

That visit hit me hard. The man I didn't remember, stuffing his hand in my pocket, haunted me. It was a struggle not to run into oblivious escape. I didn't. I kept going forward one day at a time. I instead found a beautiful apartment overlooking the lake and valley.

I'd lost a few of my long-standing clients when they tried to change their relationship to dating. They forgot they'd shared things that no woman would accept in a long-term boyfriend. At least not this woman.

One night when I was out having a bite to eat on my way home, I met Dick, a man who seemed to have what I was searching for. He was a few years older than me and attractive in a cute, almost Tom Cruise kind of way. He had a job, a house, and a truck, was well-spoken, and he asked me out.

I only saw what I wanted to see in him. A way toward a respectable life in a world I felt like a bystander. I didn't see the other pieces until too late. We went to see live bands at local bars, took day trips, and went on picnics. I warned him that if he was serious about dating me, he had to be willing to take my siblings when they came to be with me. He told me he had a daughter who was almost eight years old, and he was in the middle of a separation. He was deep in grief and loss as one of his stepfathers passed away the previous year. He hadn't been notified in time to attend the funeral. We took a road trip so that he could visit the grave and pay his respects.

One evening, as we sat enjoying the sunset, Dick asked me where we were going with our relationship. Staying as we were, we wouldn't be moving forward. In retrospect, he was fired, broke, and about to be evicted. I, however, didn't know any of this and thought his logic was sound.

He explained that for us to have a future together, we needed to leave our pasts behind and start our relationship with a clean slate. That included me having to burn every photograph and film negative I had. I hated watching my beloved photos go up in flames. I loved taking photos and documenting my adventures. Dick didn't want me to keep anything, my comfy bed, my collection of one-off bottles from the glass plant. You name it; he wanted it gone. I wanted a life different from what I had experienced bad enough that I was willing to do this.

We moved to a hick little trailer park town outside of a small city. It was his mom's trailer, and he got a job milking cows with his fourth stepdad. Dick's mom was a sober alcoholic who was trying to have a relationship with her numerous children. I didn't understand her as she was very standoffish. Her failed marriages had turned Dick off marriage, apparently.

I had a few jobs while we lived there. Every time I'd have a job for a few weeks, he'd lose his shit, thinking I was cheating or wanting someone else. We'd get into a massive fight which ended in both of us being bloody and bruised. He drank to excess, which either caused a fight or him crying. I didn't understand alcoholism and didn't have anyone to confide in. When I was little, my mother said my aunt was an alcoholic because she had a beer every day after work. My aunt was a homeowner and a traveller. She worked as a registered nurse at a well-known city hospital, so being an alcoholic didn't sound terrible.

Dick was filled with insecurities and prone to drunken rages or fits of crying and depression. I'd never been around an alcoholic or spent much time with an emotional abuser before. It was a mindset I didn't understand. I thought all he needed was time to get on his feet again, emotionally speaking, that is.

He didn't try and kill himself anymore. Not like I took his attempts seriously. When I walked into the bathroom to find him sitting on the floor below the window, his belt looped around the window knob and around his neck, I laughed from deep in my belly. I mean, how ridiculous was that? I also hugged him and asked him what the heck was going on. It's not like you can really commit suicide like that. It was a blatant act of *pay attention to me* if I ever saw one. There was no way it was anything beyond drunken narcissism.

Sadly, I didn't know what narcissism was at twenty-two years old. I thought he was going through a rough patch and needed time to heal. I was there a few times and had found my way. He would, too, right? I thought that soon he would wake up, pull up his socks and get on with life. I didn't understand that some people will always wallow and be the victim in a world of their own making. They blamed everything and everyone. I had to quit my third job, lied about my black eye, and knew it was time for a talk. This wasn't working for me.

We came to a compromise. No more hard alcohol, no more drama. He would have a six-pack in the evening, and we would build a life together. I was done with the bullshit. I wanted a life that didn't include being broke and a bum. He could get on board or say goodbye. We decided to go back west and see if we could find a job, town, and place closer to his daughter, Ava. She missed him terribly. She'd scream and sob, fighting to stay every time her mother picked her up. I can't imagine how her mother felt having to deal with that every other week.

Dick and I stopped at my mother's place for a visit, and my car died. We would have to wait a few days for the mechanic to fix whatever was wrong. The ensuing fight she had with her husband scared me. The kids told me it happened all the time. We could hear the two of them out in the woodshed, their raised voices carrying back into the house. I felt terrible my visit had caused this between them. I didn't know how common it was.

In the end, Mom let us use her minivan to sleep in. We would come back to shower and eat meals. Her husband didn't want us anywhere near the house, but Mother put her foot down. It made me so sad to see her have that kind of partner. Too bad I didn't look in the mirror.

Once we were settled in a small town, Dick went completely sideways. He must have gotten his hands on some hard booze because the next thing I knew, he was peeing in the corner on the wall of our log cabin instead of the toilet. I yelled at him. I mean, what the hell. The ensuing fight ended when the police walked in on him, strangling me to near suffocation. He was hauled off to jail and charged with assault. I was grateful that someone had called the police, for it seemed that was a fight I wouldn't have gotten up from.

I was broke, I had maxed my credit cards, and my cell phone was smashed. I trashed my life over this man and didn't even realize it. I needed to borrow enough cash to get me back east to get my stuff. I stopped by Danny's for a visit and to ask to borrow some money. He wouldn't hear of a loan, straight out giving me the money I needed.

I spent the night with Samantha so I could have a good

night's rest before the long drive. I poured my heart out as I told her about Dick. She said his behaviour wasn't anything. Her ex-husband used to drink so much that he would shit himself and not even realize it.

Alcoholism can take many shapes, and Dick's was no different or odd. Samantha encouraged me to try out this life I wanted so badly. She understood the need to build a family, to get away from the streets, and gave me her blessing. I went back to the hick town Dick and I just left. This time with a plan to get a decent job and get a handle on my finances. I had no goals further than that.

That's when I should've left or at least stayed away from Dick. I should've cut my losses, left all my material possessions, and started fresh. Instead, I let Dick sweet-talk me into forgiving him. I'm not sure why I was so gullible, so ready to stay with him. He was different after that for a while.

Dick went back to milking cows. This time the boss gave him an old farmhouse to live in instead of Dick's mom's trailer. We settled into a routine together, and things seemed to be going well. I lost the carefree financial freedom I'd become used to. I worked long days at a meat packing plant trimming fat off steaks. He worked long before the crack of dawn milking cows.

We learned to live on a tight budget. I taught Dick to be thrifty, shopping at second-hand stores and cooking from scratch. It was like growing up off the grid. You had no money and spent no money.

We weren't unhappy trying to build a life together. He would leave me love notes by the coffee pot. I'd send similar notes with the lunches I made him. We snuggled, watched endless movies together, and drove to the dump for fun and the occasional awesome find. Like an old baby blue cooler that someone didn't want anymore.

Then everything happened at once. He drank so much that he pissed into the boxes in the spare room instead of the toilet. Then I found out the one damn pill I missed the month before caused my body to be fertile as hell. I was pregnant. He took me out for dinner and got down on one knee with a ring. I didn't know what to say. Everyone was staring. He was down there looking at me expectantly. I held out my hand for him to slide the ring on.

We went to the doctor for a check-up. I was tormented by thoughts that my previous drug use would negatively affect the baby. I was pharmaceutical-free for over a year and weed-free for six months. I was blatantly honest with the doctor about the drugs I'd done over the past couple of years. I didn't want to give my child a bad start before even being born. There was no worry about my having a healthy baby from the doctor's point of view.

Within a week, we had set a wedding date and then planned a small country wedding in three months' time. I called Mom with the great news. She was going to be a grandmother, and I'd be getting married.

Mom was excited for me to have a child. Her only advice was to get some type of certificate to be able to work and not have to rely on him. It was probably the best advice she ever gave me.

That night, around three a.m., the phone rang. I was groggy from being jolted from a deep sleep. It was my little sister, Damaras, on the other end. She told me that Mom was dead. I thought I was dreaming.

"What did you say?" I asked.

"Mom is dead," was her reply.

I still didn't believe it and made her repeat it a third time. Then I realized I couldn't keep making my baby sister say it over and over again. I sat up, awake now. I'd be right there. It would take me a day to drive there, but I'd be there as soon as I could.

Before I had time to think about what kind of man Dick

was or what kind of father he would be, I had become the family matriarch.

I hadn't even considered if I really wanted a forever with him or if he was the kind of man I could raise a child with. After that phone call, there wasn't a second thought about Dick and what kind of man he was. I had much bigger issues to face.

Chapter Forty-Two:
Becoming the Family Matriarch

It turned out Mom left her husband for a second time and was killed in a car crash. She was at the religious academy, the second place I'd lived as a child. She was living in a wing of the girl's dorm with the kids. Matthias was now twelve, Damaras fourteen, and Daniel sixteen years old. We were orphans. I was twenty-three years old, newly pregnant, broke, engaged to an asshole, and about to embark on a totally different life.

Dick insisted on coming with me. We gathered up all the funds we could get our hands on, loaded our bags into my K-car, and drove to Mom's.

Aaron Tippin's song "Kiss This" was a big hit on the radio, and I loved it. It fitted where I was headed. I didn't realize the depth of the battlefield I was walking into, but I knew how I felt about the place. The trouble started the day I arrived.

The commune was no longer a commune. It was a government-accredited boarding school. They had built a large dorm on either side of the property. You guessed it, one for boys and one for girls. Many of the leaders—families I'd known growing up—were a part of this school. The man I had testified against in court a few years previously was a host family with his wife in the girl's dorm where I'd be staying. Maybe he'd outgrown his tastes in bullying young women. It was where Mom lived with my siblings, where I'd now be staying.

I stopped in town to pick up Mom's personal effects from the police station. The notebooks she carried in her purse were heartbreaking. There was absolutely no photo to be found of me, only the kids. Same for at the house, and I searched everywhere. The notebooks she carried were of notes she wrote to herself. How her husband would verbally condemn her for being a bad parent. How he condemned the demon daughter she'd allow to visit. The notes went on to describe how when he was late coming home from work, she'd get a bubble of hope that he'd had an accident and would never be coming home. These notations broke my heart. I couldn't keep reading her notes and tucked them away for a day when I'd have the strength. The extent of her unhappiness and the emotional abuse she lived with created such sadness within me for her.

To die at forty-five years of age with half her life being filled with struggle and sadness. It was almost a relief to know she wasn't struggling anymore.

I drove to the town that had the funeral home where her body was. We had to drive past the spot where her van lost control and went off the road down the embankment hitting the one tree there, smashing the roof in, and subsequently breaking her neck. Of all the shit luck or God's will, depending on how you want to look at it. She died on Valentine's Day, making sure we would never forget. It was the first time she'd left the kids alone when she went anywhere. Almost as though it was fate.

I felt she was finally free. Free from her abusive husband. Free from missing Dad. Every time she talked about him, you couldn't help but see her love for him and how she missed him.

Now she was free from the religious beliefs I strongly believed caused her health issues. She was finally free from the unhappiness in life she'd locked herself into.

At the funeral home, things did not go smoothly. They were trying to figure out who was the legal, closest living relative that could direct and claim her body. Her husband was trying to take her back to his town and bury her next to his empty plot. I knew Mom wouldn't want that. She'd want to be cremated and taken to where Dad's ashes were scattered.

After reading her notebooks about Rick, I knew without a doubt the last place she'd want to be when waking up for the second coming would be her second husband, whom she had left twice. I was a nice girl and didn't say any of those things. I did lay claim to her body. The funeral home would have to meet with their lawyer and get back to Rick and me. The funeral home's lawyer found legal precedents showing that once spouses have been separated for more than six months, they no longer are next of kin. That left me as the next of kin with the right of decision.

I tried to show my Christian spirit and direct the funeral home to give her husband a small vial of her ashes. He was with her for almost a decade. He could have a little piece to cry over. I'd be the bigger person and share a little. The rest of Mom would be given to me. I didn't want, couldn't afford a fancy urn. She'd be scattered with Dad anyway, so what did packaging matter?

I asked for a viewing to be arranged before they cremated her. Her brother, sister, mother, and others would want to say goodbye. The funeral director would be able to arrange one in a few days. That would give everyone time to arrive.

Mom didn't have a legal will. What she had was a last wish and testament, according to the legal system. That meant the children were now wards of the court until guardianship could be established. The system was willing to leave them where they were until a meeting could be arranged with social services. Mom's last wish and testament left the kids with my uncle as a guardian. They were to continue to live at the academy under the vice-principal's care until they were of age.

I didn't give a rat's ass what mother wrote. I only cared about what the kids wanted. I asked them, saying I'd go along with whatever they wished. The kids needed to think about it before giving an answer. Their answer ended up being that Daniel wanted his biological father to have full custody, with Daniel remaining at the school as a student. Damaras wanted Uncle and Auntie to share joint custody of her with me and to remain at the academy for the rest of the year. Matthias also wanted us to share joint custody, but he wanted to go back with Uncle and Auntie after the service and live with them.

Some community members offered to plan the memorial service. All I had to do was write my mother's eulogy. *All I had to do.* What a joke that line was. It took me a few nights to get it right. It was one of the hardest things I had to write. During that time, I started a love/hate relationship with Dick. I sat at my mother's desk, slept in my mother's room, and tried to write her life in a few short paragraphs. I tried to write what she'd like said about her.

Then there was Dick, butting in, needing attention. He insisted on having sex, and I had no desire for it. I'd lay there while he rutted away. I hated him. I told myself that as soon as I got through this, he would be gone. I needed him to help me face all this in the light of the day.

I arranged for the same picture of Jesus we'd used for Dad's service to be displayed at her service. I picked out hymns, some from my father's service. Her family did up a memory board with photos throughout her life. The pastor who had baptised my parents and me, who did my father's memorial, agreed to do my mother's as well. It was the little things that would have meant something to her. I know it meant something to me. We had the pastor who started it all, finish it as well.

My being at the commune really pissed off the leaders and members of the community. I was a black stain they wanted removed and forgotten. My being there front and centre was extremely uncomfortable for them. There were none of the usual welcomes or arrivals of casseroles and other funeral foods. One man did bring a huge plate of breakfast crepes. I adored his parents as a child. I had spent time in the woodworking shop with his father making things like wooden picture frames and hunting magpie eggs for his mother. The gift of food showed me thoughtfulness in my time of need. It was a kindness I will never forget. It was in such sharp contrast to how the rest of the community treated me. Few came by to offer their condolences and verify I was truly there in the flesh.

Gavina and her husband drove down to be there with me. Paula felt terrible she couldn't make it. I understood she was in the middle of exams at the university and couldn't reschedule them. In later years, I'd hear of other friends, old commune students that came to show their love and support but were told not to visit me as I couldn't see anyone. Uncle and Auntie were there, of course. Auntie was acting like we never were on the outs for the past half dozen years.

The wife of the little man I had stood witness against stopped by. She declined to enter but handed me a thick envelope. Her beautiful cursive writing was in sharp contrast to the message within. I glanced through it, reading the odd line. She wrote that she didn't understand what had happened. She forgave me for all the transgressions I made. She asked God to give her the strength to see past the error of my ways and love me as one of his children. I stopped reading and tossed it in the trash.

I shouldn't have felt anger, hurt, and betrayal, but I did. I didn't need or want her forgiveness. I knew she couldn't face the kind of man she married and had children with. She needed someone to blame for the stories about him. I was the perfect scapegoat. The letter wasn't about forgiving me, and I knew that. It was for her. To make her feel holy and God-like. She did it to feel she was worthy of Heaven for saying those things to me. There was no acknowledgement of wrongdoing by her husband. There was no justice to be had for me, as in her mind, he was my victim. He was protected by his religion and communal family.

I couldn't think about that. I had a eulogy to write, a custody battle to iron out, and I needed to be careful not to lose my baby. I was only two months pregnant, and there was concern I'd miscarry due to stress. Whether I should have had a child with Dick never crossed my mind.

Mom's viewing was coming up, and I had to bring the funeral home clothes for her to wear. Picking out the clothing for mom's viewing was difficult at best. I mean, what is appropriate to be the last outfit you are seen in? What would she have wanted?

At the viewing, I sat there. I mean, I just sat there and didn't want to leave. She looked so peaceful lying there. Her skin didn't have the yellow tinge it usually had. Her smile lines were missing in this relaxed state. I kept thinking about how this would be the last time I'd ever see her. I'd never see my mother again. I didn't want to leave her. I wanted to talk to her, hug her. I knew it was just her shell, but I wanted to throw myself down next to her. For all that she had done, she was still my mother.

Dick told me we had to go, that everyone was waiting outside. I didn't give a shit about everyone. It took everything I had in me not to pick up a chair and send him through the eternal gates, too. Instead, I forced my body to rise from the chair and walk out into the parking lot, where others waited for me.

My uncle and aunt, the same ones I had lived with years before, called a meeting with me. Just the three of us, but I brought Dick. We all sat down at the dinner table, and they addressed the problem.

Me, I was the problem. That isn't how they started it mind you. My aunt expressed her love for me, for my unborn child. She'd be a grandmother to my child. I smiled, nodded, and thanked her. I knew this wasn't the reason I was seated here before them. Then the question of why I was petitioning to be involved in the legal documentation of the kid's guardianship was raised. This was the real issue.

They didn't want me to have legal rights to my siblings. It didn't matter to them what the kids wanted. Or that Damaras and Matthias had asked me to share custody and guardianship with them. Auntie and Uncle weren't having a meeting with Daniel's father about his involvement. Daniel, my adopted brother, wanted his biological father to have sole guardianship against Mother's will, and that was acceptable. Respectable even. My involvement would be scandalous. Say what they would it wasn't about what mother would have wanted but what they wanted.

I sat at that table and faced the woman who had accused me of incestuous thoughts about my uncle. Now she wanted to be a grandmother to my child. This was a woman who locked her own husband out of the house for talking to me. I knew the truth about this woman who now smiled and acted lovingly. I hadn't forgotten what she'd done. They wanted me to walk away from my remaining family and abandon them to all those wonderful people who had treated me so Christian-like.

As the conversation progressed and I refused to back down, they were more and more frustrated with me. They were not used to me standing my ground. The longer I refused to cave and give up my claim to joint guardianship, the less civil the discussion became. It was probably the only time they both raised their voices at me. They were almost yelling. They disparaged my character and attacked me because I had the audacity to think I should have anything to do with the kids. They told me I was a drug addict and a whore who had no right to her family. That's when Dick lost his cool.

"How dare you talk to her like that," he yelled. "You're family. You claim to be church-going folk, and yet you would say these things! This is how you talk to her in a time like this?"

Dick turned to me and said, "They have no right to talk to you like that. You don't have to listen to this garbage. We're leaving." He took my hand, and we left.

I was shaking as tears streamed down my cheeks. Outside, Dick lit a cigarette and passed it to me for a quick calming puff. I didn't smoke anymore, not only because of my pregnancy but for personal preference. However, I needed to calm down. The action of taking a slow breath started to calm me, breathing in and out instead of hyperventilating with anxiety.

I wouldn't be backing down from this fight. I only wanted to do what the kids wanted. They were old enough to decide, and I'd do what they asked. It wasn't about my aunt and uncle. I'd stand my ground.

* * *

I walked the hallway, sometimes to go and get a glass of water, other times to stretch my legs. Most times, when I passed the living room, I'd see the two youngest, Damaras and Matthias, sitting on the couch together. They had stretched out their feet toward each other as they watched the tiny television. This kind of worldly access had never been allowed when I was young. I was glad they had something to distract them. It warmed my heart to see their bond and how they had each other. The two of them were wrapped up in their mother's blanket, secure with each other. It had a lasting effect on me. They were a team facing the unknown future together.

Dick and I took Damaras and Matthias for meals in the nearby town. We went to town to eat because I knew we should stay away from those in the community. Using the cafeteria wouldn't have been wise. I didn't want the kids to see how unwelcome I was. They didn't ask, and I didn't tell. I knew getting out, going for a drive, walking by the river, and going to a restaurant would be good for them. It was a respite from the constant reminder that Mom was gone.

I remember having lunch at a local diner. We all had sandwiches and fries. The kids weren't accustomed to eating out. The ordering was a little difficult at first, but they got the hang of it. Sitting for that long was something my baby brother Matthias couldn't do. He was used to running about. Sitting still for an hour without reason wasn't something he was trained to do. He cavorted, wiggled, chatted up the waitress, and paced behind the seats. It did my heart good to see his boundless energy.

The oldest, Daniel, stuck with his father most of the time. He may have lost his last adopted parent, but he still had his biological father. Now that Mom was dead, Daniel wanted to be with the family he still had. I understood this; his personality was more like his family than ours.

We all went to a meeting with social services a couple of days before the memorial service. When I say we, I mean everyone involved with and including the kids.

Daniel's father and stepmother were there since he wanted his father to have custody. I was there for Damaras and Matthias. Dick was there for my support. Auntie and Uncle were there, wanting sole custody of Damaras and Matthias. Once we were all seated at the boardroom table, the worker explained how it would work and what was required of each of us. Auntie and Uncle tried to take control of the meeting and push toward excluding me from being a part of the process and paperwork. They began to disparage my character based on their opinions.

The social worker didn't hand over the reins of the meeting. She wasn't there to mediate. She refused to give ground for hearsay and opinions of one set of adults toward another. The care and concern were for the children. There was no issue with giving shared custody to us both. The kids had asked for a primary residence to be with Auntie and Uncle. Matthias wanted to go with them once the funeral was over. There was a set amount of paperwork to be signed and stamped. Everyone but Auntie and Uncle wanted the same thing. They had to agree and sign or look like the childish asses they were. Before we went to the courthouse to sign the last set of documents, we all stood outside for a photo. It would be the last time we were all together. I was twenty-three years old, two months pregnant, an orphan, and now had joint custody of a twelve and fourteen-year-old. My life was forever changed.

Chapter Forty-Three: Life After Mom

Dick and I were running on financial fumes. We borrowed on upcoming paycheques what we could, but even that was almost gone. Mom's family wouldn't help cover her cremation costs. Gavina paid for her cremation and gave us enough to get home and back to work. We had a couple of more days to wait as we couldn't leave until after her memorial. I arranged to pick up Mom's ashes after the service was over.

Everything I had to do to settle Mom's estate cost money. There was the fee for storage of her totalled van at the junkyard. The towing fees, and the selling of her vehicle unless I took it. The cancellation of her insurance. Fees to get the death certificate and notarized copies. There were fees for documents and filing court forms.

She had no savings, life insurance, or education fund for the kids, and the bills were piling high. Thankfully debt was deemed sinful, so there were no big credit card or vehicle debts outstanding. It was still a daunting task.

Rhena, my old roommate from before Dad's death, was there and willing to take on what she could. She offered to pack up all Mom's stuff for us to come back for in a few months.

Little did I know then that Mom's POS husband would come and take everything of value. It didn't matter how she'd acquired it. He took any furniture he had made for her and the kids and all the appliances she owned. All of that was gone when I came back with a truck to pick up her belongings.

The day before Mom's memorial service, I was asked to come to another meeting. This time not only was Auntie and Uncle there, but a few others. Daniel's father and stepmother were there to represent Daniel. The vice president of the school was there. The local pastor was there to lend a spiritual tone to the meeting. It was no different from any other time I was cornered by well-meaning Christians.

It was almost an intervention, except instead of taking turns reading letters to me about how they cared, I was questioned. Why was I there? What right did I have to be involving myself like I was? What did I think I could do or had the right to do for my siblings? What would my mother think of me being like this? How dare I go against her wishes. I think they thought that mentioning what Mother would think was a strong argument.

I'm not a betting woman, but I would bet none of those pious jerks had ever been turned upon and hurt like I had by the church or by my own mother. The wounds she and the church had inflicted were the reason I'd fight tooth and nail for those kids and stand beside them no matter what. The way those Christians treated me was the reason I fought for the kids.

I sat silently as the meeting went on, with each person or family representative taking their turn to speak or read to me their opinion. It was their opinion of what Mother, Father, and God would want. Then it came round to my turn to respond. I didn't waste my breath trying to convince them. I knew there wasn't anything I could say to change their opinion of me, of why I wasn't going to walk away from the kids. I looked around the room at each of them and simply said, "no," and I walked out.

I went to Gavina for reassurance and support while they all

dispersed from the sitting room. Gavina, of course, hadn't been aware of the meeting. She'd have given them all a piece of her mind. One of the many reasons I loved her. Gavina would have ripped a strip off Auntie and Uncle and the rest for being like that. She is one of the few people I have ever met who is a good Christian person.

The next day at the memorial service, I sat in dry-eyed shock, my siblings so little and vulnerable on either side of me. My heart broke for them. Knowing the sorrow they felt hurt me more than the loss of our mother. Tears streamed down my cheeks as I wondered what their future would be.

The memory board filled with photos of Mom's younger life was displayed on a side table, thanks to her family. I had bare minimum contact with any of Mom's family since arriving at the commune. Between the poison Mom spread about me, the lack of trust I had for family, and us being housed at a different end of the commune, we saw little of each other.

They were happy to cut me a wide path. The sepia-toned picture of Jesus that was lacquered onto a piece of plywood was in front of the pulpit, just as it was at Dad's service. The songs were a sad reminder of my childhood. Silent tears leaked down my cheeks.

The discomfort of sitting in a large auditorium filled with people who didn't welcome my presence was as overwhelming as listening to her service to commemorate her passing. As her eulogy was read, I wondered if I had done her justice. I didn't even attempt to read it. I asked the pastor to read it for me.

It was so hard to write her life in a few short paragraphs. I'd tried to be kind and just to her life—to not leave out the important bits or have a trace of bitterness. I knew I was lacking in experience in writing one and only hoped I had done the eulogy the best it could be done.

The open mic brought about laughs thanks to Grandma sharing funny antidotes about Mother growing up. Whenever a sad story was shared, Grandma would get back up to that mic to share another funny story about Mom. Grandma knew Mom wouldn't want it to be a terribly depressing service and did her best to keep it focused on better memories to keep with us.

There was a potluck meal put on for everyone afterwards. I wasn't sure where the cafeteria was and felt extremely unwelcome. I wasn't sure I was up to all the fake smiles, empty words of sympathy, and small talk. So instead, Dick, the kids, and I went to town to finish the last bits of Mom's estate before we headed home the next morning.

I packed a few of Mom's mementoes that would fit in the car: her photo album, her Bible, Dad's Bible, and a few other little things of sentimental value. I said my goodbyes to my siblings. They wouldn't be coming with me. Daniel and Damaris wanted to stay at the boarding school until the school year ended. Matthias would be going north with Auntie and Uncle to attend the private non-denominational Christian school there.

It was arranged that Matthias and Damaris would come to visit me over spring break and then fly back. Daniel wanted to visit his father instead of coming with them to me. Daniel wanted to spend his breaks with his father and stay at the commune as a student.

The school had changed in the ten years I was away. It was now an accredited government school with an award-winning choir. There was a dorm for boys and for girls. The students ate in a cafeteria instead of with families and would graduate with a dogwood diploma and be able to attend post-secondary education without having to upgrade. Religion, rules, and segregation were still first and foremost. Daniel was comfortable with this type of lifestyle and felt at home with it.

Chapter Forty-Four: An Overnight Mom

When Dick and I got home, my poor cat was angry and happy to finally see me. He'd eaten the entire bag of cat food I had left out for him. Dick and I both went back to work as though life hadn't changed.

In the back of my mind, I realized some things needed to change. We fell back into our routine of both of us working while I also played housewife. I baked bread from scratch, and the flower-patterned carpet in the kitchen sucked up the flour that I spilled. I'd never seen a kitchen and bathroom that were fully carpeted before we moved into that farmhouse.

I made meat and potato dinners for Dick. I accidentally gave him food poisoning a few times. After that, all meat was cooked beyond well into a tasteless chunk. Dick continued to woo me with love notes hidden in the kitchen and bunches of wildflowers picked on his way back from milking the cows. He also continued to be jealous and possessive. He would go into rants about me wanting someone other than him. He had no examples. It was his own inadequacy and insecurity that he put upon me.

The kids' arrival was upon us in no time. I was so happy to see them. We watched movies on the little TV/VCR combo I had. They stayed up late as teenagers did and ate ice cream and snacks. I'd join them, standing in the kitchen, eating ice cream, and visiting. It was nice to spend uninterrupted time in a relaxed environment with them. It was something we had never had before. A camaraderie formed—a closeness we felt but hadn't experienced before. I adored them. These were the brother and sister I hadn't been welcomed to know since they were toddlers. We went to town for slushies, to buy clothes, and to the public pool. All too soon, the week was over, and they had to go back. Matthias back to my aunt and uncle, and Damaras back to the boarding school.

After Damaras and Matthias left, I decided to move closer to them. I wanted to live close enough so I could drive and pick Damaris and Ava up for a weekend. We decided to move halfway between Dick's daughter Ava and the community where Daniel and Damaras lived. Living geographically between Ava and the academy, we could drive to pick up Dick's daughter Ava one weekend and my siblings the next. I'd have moved with or without Dick, but somewhere along the way, he and I became a team. We were two adults set to have a family, with all else becoming minor trivialities.

We bought a little pickup, rented a U-Haul, and gave away anything that wouldn't fit. We hit the road where Dick had a line on a job, not milking cows. He was happy to never see another cow. We could crash at his sister's place for a day or two until we got a place. Within forty-eight hours, we'd found an affordable apartment in an adult-only building. I have no idea how Dick sweet-talked the landlord into letting us rent in a seniors' building, but he did.

Dick got a job nearby, and I was back to work in the hospitality field. That's a fancy way of saying I cleaned hotel rooms. My work didn't last long because Dick constantly harped about me being unfaithful instead of working. I quit my job in a fit of anger.

"Fine!" I yelled at him. "You want to yell and accuse me when I go to work. Then you can earn all the bacon!"

We didn't physically fight anymore, but he was still prone to tantrums. I preferred to avoid conflict. I felt less and less as though I could handle any sort of stress or dispute. I tended to ignore Dick when he went off the handle. I tried to become invisible as time went on.

I had creditors hounding me since I had racked up debt while with Dick. My parents' families were mad at me for standing up for the kids. I had friends of both Mother and Father reach out to me in their time of loss to share their grief. I couldn't face the phone calls, the grief, the questions, or the creditors' threats. I stopped answering the phone. It was a struggle to eat. I couldn't disappear in books like I used to. Life began to blur out of focus as I struggled to get through each day.

Once we moved, I drove out to get Daniel and Damaris every second Friday, returning them Sunday afternoon. I'd go up and take a truckload of Mother's belonging back with me. I'd then have two weeks to sort and deal with her material possessions before going back.

There wasn't anything the kids wanted of hers that they hadn't already taken. I took most of her clothing and kitchen items to the local thrift shop. I gave them back to the same type of store she bought them from. There was such nostalgia as I boxed the jean skirts and jumpers that I knew I'd never wear. As I folded the bulky wool sweaters and high turtlenecks, I could see her wearing them in my mind's eye. I swallowed past the lump in my throat. It was hard to let them go, but it would have been foolish to keep them. Many of the kitchen items I kept because I didn't have a full kitchen set up to cook for a family.

I held garage sales to sell off the rest of the household goods, which barely covered the cost of gas to drive and get it. There was a story on the radio about a woman and her child who had lost everything they owned in a house fire. I offered some of Mom's stuff to help them. Her response stayed with me forever. She said she didn't want gently loved things. She wanted brand new pieces to set up her house. What kind of person asks for help and expects cash or newly purchased gifts? I was raised to give the shirt off my back to those in need. If I have two and you have none, I will give you one, that is how I was raised.

I learned many people feel they need the best they can get. Not because they need new stuff but because they want it. I was shocked and offended by this kind of mindset.

I spent hours taping videos of funny cartoons like Bugs Bunny, Road Runner, Betty Boop, Wylie Coyote, and other great classics for Matthias. I'd make up shoe box care packages with videotapes, comics, and treats that I mailed to him. We talked on the phone, but he was young and not big into talking on the telephone. I understood. I knew the care packages would mean more. It let him know I cared and that he was loved.

I let go of most of my collections: my movies and my Loony Tunes collection of stuffies and mugs. After one good flea market, a gentleman came by and offered to buy the entire lot I had left. He named a number, and it was sold. No more dealing with all the extras.

The bedroom was piled high with boxes of items that had to be kept. The entire set of Ellen G White books, adult and youth series. The series of children's Bible stories that I had grown up on. Much of Mother's household knickknacks and decorations made a house homey.

There was the wall art that hung on the wall when I was a little girl. There were boxes of slides from when Dad used to take photos. So much to save for when we had a house, not a one-bedroom apartment.

The Canon camera was missing. The blender, food processor, dressers, beds, and bedding were all taken by Rick.

He didn't offer any financial support to the kids he had raised for eight years. He sent the kids a care package of vegan treats once near the end of the school year, but no note. It felt like a good riddance to the kids, and don't dare ask for help with them.

The only furniture he left was the couch set Mom bought after Dad died. That became our living room furniture. The futon we brought was the spare bed when the kids visited.

Dick hadn't drank hard alcohol in almost a year. He could still be unpredictable, but it was becoming less and less. When he did get drunk off his six-pack, I'd go to bed so that he would, too. I'd lie there rubbing his back, hoping to God he would fall asleep. I'd tell myself that I needed him and this would get better.

I was embarrassed by the man I was with. I told no one of the troubles I faced with him. I couldn't, really. I didn't feel I had anyone to talk to about my fears.

Paula and Gavina had done so much for me already that I could never repay. I didn't want to burden them with this, too.

They were the only adults I knew I could really talk to. I lay there hating him and myself. I prayed he would fall asleep and stay asleep. I told myself he would stop being like this, to wait it out because I needed him.

I truly believed I needed him to help me create a family and raise all the kids. Oh, how I wish I could go back and tell myself how strong I really was.

* * *

I was now six months pregnant and barely showing. The doctor was concerned with how little weight I was gaining—how little weight the baby was gaining. I didn't know what to do. I was doing my best to eat. I didn't drink or smoke. I was trying to stay calm and happy, not be overly emotional or sad. Not an easy feat when dealing with my dead mother's belongings. I bought a cheesecake that I choked down. Dick and I went out for Chinese, buffet dinners, and Greek meals trying to find things I'd eat. I slowly gained a little more. Heartburn became my newfound friend. I didn't even know what heartburn was until then.

We had kids every weekend. Ava one weekend and Daniel and Damaras the next. We spent Fridays driving to pick up the kids. Saturdays were spent getting used to being together and learning what we enjoyed doing together. Sundays were the return drive. Damaras and Daniel did well with the visits, having little issue adjusting to our home and spending time together. Maybe it was because of our upbringing or our deep loss. Maybe it was the sense of family clinging together, but we never had issues, no matter the situation.

Ava was always a bit more difficult. She took the separation of her parents badly and had meltdowns every time she had to leave her father. The first day we had her with us was always a little awkward, as though she needed to find her footing with us again. Once she settled into the apartment and made sure to have her father's attention, things usually went well until the drive back when she acted out. I felt terrible for her situation but didn't know how to help. I thought time would heal her wounds.

Saturdays, we always tried to get out and do something together. We went for bike rides along the river. There was beach access, trails, and a public pool, all within a few minutes' drive or bike ride. I was becoming a mother without even realizing it. I just did what needed to be done, what any family would do for their own.

Before I knew it, summer had arrived. Matthias came down from Auntie and Uncle's to spend a few weeks with me. I picked him up from the airport, and then we drove to the boarding school to pick up Damaras. Daniel wasn't coming with us as he was going to his dad's. After a couple of weeks with me, Damaras and Matthias would visit Mom's best friend, Nina, and her children for a week. After that, the plan was that they would both go live with Auntie and Uncle.

While Damaras and Matthias were at Nina's, they phoned me. They called with a question for me to think about before they came back at the end of the week. They wanted to know if they could stay and live with me instead of going back to Auntie and Uncle's. Their request knocked the wind out of me. I asked them why they wanted to stay with me instead of the Christian boarding school or with Auntie and Uncle.

I didn't want to agree just because they liked how unreligious I was or because I let them eat candy and ice cream. I didn't want them to come if it was just because I let them ride their bikes to the store, swim in bathing suits at the public pool, watch television and stay up past nine p.m. Their answer brought tears to my eyes. I choked up as I listened to their young voices explain why they wanted to stay with me.

It was simple, they said, they felt at home with me. They liked how we spent time together doing things. They liked how I let them eat fruit and veggies between meals. They liked that I let them eat an entire apple and didn't make them save half for later. They said their main reason was they missed Mom, and being with me felt like being home.

That was all I needed. I understood their wanting to feel safe and at home. That's something hard to feel once you lose your parents and don't really belong to anyone. That was all I'd ever wanted since losing Dad. If being with me made them feel like they belonged, then I'd do everything in my power to make that happen for them.

* * *

I knew I faced a battle and had little time to set the paperwork in motion before school began. If Auntie and Uncle hadn't liked me having joint custody, they sure wouldn't like me asking for a primary residence. I petitioned for an interim order that granted them to stay with me until we could be heard in court. I also petitioned to have the court case moved to where we lived instead of the small town where the case originated. The courts had no issue moving the court file.

Setting a court date at its earliest opening down the road was easily decided. I had no clue what to expect or if I should bring the kids. Dick and I sat in the back, waiting our turn. My dress hung out in front of my swollen belly like a small tent. I was now eight months pregnant, and it showed. When our case was called, the judge asked where the kids were. They were at home, and he wanted to talk to them. We raced home and brought the kids back.

When we walked back into the courtroom, I wondered what sort of picture we presented. I felt like my walk was more like a waddling duck. I had a kid on either side, my sister a tad shorter than me, and my brother barely to my shoulders. I sat on a bench, and the kids were asked to sit at the table right in front of the judge.

The judge asked them if they wanted to live with me full-time. Damaras and Matthias both answered yes in their quiet but confident voices. The judge then asked if they were going to listen to their big sister, and they both nodded and said, "Yes, sir."

My heart ached as I watched these youngsters be strong and ask for me to raise them. My aunt and uncle were livid when they were given the interim order. They sent the kids a few belongings down with my cousin. She declined to even enter the apartment. She chose to stay in the hallway and have the kids go out into the hallway to get their things from her. She only brought them their backpacks. A lawyer was hired to fight me in court. The lines were drawn even deeper than before.

I knew the kids probably had spotty immunization. We were only immunized partially or for the first year or two, then nothing. The kids and I all went down to get them caught up on their immunizations. One more thing was checked off the list of trying to get them caught up and comfortable living in a world they knew little to nothing of. They needed to be able to navigate and live as successful adults. I hoped with every fibre of my being that I'd guide them right. New clothes, three meals a day, freedom to explore, and love only goes so far.

We needed a larger place but couldn't afford much. I wasn't working, and Dick was in an apprentice position. We found a two-bedroom upper floor for rent on the outskirts of town in a nice little subdivision. Damaras got the second bedroom but had to share when Ava was over for the weekend. Matthias's bedroom was behind the couch in the alcove that normally would house the dining room table. It was the best we could do, especially without knowing if we would win in court in a couple of months. Auntie and Uncle weren't talking to me, but I heard about the fund-raising dinner they had to help with funds for caring for Damaras and Matthias. Care they weren't providing and fighting me every step of the way.

My grandma phoned to tell me she was disappointed, in fact, downright angry with me. She called to try to talk sense into me. What was I thinking trying to keep the kids? How could I do this to my mother's memory? She said my fiancé was a worthless bum and would leave me within a few years. Then what would I do? How dare I cause these problems. She told me she had to pay for my uncle's lawyer to help him fight me in court. I was astounded at her barrage. I was taught not to be disrespectful to my elders, but this pushed my patience. I was shaking and tried not to cry when I got off the phone. I hadn't expected this kind of response from my family. I was shocked that my uncle, who worked a good job, as did his wife, would ask a senior citizen to help pay for a lawyer. Did he have no ethics? No pride?

I had written letters to Mom's brother and sister asking for them to disregard what they may have heard or thought of me. I even sent Grandma a similar letter. I asked they be there for the kids, for they were in a time of need like no other. Becoming orphans, transitioning into the world, the school system, everything about it was foreign.

Damaras and Matthias deserved all the love and support they could get from their family. I explained in the letters how hard it was to be raised in a community like we were and then to try and adjust to life in the world. I never heard back from either of Mom's siblings. Grandma's phone call showed the support she'd give.

I felt an overwhelming sadness and loss for myself and for the kids. They were young and so innocent. To lose any family ties we may have had was one more blow to add to the list. I never told them I'd reached out. They didn't need to know that. I wanted to protect them from as much hurt as I could.

The day for our case to be heard in family court came with much trepidation. I didn't hire a lawyer as I couldn't afford one. The judge, my uncle and aunt's lawyer, Dick, and I all sat at a large conference table in a side room. We were logged onto a spaceship-looking telephone to conference call my uncle into the hearing.

They had declined to make the twelve-hour drive for the court case. After all the polite pleasantries, we sat waiting. Two minutes, six minutes, eight minutes, twelve minutes: the time slowly ticked by. Still no call from Uncle.

The judge was done waiting. He began to discuss finalizing the court order when the automated voice announced Uncle and Auntie had joined the call. They barely made their greetings to us when Uncle began a rehearsed attack upon my person as a "drug user and addict, a no-good street person who would only cause—"

He didn't get to finish his attack before the judge set him right. "How dare you come on and start talking like that to this young lady? We have been sitting here waiting for almost fifteen minutes because you couldn't bother to be on time, and you want to start like that?" The judge wasn't done yet. "This young lady came in on time, prepared and properly representing herself in a manner befitting an adult. You, sir, need to watch your tongue."

After that, things went rather smoothly, with the lawyer and me answering a few questions. I was granted primary residence and joint custody of Damaras and Matthias, with Uncle and Auntie getting visitation.

Without any ado, the judge wished us all luck and stamped a new custody order. The judge's faith in me, what he must have seen in me, meant a lot. I'd do my very best for the kids. I was almost twenty-four years old and had custody of two adolescents, was a part-time stepmother to an angry eight-year child, and was pregnant with my own. It would have been overwhelming if I had let myself think about it.

Epilogue

I spent the next ten years raising my siblings and children. I grew up with them. My troubles were not over, but that is for another book.

The tale of my marriage, divorce, raising five children, going back to school, and travelling to Africa is in my next book: *Is This Really my Life.*

Acknowledgements

Thank you, Koby. Your immediate welcoming of me into your life and your home, when I was a homeless teen, changed my life's trajectory. Your support against those who tried to keep me down meant more than words can ever express. Knowing you were there for me saved me many times as I struggled with depression. Your strength always inspired me to be better, stronger, and more.

I want to thank all the other people who helped me and kept me safe over the years. To all those who gave me a helping hand: the family friends, friends, and strangers who saw what I was facing. There are many people who gave me a couch, a toothbrush, a ride, a hot meal, a hug, or a listening ear.

To my siblings and my children. Without you, life would have been harder. I'm so glad that you chose me to be your mother, your sister, and your family. Every day I'm grateful you chose me.

Thank you to my friends as they listened to me worry and vent as I wrote the book.

To my beta readers, Audrey and Nelson, thank you for all your input.

Thank you, Darcy Nybo, for being my editor and writing coach. This wouldn't be a book if it wasn't for your unending support and encouragement as I struggled to put my past into words.

Last but not least, my partner for supporting and encouraging me to tell my story.

About the Author

Sarah Carrington is a born and raised Canadian. Lover of nature, the underdog, and learning. She's a believer in saving our planet and helping the innocent and less fortunate.

Sarah became a blogger about her childhood while writing her memoir, *Where Do I Belong.* An avid reader of memoirs and fiction, Sarah has future writing plans for books involving subjects such as depression, homelessness, sex work, the LGBTQ+ community, and the humour and exhaustion of parenting.

Sarah is writing her second book, *Is This Really My Life*, sharing her journey as a young mother figure to five children at the age of twenty-five. Her journey through parenting, being married to an alcoholic, raising teens, and going back to school.

At the time of this writing, she was in school to become a practical nurse. She wants to work in geriatric and end-of-life care.

You will find her exploring nature and adventuring with her besties when she isn't writing or working.

A Message For My Readers

This story is my story how I remember it, how it affected me. This story is not meant to show any side other than mine, the child who asked questions, who was pushed to the side when she was inconvenient.

I know my parents loved me. I know my mother didn't intend to be the parent she was to me. I know that not all religions and God-loving people are like the ones who were in my life. This story is not about them. This is a recount of how the best of intentions, ideals, and fears created a chain of travesty for an innocent child: me.

I love the woman I am and am thankful I was given the tools that I was for they helped me become who I am. Be it genetic or childhood lessons, I'm grateful for those things that helped me become the strong, resilient, independent, and fun, woman that I am.

It took me decades to be in a safe enough space that I could try to revisit the pain and trauma I went through. In writing my story I hope I give others the courage to make it for one more hour, one more day. To give them the courage to live their life, to love themselves just as they are. And the courage to look past the bad, the pain, the fear, and look toward tomorrow.

Be kind, be humble, be true. Live your life with no fucks but those that you want to give. As I said to myself all those years ago: feel the fear and do it anyway.

Made in the USA
Columbia, SC
20 July 2023

20639186R00205